IMAGES
of America

SHELBY COUNTY

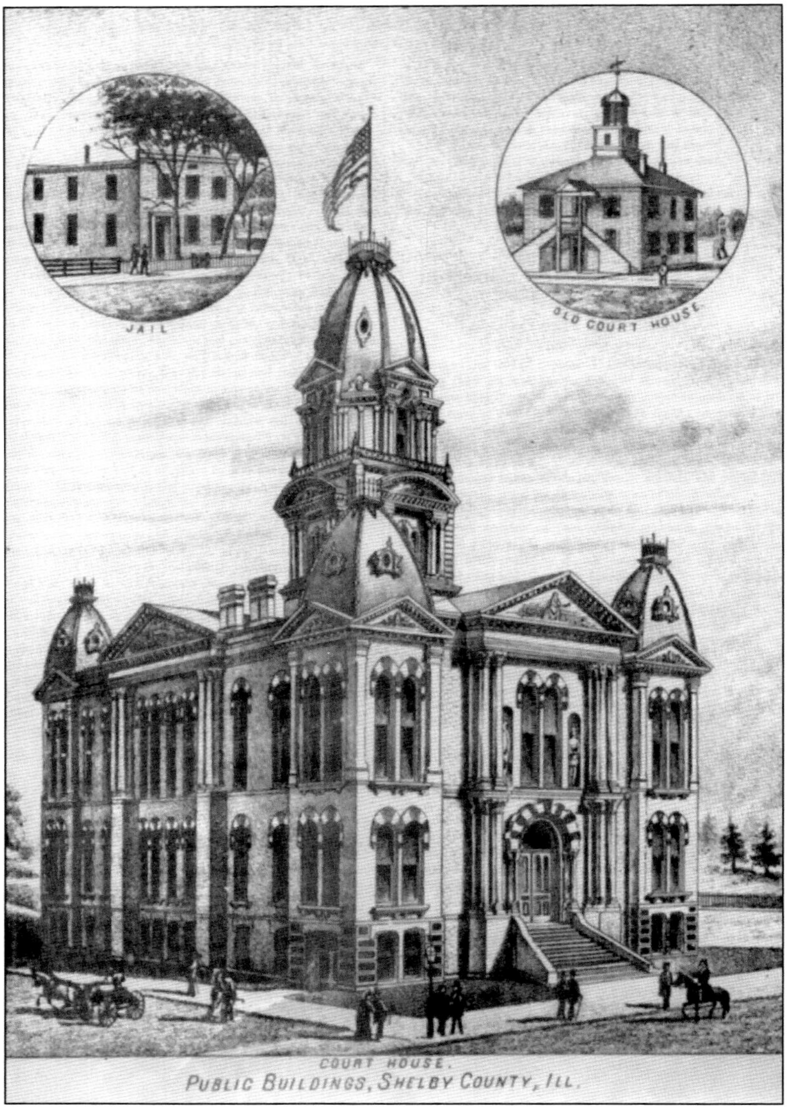

This is a drawing of the current courthouse as it looked not long after it was built. In addition there are insets of the second courthouse and the third jail. The inset shows the cupola on the second courthouse that was removed. The clocks have not been added yet to the third courthouse and the shingles are still slate. A set of pillars is missing on the front. The goddess above the doors is missing and its' location is unknown. The three pediments on each side of the courthouse have decorations in the tympanum or triangle within the pediment. The Goddess of Justice was in the triangle above the south door. It is difficult to see the decorations today that are easily seen in this drawing. This type of architecture is classical, Parthenon style.

ON THE COVER: This photograph was taken in 1918 at the Middlesworth Farm east of Tower Hill. The steam engine, resembling a tractor, furnished the power for the threshing machine. Wagons usually brought coal to run the engines. One of those wagons can be seen in the middle, just under the belt. The farmer was responsible for furnishing the coal, not the threshing crew. (Courtesy of the Shelby County Historical and Genealogical Society.)

IMAGES
of America

SHELBY COUNTY

Julie A. Elbert

ARCADIA
PUBLISHING

ISBN 978-0-7385-7797-5

Published by Arcadia Publishing
Charleston SC, Chicago IL, Portsmouth NH, San Francisco CA

Printed in the United States of America

Library of Congress Control Number: 2009940415

For all general information contact Arcadia Publishing at:
Telephone 843-853-2070
Fax 843-853-0044
E-mail sales@arcadiapublishing.com
For customer service and orders:
Toll-Free 1-888-313-2665

Visit us on the Internet at www.arcadiapublishing.com

Dedicated to the people of Shelby County. The past and the present will shape the future of rural America.

Contents

Acknowledgments

The Shelby County Historical and Genealogical Society made this project possible by opening up its collections for inclusion in this book. All photographs are courtesy of the Historical Society unless otherwise noted. I also wish to thank everyone who allowed us to use their photographs.

I wish to give a big thanks to Donna Lupton for her tireless scanning efforts. She helped to get the best images possible and keep them organized. I wish to thank Jeff Ruetsche of Arcadia Publishing for his support in this project. Most of the information for this book was provided by the histories and centennial publications for the villages in Shelby County, *Here and There in Shelby County* by Beulah Gordon, *Shelbyville Past and Present,* and Shelby County history books. Last, but certainly never least: Thanks Mom for your support and patience in all of my projects.

INTRODUCTION

Native Americans were the first known settlers of Shelby County. Many of the Native American names in Shelby are a testament to their influence in the county. These early Native Americans were Mound Builders and there is evidence that they were located near Williamsburg Hill. At the time there were buffalo herds and large herds of deer roaming the area. The Mound Builders were run out of the area by numerous individual warring tribes. In 1863, Louis Joliet and Jacques Marquette claimed territory for France. They called the area "Illinois Country." In 1717, the territory of what will become the state of Illinois was annexed to the French Province of Louisiana. At the end of the French and Indian War in 1763, the British received "Illinois" as a result of the Treaty of Paris. In 1778, Gen. George Rogers Clark led the Illinois campaign to take over the British outposts during the Revolutionary War. With that success, it was called Illinois County, Virginia. In 1787, it became part of the Northwest Territory. In 1809, it was renamed the Illinois Territory.

In 1818, Illinois was admitted to the Union, and Shelby County was created on January 23, 1827. The county was named for Isaac Shelby, a soldier in the Revolutionary and Indian Wars. He was governor of Kentucky from 1792 to 1796 and from 1812 to 1816. In the War of 1812 Shelby commanded Kentucky troops in the Battle of Thames. In 1827 Shelby County contained most of present day Moultrie County, Pana, Assumption, and most of Prairieton Township in Christian County. In order to more accurately depict the 1827 version of Shelby County here is what happened; the present courthouse location on would have been in Knox County, Northwest Territory, St. Clair County of Territory of Indiana, Madison County Illinois Territory, Edwards County Illinois Territory, Crawford County Illinois Territory, Clark County State of Illinois, Fayette County, and finally Shelby County.

According to the U.S. Census Bureau, the county is 768 square miles of which 759 square miles are land and the remaining are water. Shelby County ranks 18th in size and 55th in population out of the 102 Illinois counties.

The settlement followed the geography of the county based on the needs of the settlers. The settlers needed dry land for their homes, a close water source, and forests nearby for hunting game. Cold Spring, Shelbyville, and Henton were those areas that first met these requirements. Later as farmers moved in, their needs changed and Moweaqua and Richland townships opened up. Railroads influenced the development of the county, rather the other way around. Swampy areas like Prairie Township were some of the last areas to be settled.

The first permanent settlement in Shelby County began on Williamsburg Hill in 1818 and was named Cold Spring. Tombstones for "H. O. Preston 1815" and "wife of F. F. Donnell 1801" were found in this area. In order to keep wolves from the graves, large pieces of sandstone were placed on top of them, so the graves in this area are better preserved. At this time the three most prosperous villages were Cold Spring, Shelbyville, and Prairie Bird (Henton). There was quite a rivalry between Cold Spring and Shelbyville, as to which would be the dominant village in the county. The arrival of the railroad settled the contest in favor of Shelbyville and the Williamsburg community went into decline.

The first pioneer to settle in Moweaqua Township in 1831 was Jacob Traughber. There were few settlers, so they would get together to socialize by singing play songs and forfeit songs. The Moweaqua

Centennial Booklet provides an example of a forfeit song: "The needles eye that doth supply, The thread that runs so truly through, How many a lass have I let pass, Because I wanted You." Reading was a popular activity as well, but only three books were common—the Bible, Pilgrim's Progress, and a hymnbook.

In the 1830s corn was 15¢ a bushel, wheat was 25¢ a bushel, hogs were 1¢ a pound, and cows sold for $5. The style was different as well. Caps made of coon or squirrel skin were commonplace, and people were regarded as "well dressed" when they wore a buckskin shirt and pants with moccasins. The climate was somewhat different as well. The reflective properties of the thick prairie grass and timber were significantly different from the nearly bare soil of planted crops. This was also during the time known as the Little Ice Age that lasted from the 16th century to the 19th century. North America and Europe experienced colder winters with much heavier snowfall, which resulted in the snow staying on the ground for months.

Two important storms impacted the whole county. In the winter of 1830¬¬–1831, there was extremely deep snow. The snow began falling in December and continued throughout the winter. The snow was 4 or 5 feet deep, and for weeks everything was buried by snow. The snowfall was so extreme that livestock and even wildlife perished. In January 1836, the "sudden freeze" occurred when a Manitoba Wave swept in just after midday. Ponds and streams froze instantly. Boiling water thrown in the air came down as a sheet of ice. Meteorologically, a cold wave is when the temperature falls rapidly within a 24-hour period. The Manitoba Wave would be named after a cold area of the country, and the temperature would fall precipitously and almost instantly, in what is usually an unusual event. Under the proper conditions, water can freeze instantly, but recall from science class that boiling water freezes faster than cold water does. This is usually a way to demonstrate how cold it is,

The first reported settler in Richland Township was David Elliot in 1825. His brother John Elliot had twin daughters, and the Indians in the area were so fascinated by the girls that they built them a double papoose cradle. Pioneers cut trails from Centralia, north into central Illinois. Strasburg was built on the Grand Prairie Trail. Located in the middle of Strasburg, Richland Creek was a popular place to stop and water livestock. Some of the wagons that went on the Oregon Trail in 1847 passed through Strasburg. As the pioneers moved west, the Germans moved into the area in the 1850s.

The Southeastern part of Shelby County was one of the last areas to be settled. Prairie Township was described in the Stewardson Centennial book as wet and swampy land with prairie grass "high as a horse and rider" and as "thick as quills on a porcupine's back." People settled in the slightly wooded areas. They built houses and proceeded to break in the prairie in spite of the flies, rattlesnakes, and malaria. The Germans that moved in broke the sod by hand using spades when plows would not work. One plow, the "prairie breaker," made some progress, because it had a stronger wood frame with a steel shear and a front wheel to regulate depth. Two stagecoach roads passed through this part of Prairie Township. When the railroads arrived in 1873, more settlers moved in.

After the law establishing Shelby County was passed, the men had to build an infrastructure and organize a government. In April 1827 a meeting was held at the home of Barnett Bone. At this meeting John Whitley, Levi Casey, and William Weger were elected commissioners, William Williamson was elected as sheriff, Isaac Martin as coroner, and Williamson was also appointed as constable and surveyor. Williamson was paid $20 to lay out the county seat. Joseph Oliver was appointed as county clerk in addition to his positions as county recorder and circuit clerk. He was also the first probate judge, master in chancery, justice of the peace, and school commissioner. In addition, Oliver was one of the first trustees of the village of Shelbyville, and the first merchant, schoolteacher, and postmaster. While the first courthouse was being built, court was held in Joseph Oliver's home. His daughter Mary Jane was the first white child born in Shelbyville. These first commissioners levied taxes to build the infrastructure of the county. One half percent was levied on personal property such as slaves, servants, pleasure carriages, "distilleries", mules, horses, meat cattle three years or older, watches, and all other personal property except for household furniture.

Shelby County has had three forms of county government. From 1827 to 1849 there was a county commissioners' court, and from 1849 to 1860 it was a county court. Finally in 1860 it changed to the present form, the county board of supervisors (more commonly the county board). In 1859 the county was divided into townships and the township roads were laid along the first section line. Six new townships have been created from the splitting of others: Clarksburg from Holland in 1918, Herrick from Cold Spring before 1921, Lakewood from Dry Point in 1911, Penn from Pickaway before 1911, Sigel from Big Spring before 1921, and Todds Point from Okaw before 1921. The growth of villages caused the townships to form more efficient governmental units.

In 1858 the Illinois Free Public School System was established. Shelbyville attorney Samuel Moulton, a state representative and later a U.S. Congressman, introduced this law several years before and fought until he got it passed.

Shelby County has had three courthouses. The first was a log cabin. It was 20-feet-by-24-feet with two stories and cost $110 when it was completed in April 1828. The second courthouse, completed in March 1832, was located on the square. It had two floors and was made of brick. It was a 40-foot square and cost $1,094. The second floor could only be reached by the outside stairs shown in the photograph on page 12. A cupola was added in 1837. The courtroom was on the first floor and offices were on the second floor.

Beulah Gordon told an interesting story about the construction of the second courthouse. A column was needed to support the ceiling in the courtroom, and the only man that would volunteer to round the column was Col. Peter Warren. He chose a black walnut tree north of town for the column. Colonel Warren felled the tree and held the chisel against the trunk while a helper turned it. The column was 20 inches in diameter. In 1879 when this second courthouse was dismantled the wood from the famous column was used to make chairs. Circuit court judges used the chairs. This is the courthouse where Abraham Lincoln argued cases while he was on the 8th Circuit. The famous Lincoln-Thornton debate took place on August 9, 1856, at this courthouse. Beyond it being a part of Shelby County history, the courthouse was noted for its national significance. This was the first time that the topic of slavery came up in a Lincoln debate.

Robert Root completed a painting of the historic Lincoln debate in 1918. For their class project, the Shelbyville High School class of 1920 raised money by doing chores around the community and accepted donations to purchase the painting. The school board paid the remainder of the debt. The painting hung in the high school auditorium for many years. In the late 1970s the Shelbyville School Board voted to loan the painting to the county for display in the courthouse with the provision that a plaque would be attached to the painting as proof of ownership. Its location in the courtroom is ideal and is a constant reminder of the history of Shelby County. Statues of Abraham Lincoln and Anthony Thornton are located on the south side of the current courthouse to commemorate this historic event.

In 1871 it was determined that the third courthouse building was no longer safe. The next year the voters approved the special tax for a new courthouse, not to exceed $100,000. Five architects submitted plans, and the plans drawn by J. C. Cochran of Chicago were accepted. When the cost of Cochran's plans would greatly exceed the $70,000 appropriated, the board cancelled his contract. He would later sue the county. At the advisement of Anthony Thornton the county board voted to pay Cochran $1,470.30. It would be interesting to see those plans. On January 8, 1880, the board accepted the plans by Chicago architect O. H. Placey. The first site proposed for the new courthouse was the old seminary ground, the approximate location of the current Shelbyville Public Library. The county board accepted this land from the "Shelbyville Graded Schools." Thomas Thornton proposed another site, the location of Charles Dexters's store, just north of the second courthouse. This lot was purchased at a cost of $800 and the board made a trade with the city in 1880 that added 40 feet to the north end of the courthouse square. The new courthouse was 76-feet-by-105-feet and it extended into North Washington Street. Moses Flanders Brickyard was awarded the contract for 1,750,000 bricks at a cost of $6 per thousand or $10,500 total and building began. Flanders employed 40 men at his brickyard to make the bricks for the courthouse. A sign at his brickyard read "no one who drinks, plays cards, or swears need apply." In April 1880, the groundbreaking ceremony was held and the building was completed by December 1881 at a total cost of $72,987.

The unsafe, second court house was sold on December 17, 1881 for $101, and it was "in ruins" on February 16, 1882. For several weeks there would have actually been two courthouses. On January 26, 1882, there was an effort made to macadamize Main Street at Broadway to the top of Bruster Hill. This is a type of road construction where 2-inch pieces of rock are laid 6 to 10 inches deep on top of the soil. Although this is very labor intensive, it results in a better road than using massive amounts of rock alone. A dedication ceremony was held April 3, 1883, and the first court session was held that day.

There have been several changes to the third courthouse, including the following: a statue of the Goddess of Justice was removed and her whereabouts are unknown, and two pillars on either side of the south door were also removed. In 1904 lightning struck the flagpole, which is no longer on top of the courthouse. County board member Jacob E. Gallagher moved the motion to purchase the clocks from the Old Main Street School and add them to the tower. In 1896 it was wired for electricity and the building was heated. In 1955 the original slate roof was replaced with asphalt. An elevator was added in 1965, followed by an air conditioning installation in 1987. The Shelby County Courthouse is an impressive building, and it was a common backdrop for important photographs.

Agriculture has been and continues to be an important part of Shelby County history. When the plows broke in the prairies, trees were cut down, and the marshes were tiled, what emerged was a fertile land capable of significant agricultural production. Productivity varies throughout the county. Those areas north of the Shelbyville Moraine are much more productive. However, even the least productive soils in Shelby County are productive from a national or even international perspective. In the April 2009 issue of Farm Futures, Shelby County was ranked as one of the top 500 counties in the United States for farming. The four factors involved in the decision were: return on assets, profit margin, asset turnover, and average net farm income.

The population has fluctuated with the introduction of cash crops and the mechanization of agriculture. Agricultural labor efficiency went from 27.5 acres per worker in 1890 to 740 acres per worker in 1990. In the early agricultural history of the county wheat was extremely popular, followed by corn, and then much later soybeans. Although soybeans are a more recent cash crop than wheat or corn, soybeans were adopted much earlier in Shelby County and Central Illinois than the rest of Illinois or the other states. After the arrival of the railroads, wheat, corn, and corn-fed livestock could be shipped to markets like Chicago, St. Louis, and beyond.

Soybeans emerged as a cash crop in Shelby County because of the county's proximity to the soybean processors in Decatur. Decatur was the center of soybean processing and relied on the surrounding area to provide its raw material. Today the average farm size in the county is 342 acres. Around 100 or even 50 years ago that figure would have been unmanageable for the average farmer. In 2008 farmers grew 166,704 acres of corn for grain, 168,378 acres of soybeans, and 13,080 acres of wheat. Shelby County produces near equal amounts of corn and soybeans, and it is one of the top producers of each of these commodities. If county farmers chose to focus on producing one instead of both corn and soybeans, it would be in the top 10 for total production in the nation. Livestock makes up only 22 percent of the value of agricultural products; 78 percent are from crops. These figures are dramatically different from what we would have found in the early 1900s or even the 1950s. Livestock producers did well or had to get out and the larger numbers did not offset those who needed to get out.

In Shelby County, about 9 percent of the population are farmers with only construction having a larger percentage at 13. This is still well above the national percentage of less than one percent farmers. In 1935 the number of farms in the United States peaked at 6.8 million, and in 2002 there are approximately 2 million.

PLACE NAMES OF SHELBY COUNTY. This map shows the location of all the cities, towns, and villages in this book. The map also shows how many places were not included. There were at least 54 named places in Shelby County.

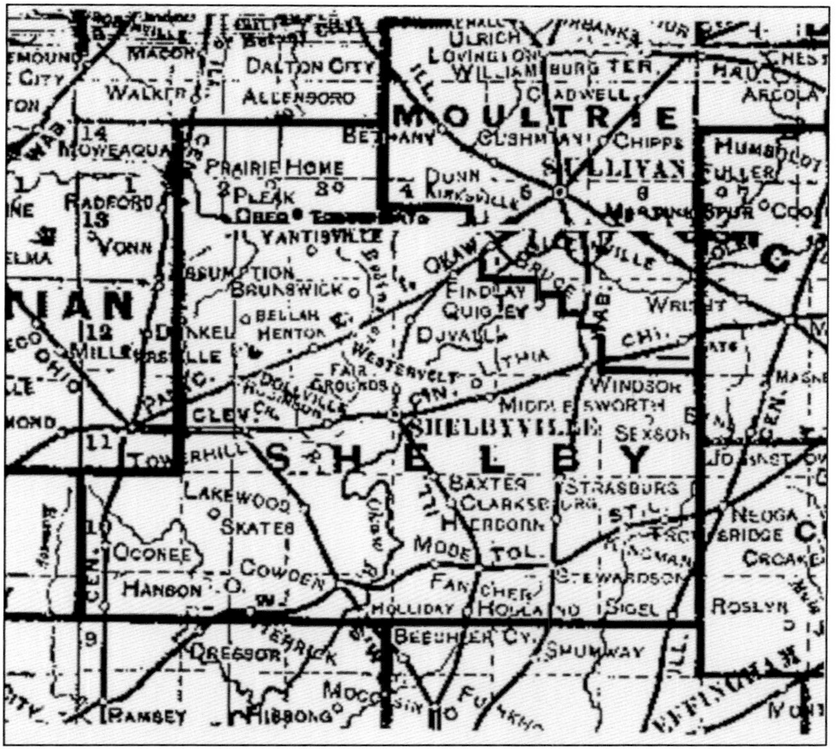

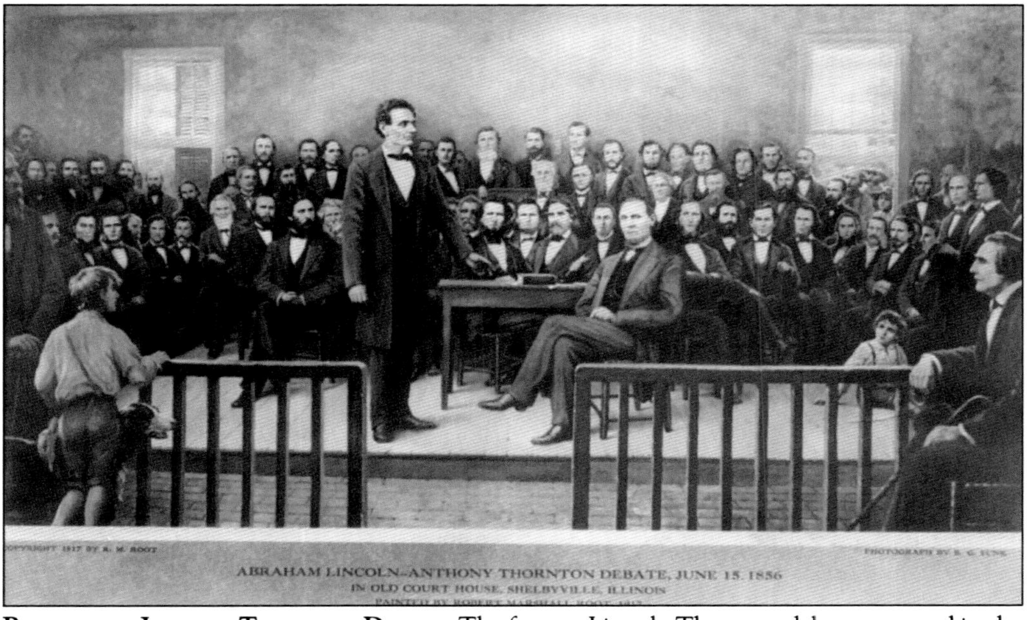

PAINTING OF LINCOLN-THORNTON DEBATE. The famous Lincoln-Thornton debate occurred in the second Shelby County Courthouse on June 15, 1856. It took Robert Marshall Root over four years to research and complete the large painting. Almost all of the men in the painting are identified. Robert Root also painted the Lincoln-Douglas debate and famous portraits such as the second president of Eastern Illinois University, Livingston C. Lord.

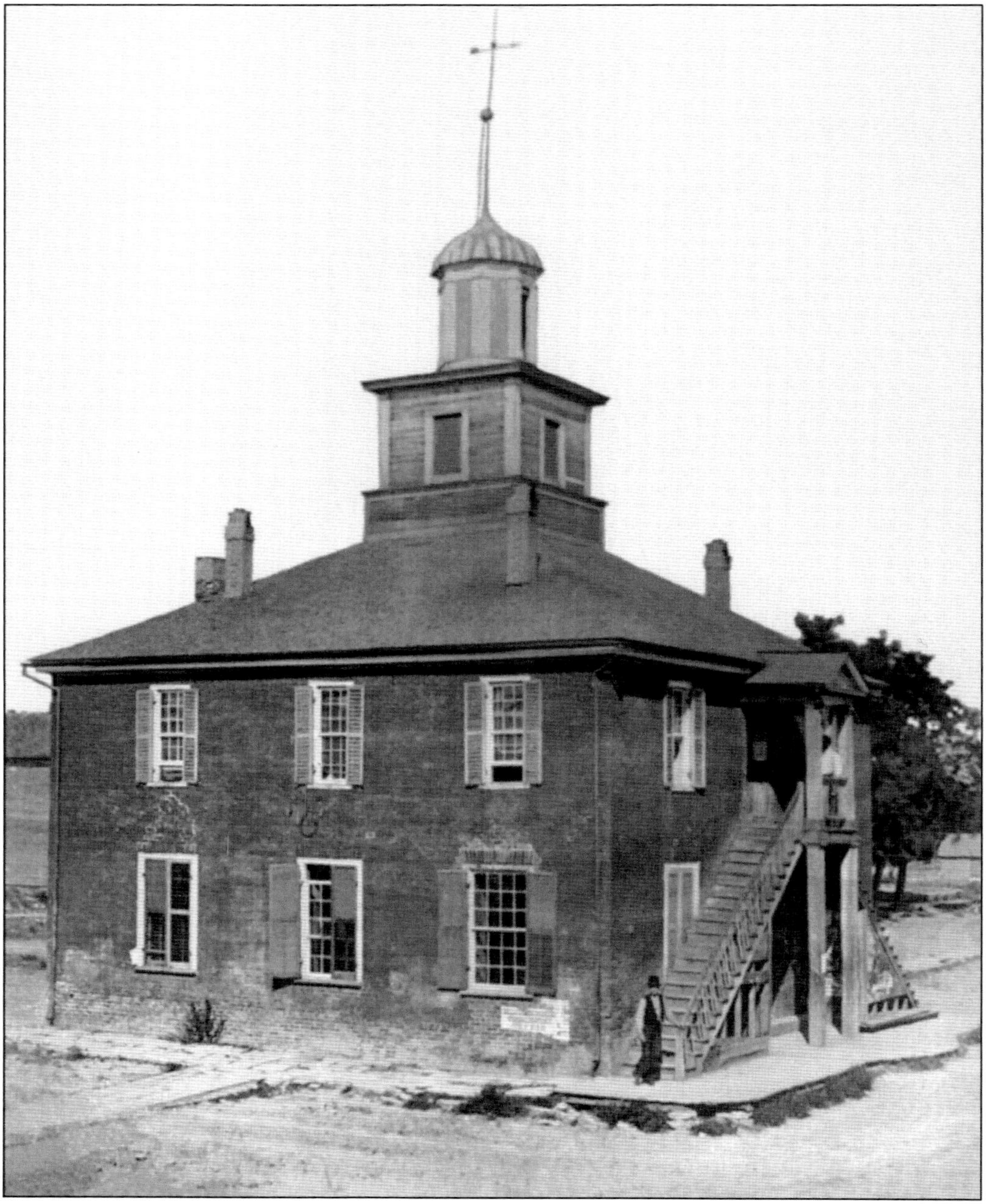

SHELBY COUNTY'S SECOND COURTHOUSE. This courthouse was built in 1832 and was located just south of the current courthouse. The famous Lincoln-Thornton debate occurred here on June 15, 1856. The second floor can only be accessed by the outside stairs, shown here.

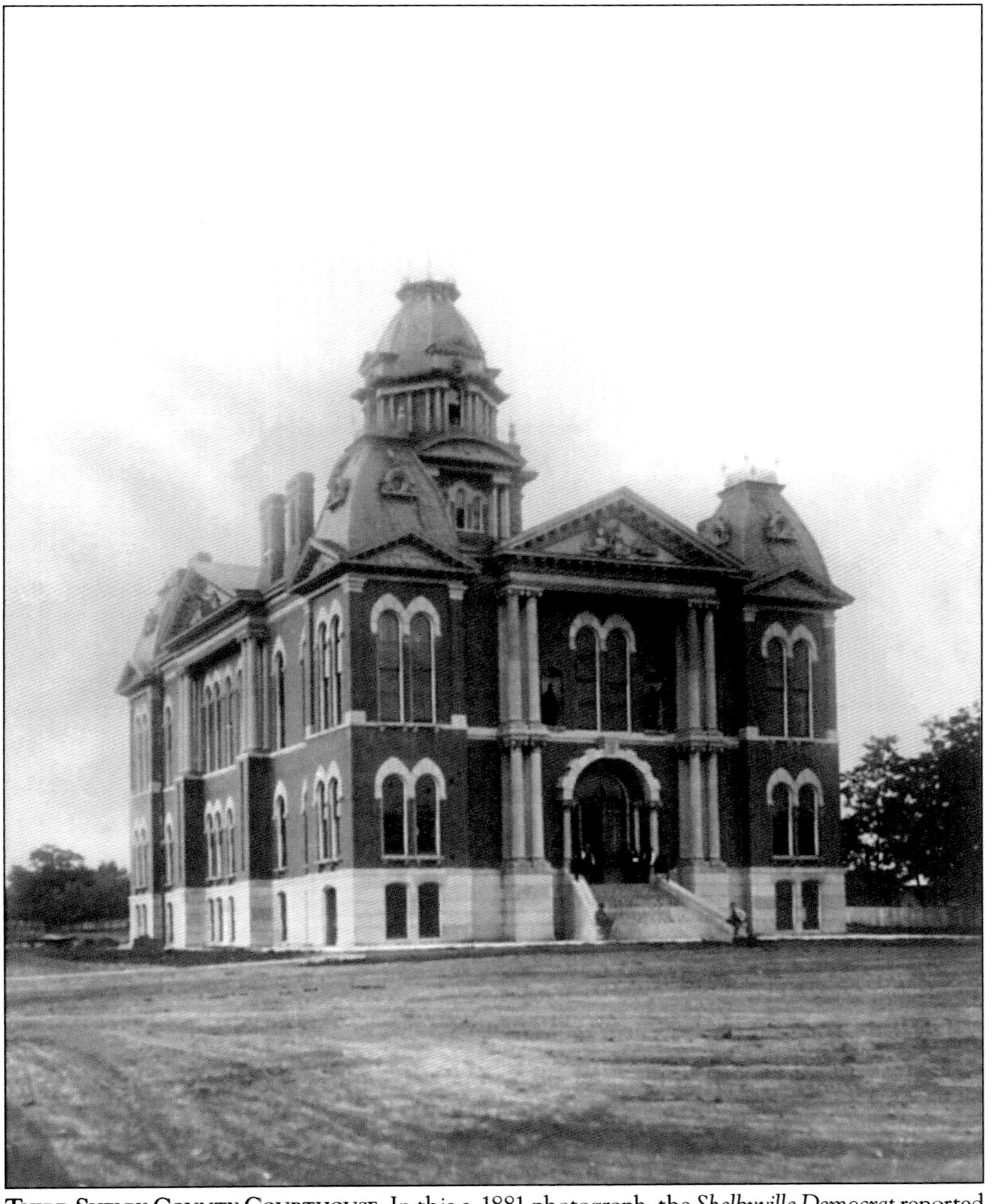

Third Shelby County Courthouse. In this *c.* 1881 photograph, the *Shelbyville Democrat* reported that the courthouse was almost complete on August 18, 1881. There is a pile of bricks on the side of the courthouse, and the dirt looks freshly graded. The photograph had to be taken near the completion of construction. The detail of the Goddess of Justice is easily seen in this image.

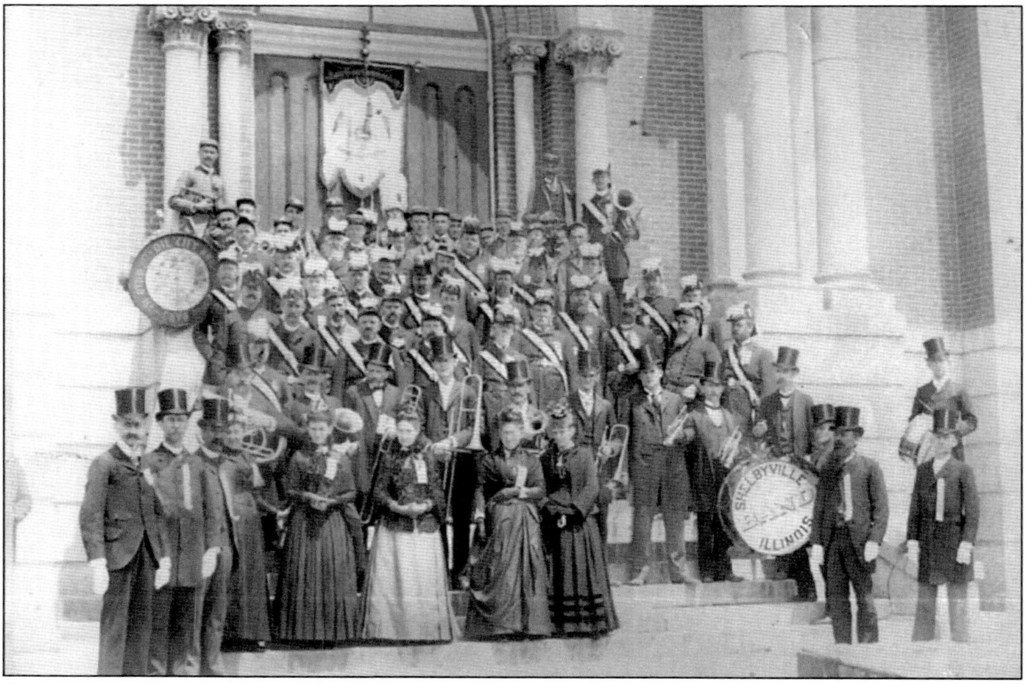

COURTHOUSE DEDICATION. The dedication ceremony was held in 1883. This is the photograph that started the trend to be photographed on the courthouse steps. The dedication ceremony was attended by people from surrounding communities. Shown in this photograph are members of the Shelbyville and Mattoon Masonic Lodges and the Oil City Knights from Litchfield.

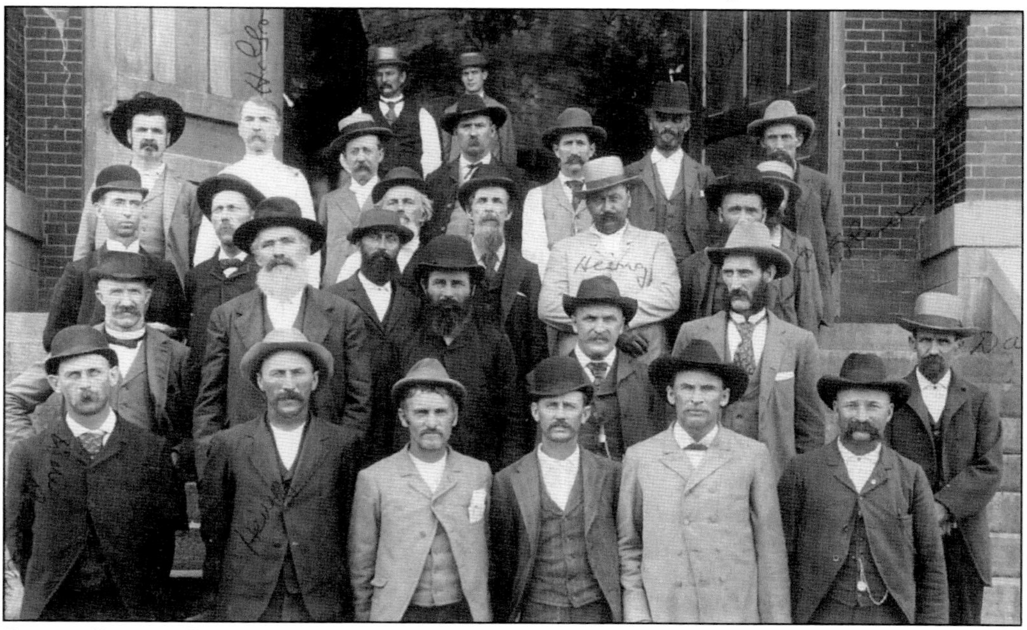

SHELBY COUNTY BOARD OF SUPERVISORS. Members of the 1894 Shelby County Board pose for a photograph on the courthouse steps. Pictured along with members of the county board are other elected county officers and even a schoolboy, Earl Wilson.

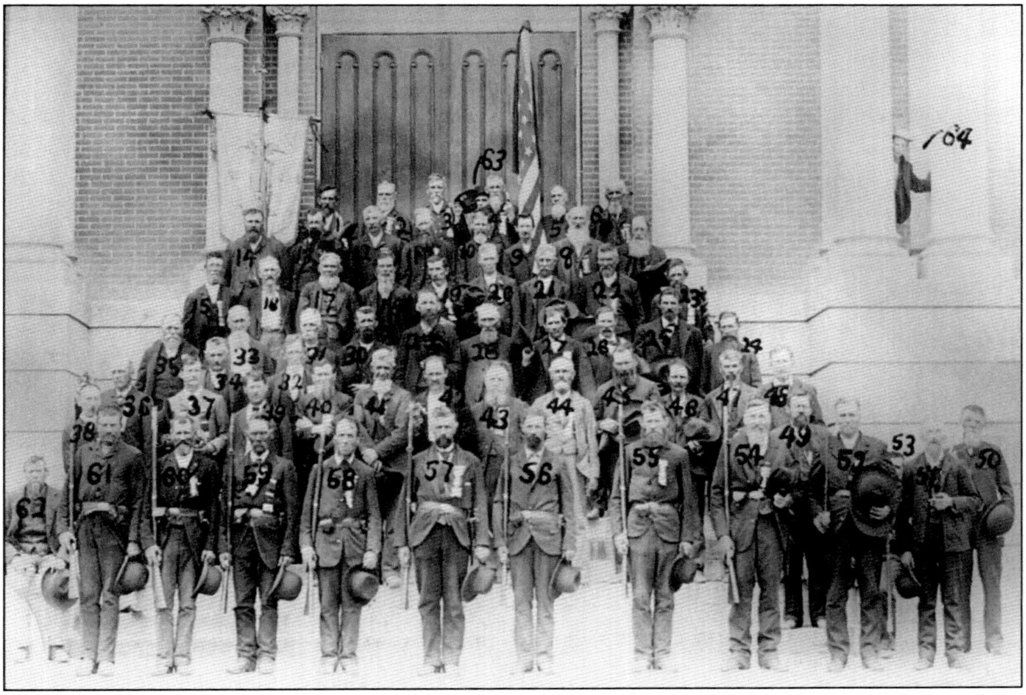

SHELBYVILLE CHAPTER OF THE GAR. This is the Shelbyville Chapter of the Grand Army of the Republic. It is composed of former Union Civil War veterans. The photograph was taken around 1900. Several of the veterans are shown with their guns and cartridge belts. There are 64 veterans who fought from Shelby County in the photograph, and only 15 are unidentified.

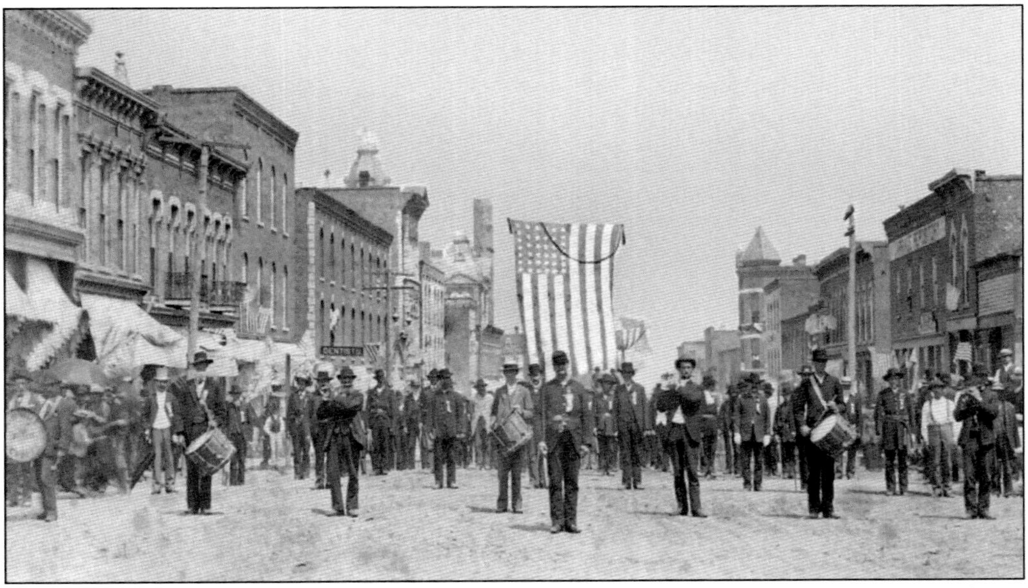

GAR ON PARADE. The same 64 members of the GAR who gathered for the top photograph are pictured marching down Main Street in Shelbyville. The courthouse can be seen in the background along with the old water tower. The streets were paved around 1900, but in this photograph they are still dirt. Note the flag has 48 stars.

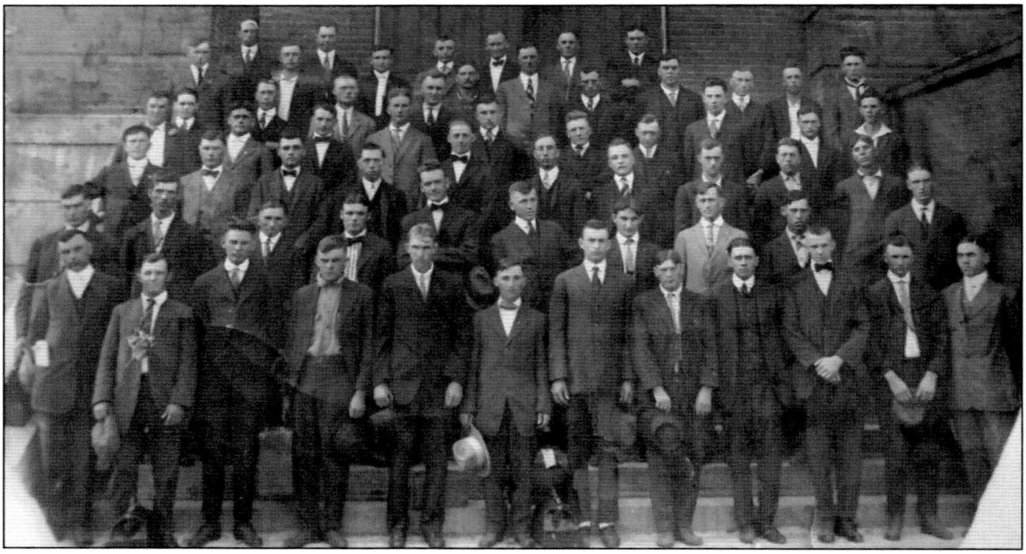

World War I Recruits. These men posed on the Shelby County Courthouse steps on September 18, 1917. They are being shipped out to Camp Taylor in preparation for joining the war effort. At least one soldier in this group will not return to Shelby County alive.

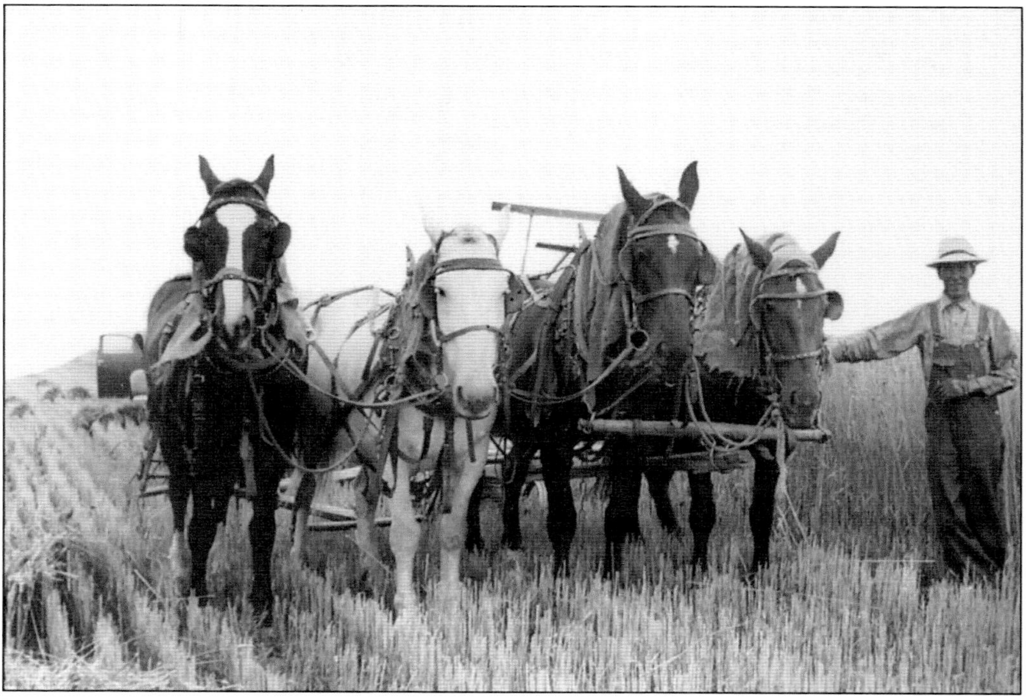

Farming with Horses. This is an example of the horsepower that Shelby County farmers used to depend on to raise their crops. An unidentified Shelby County farmer poses in a wheat field with his team of horses. The horses are pulling some implement, possibly a reaper. All the horses have blinders and covers on their necks. The right two horses are joined with a single tree.

One

The City of Shelbyville

Shelbyville really began when Barnett Bone built a cabin along the Kaskaskia River just south of town in 1835. His canoe was the primary way to cross the river, and his house was the hub of activity. The first Shelby County election was held in his cabin in April 1827. The first business in Shelbyville was that of a blacksmith, as horseshoes were a necessity at the time. In 1827 Jacob Cutler and his son opened a small general store that later became the Stage Coach stop. Shelbyville was incorporated as a village on May 22, 1839, in the same year taxes were levied on property. In addition, all able-bodied men between the ages of 21 and 50 were required to labor on the roads, streets, or alleys for five days a year or pay $1 a day. In 1863 the village was incorporated as the City of Shelbyville. In 1877 the Town of Moulton was annexed to Shelbyville and became known as the "citizen's addition." Michael Gregory purchased land and built a cabin (near the current Veterans of Foreign Wars Post 4829) in anticipation of the Big Four Railroads arrival. In 1850, Gregory, along with speculators Samuel Moulton and William Thornton, drew straws to name the town. Samuel Moulton drew the long straw and named the town Moulton.

The Chautauqua Auditorium is a unique and historic building. H. B. Trout, a local bridge builder, constructed the auditorium in 1903. It was patterned after the Chautauqua in Dixon, Illinois. It is unique because it is a clear span, the outer walls support the building, and there are no posts to obstruct the view. We are familiar with clear-span buildings like the Assembly Hall or the Superdome, so to have this type of engineering technology this early was impressive. Chautauqua is not only a building but also a movement. From the 1870s to the 1930s people in many areas of the country met there for entertainment and enrichment. The Chautauquas were the early version of the multichannel television, the Internet, and computers; they taught, entertained, and provided information on current events.

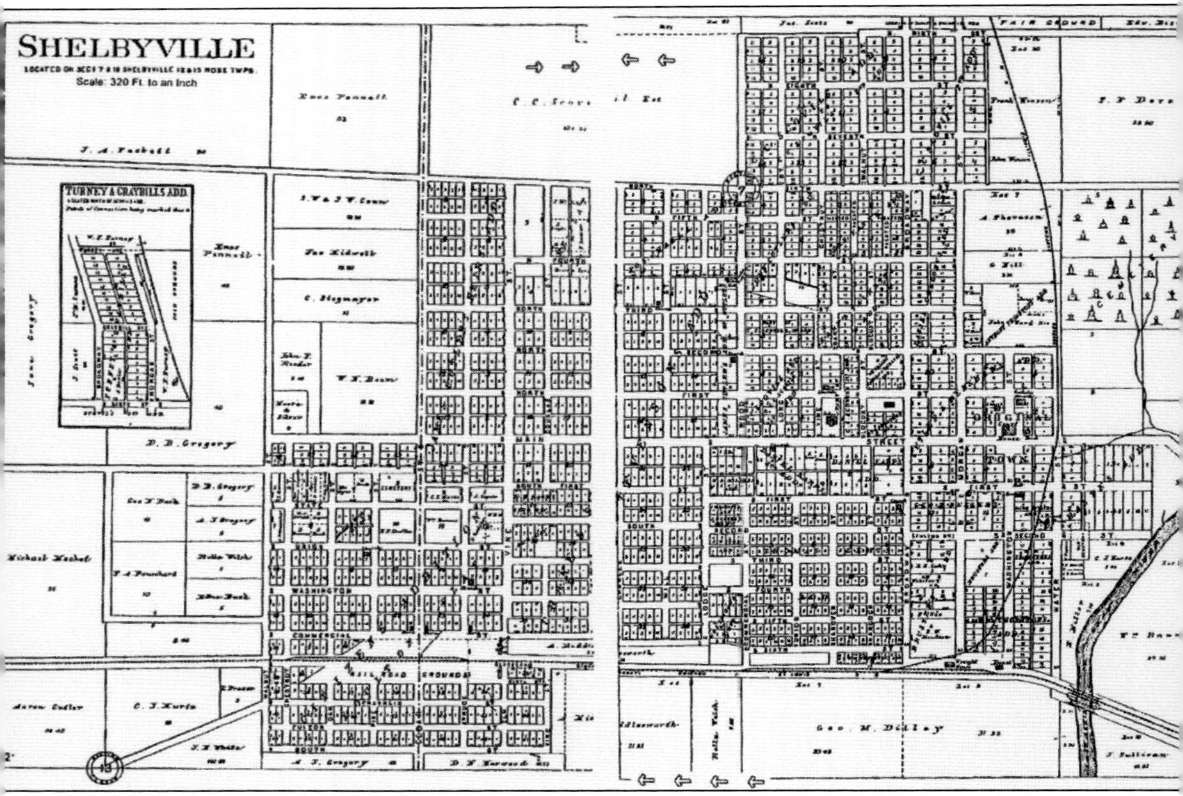

Shelbyville Platt Map 1914. This map provides a very detailed look at the size and layout of the city. It also includes areas such as Glenwood Cemetery that were not in the city limits at the time. Most of these additions to the city limits are labeled. The only time most people find out if they live in an addition to the city is during legal transactions. South Vine Street was the dividing line between Moulton (Citizen's Addition) and Shelbyville. South First and Second Streets do not go across Vine to the other side because this was the north part of Moulton, the zone where the two towns "meshed" together, and it was not a perfect fit. Cemeteries mark the edges of the city. As the city grows, a cemetery—like Glenwood Cemetery—will mark the former edges of the city.

SOLDIERS AND SAILORS MONUMENT. In 1906 the voters of Shelby County approved the building of a monument. The Shelby County Board appropriated $10,000 for the monument. Designed by Robert Root, 6-foot-tall statues made of Barre Vermont granite were placed on the corners of the monument. They represent the U.S. Infantry, Navy, Cavalry, and Artillery. A 12-foot-high, bronze statue of a color-bearer and flag rests on top of the monument.

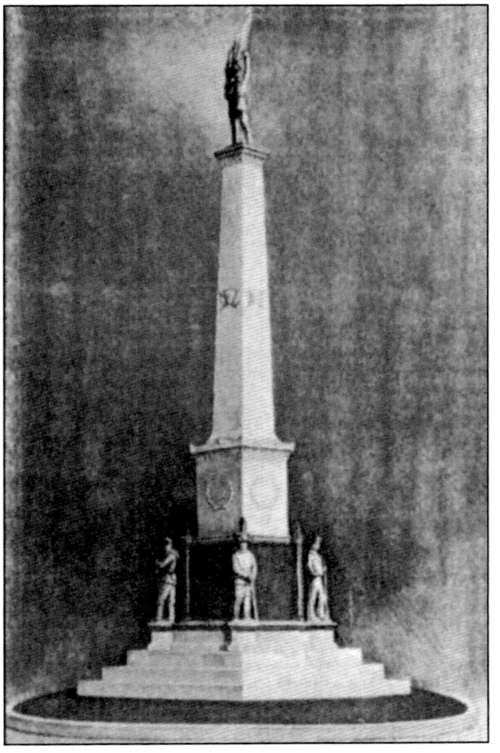

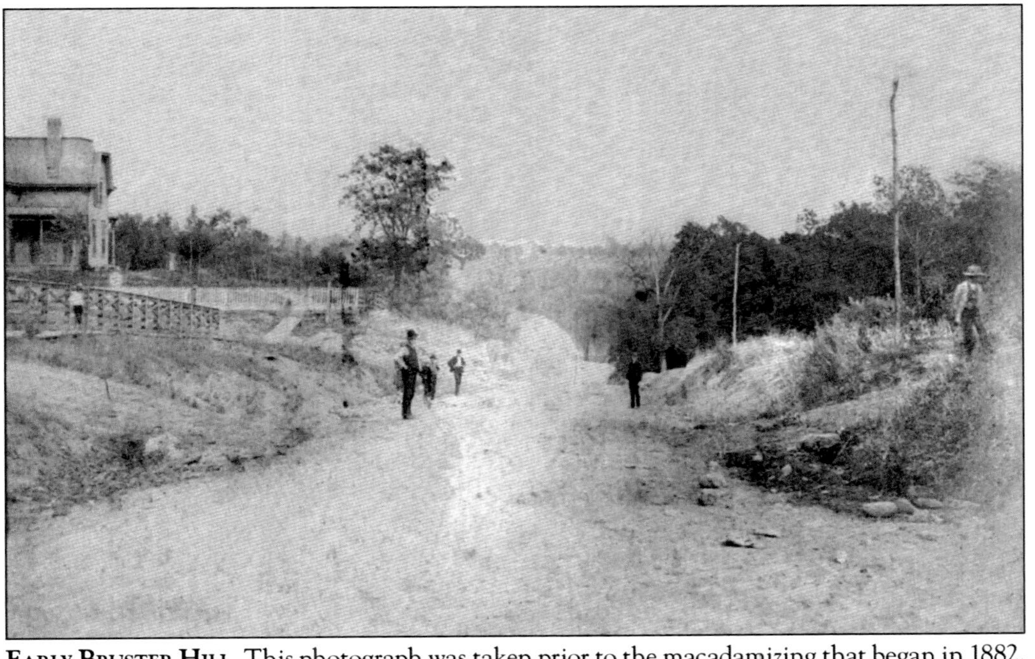

EARLY BRUSTER HILL. This photograph was taken prior to the macadamizing that began in 1882. The narrow, winding dirt road led down to a wooden bridge that was built over the Kaskaskiswatikaa River. In 1881, an iron bridge was built. Bruster Hill got its name from John Bruster who ran a tanning yard at the top of the hill.

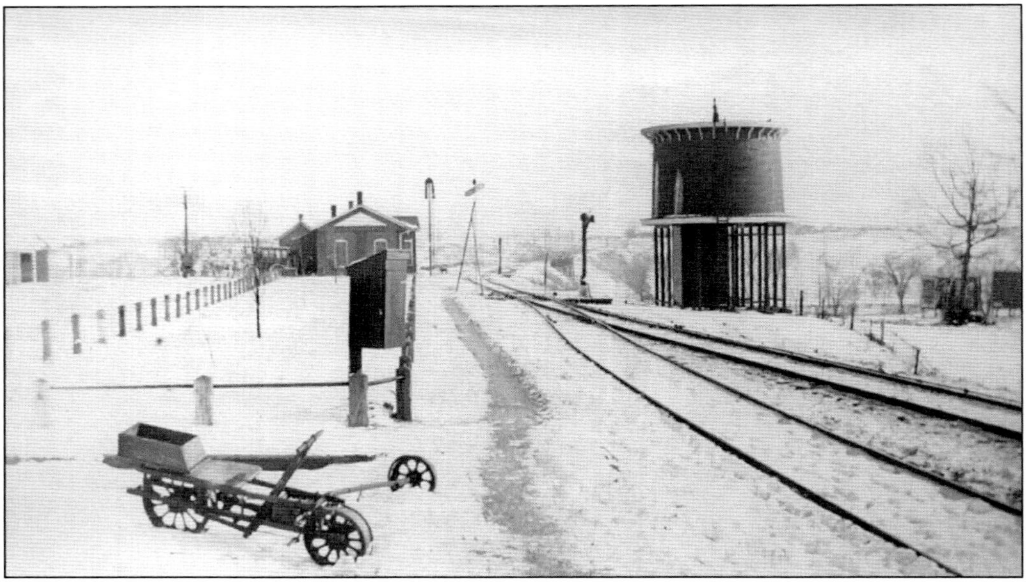

TWO WINTER VIEWS. In the top photograph, the Shelbyville, New York Central Depot with switches can be seen. A horse and buggy dates this photograph in the late 1800s. This depot was originally located in the town of Moulton when it was built. The following companies operated the railroad: Terre Haute, Alton and St. Louis, the CCC (Cleveland, Cincinnati, and Chicago), and St. Louis (The Big Four), the New York Central, and the Penn Central. The bottom photograph shows the C&EI Depot at the east edge of the city. The cylindrical water tower was in place before 1915. The courthouse does not have a clock yet. The Catholic church and the Lincoln Hotel are in the background as well.

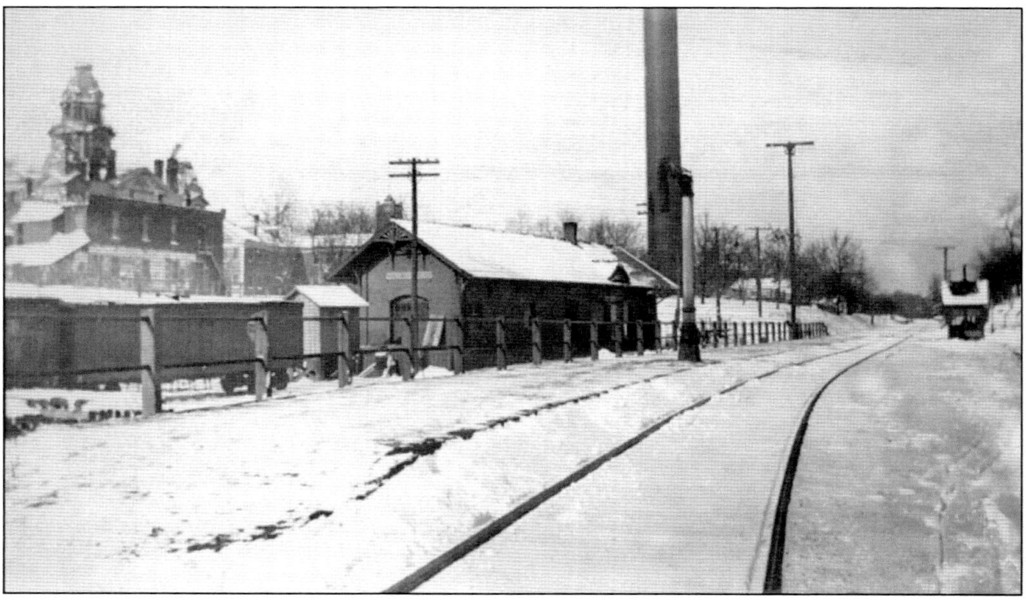

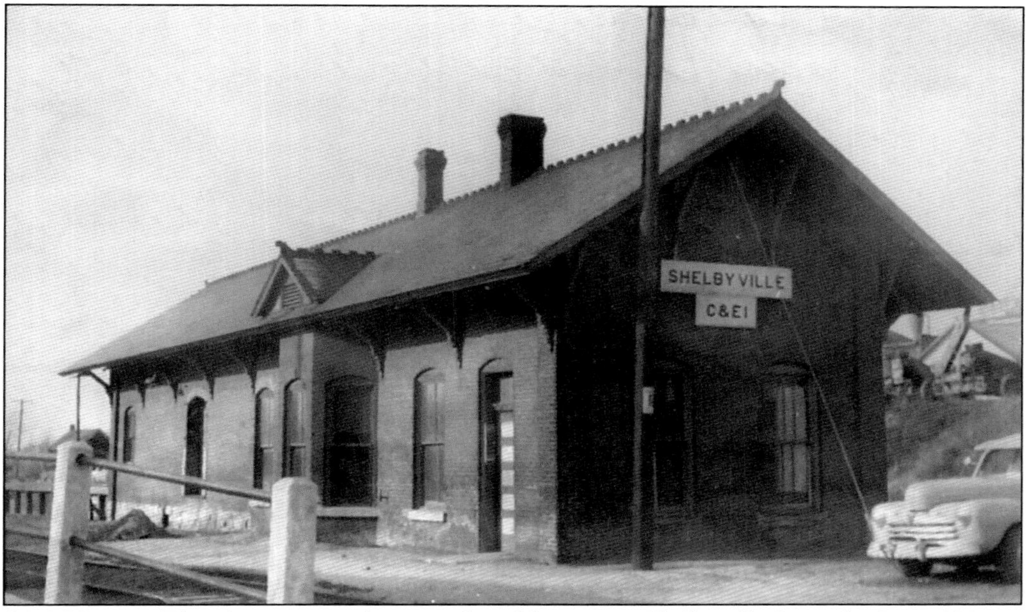

C&EI Depot. This depot was at the east edge of downtown Shelbyville. It was built in 1892 at a cost of $4,000 after the railroad reached Shelbyville in 1891. John Tackett owned the land north of Shelbyville that the railroad crossed. A railroad crossing was called Tackett's Crossing in his honor. Today that crossing is where Country Club Road crosses the tracks northeast of Shelbyville.

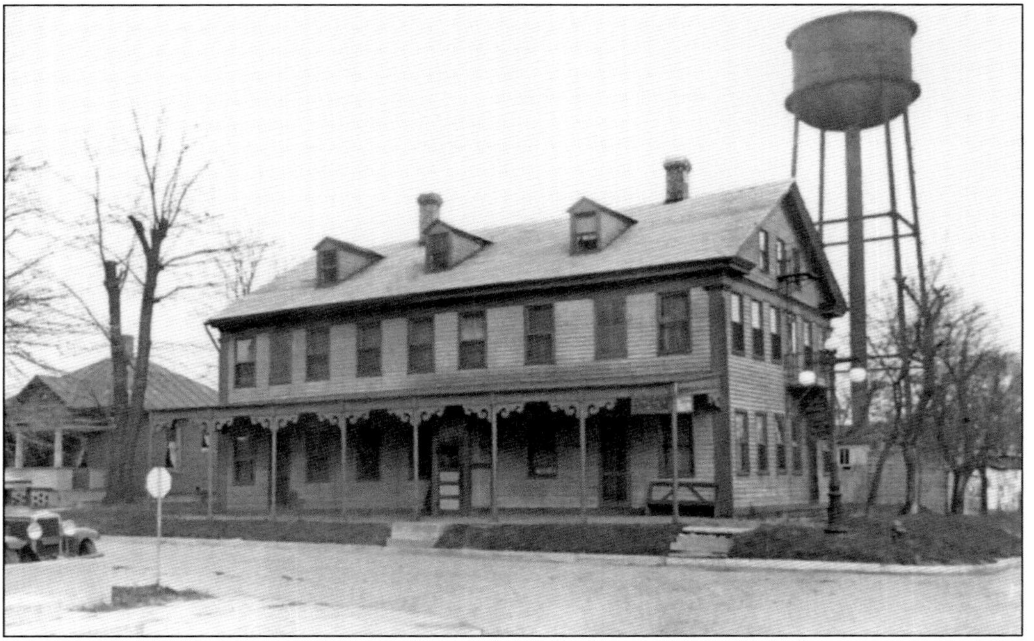

Lincoln Hotel. In 1856 Benjamin Tallman built a new hotel on the square. It became a favorite landmark because Abraham Lincoln slept in the corner room on the second floor. This was during his circuit riding days. The hotel had many names, but it was called Lincoln in 1915. It was torn down in February 1930, and Morgan Quigley sold the lot to the Lincoln Oil Refining Company.

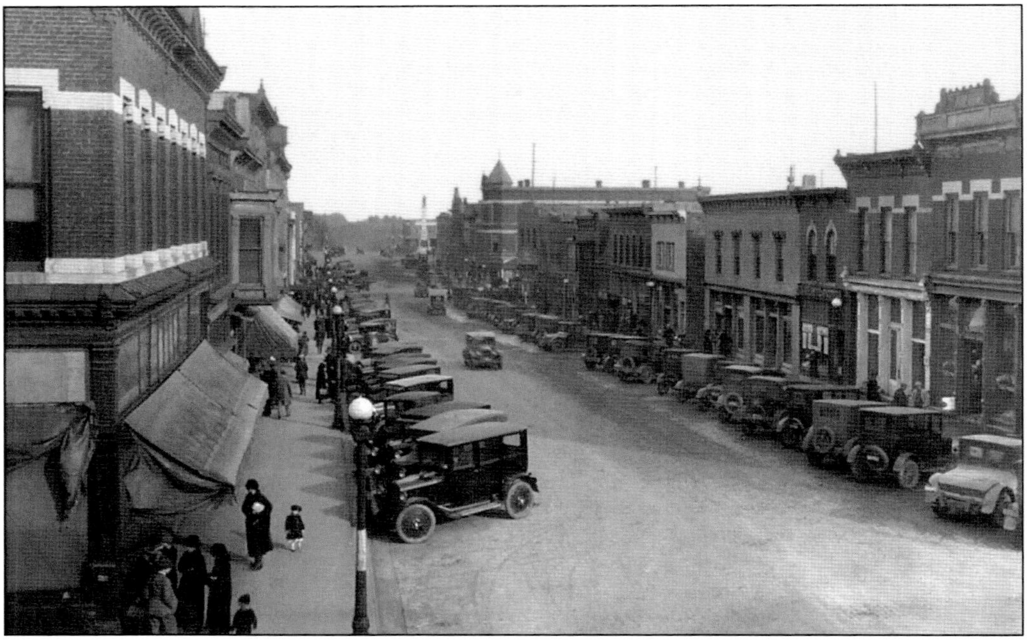

DOWNTOWN SHELBYVILLE, 1930S. This view looks east down Main Street at the corner of Broadway. The Soldiers and Sailors Monument can be seen in the distance. In this photograph, the "corner drug store" building has not yet burned in the fire that will remove its third story. The same fire damaged Robert Root's studio.

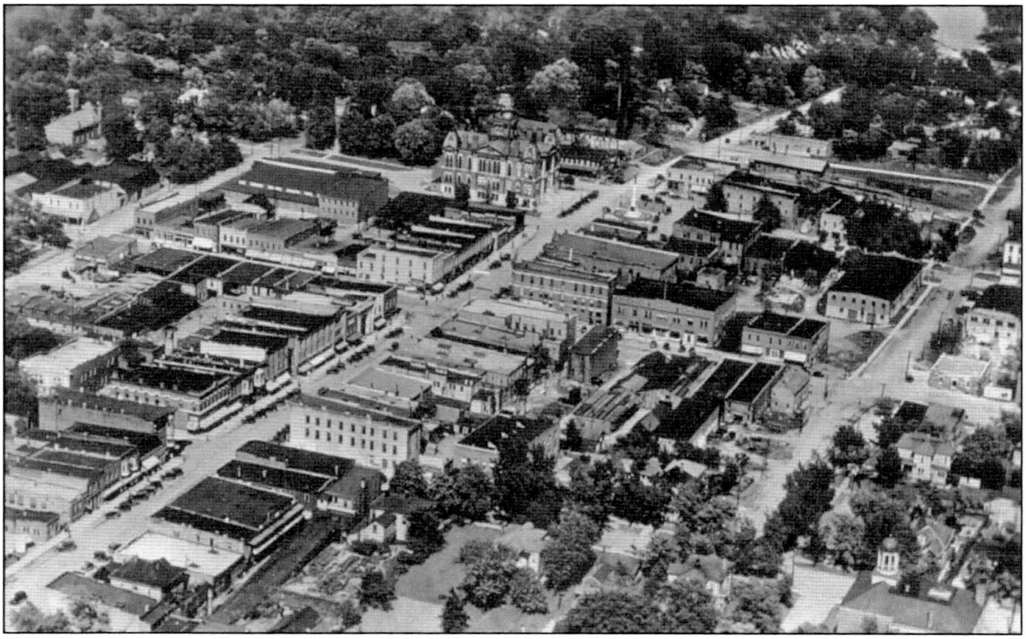

AERIAL VIEW OF DOWNTOWN, 1900S. Many buildings along Main Street still exist. However, the south half of the block between South Morgan and South Broadway has changed drastically. There were at least a dozen buildings crowded into the current locations of the Shelby County State Bank and the Shelbyville Mutual Insurance Company.

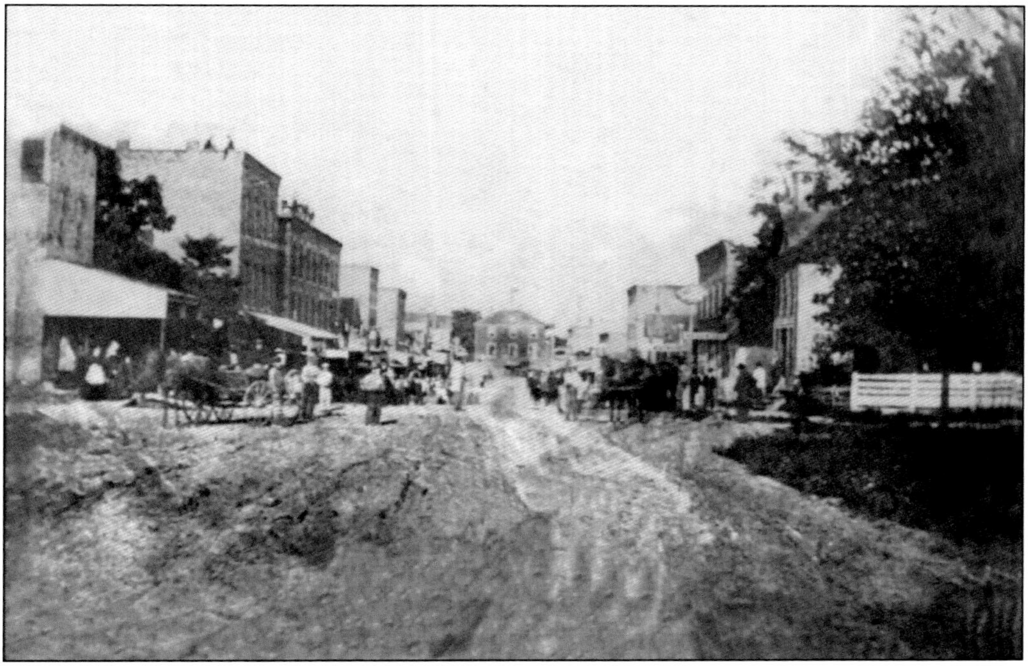

MAIN STREET, 1867. This view looks east down Main Street. Nearly in the middle of the street is the second courthouse. The occasion for the photograph was the partial solar eclipse on May 24, 1867. Historically, this was the largest partial eclipse.

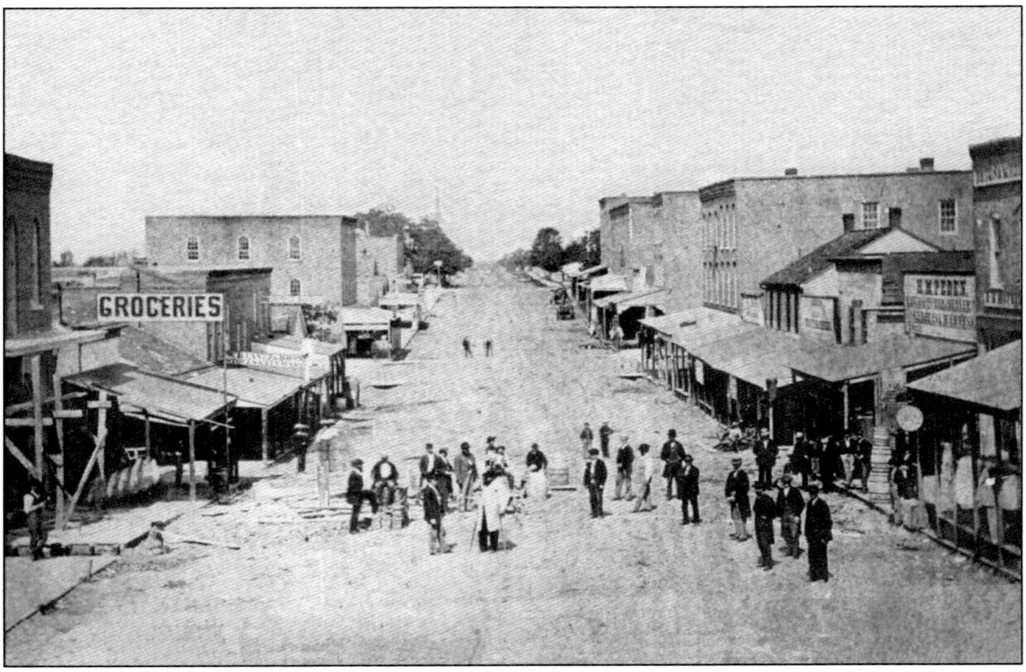

MAIN STREET, 1860S. This view is looking west down Main Street. Something is going on in the middle of the street. The barrels and stacks of material do not give much of a clue. One of the signs reads, "W. B. Lantz Furniture, tinware, and coffins."

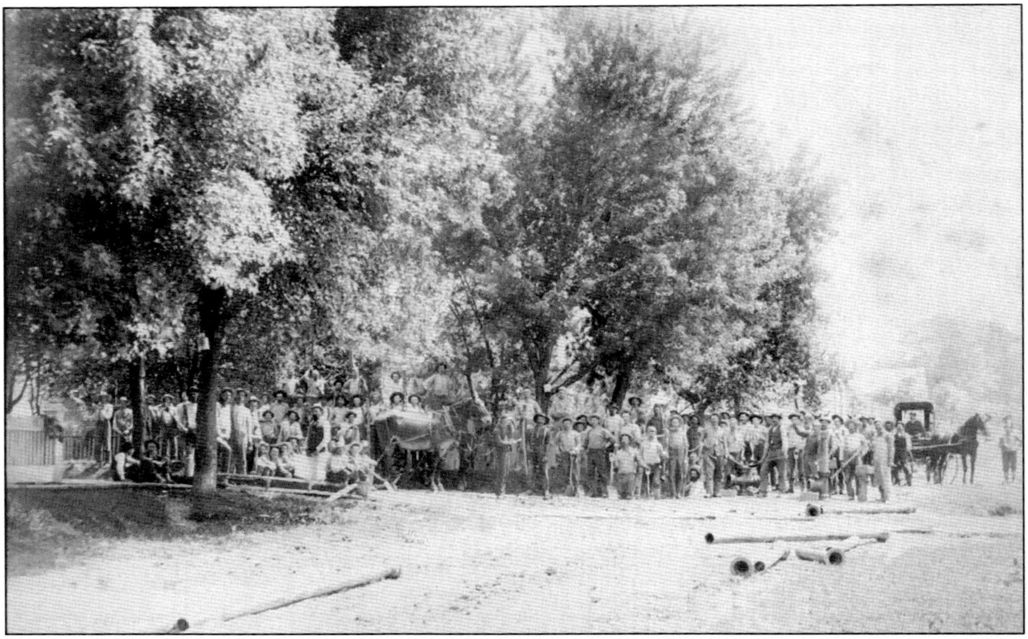

Laying Water Lines in Shelbyville. The work crew poses on West North Third Street at "Aulds Corner," for a photograph taken prior to 1886. The Auld family purchased their home, located at 413 West North Third Street, in 1872. After 1886, six miles of water main was laid with 50 fire hydrants and four combined spray and drinking fountains.

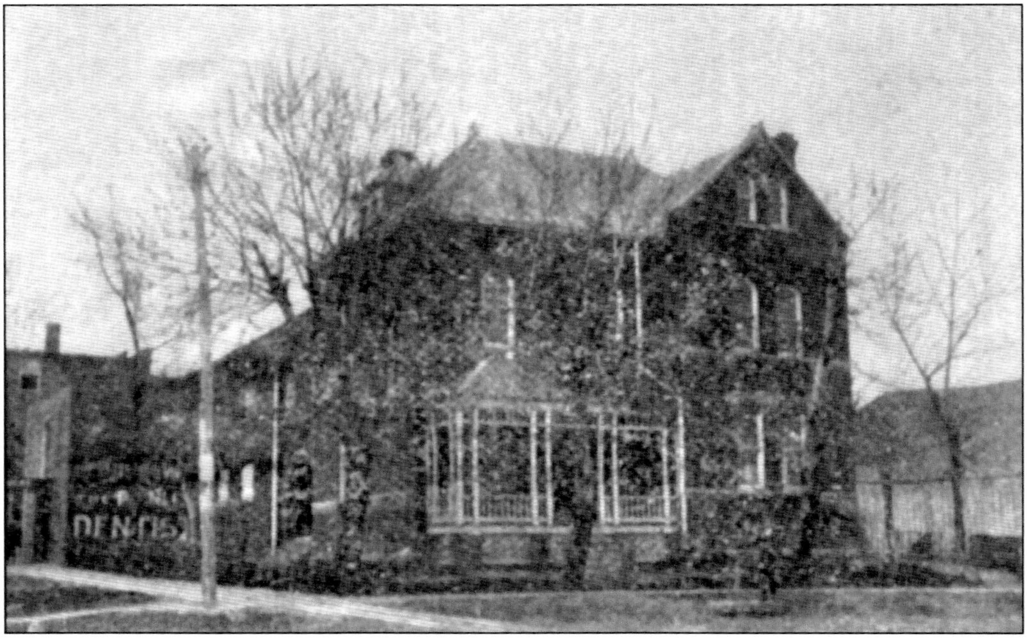

Fourth Shelby County Jail. In January 1892, the Shelby County Board approved a resolution to find a new site and build a new jail. This building cost $22,952 with an additional $850 for the steam heating. It was completed on January 4, 1893. This jail sold for $7,500 by sealed bid in October 1987 to the Shelby County Historical and Genealogical Society.

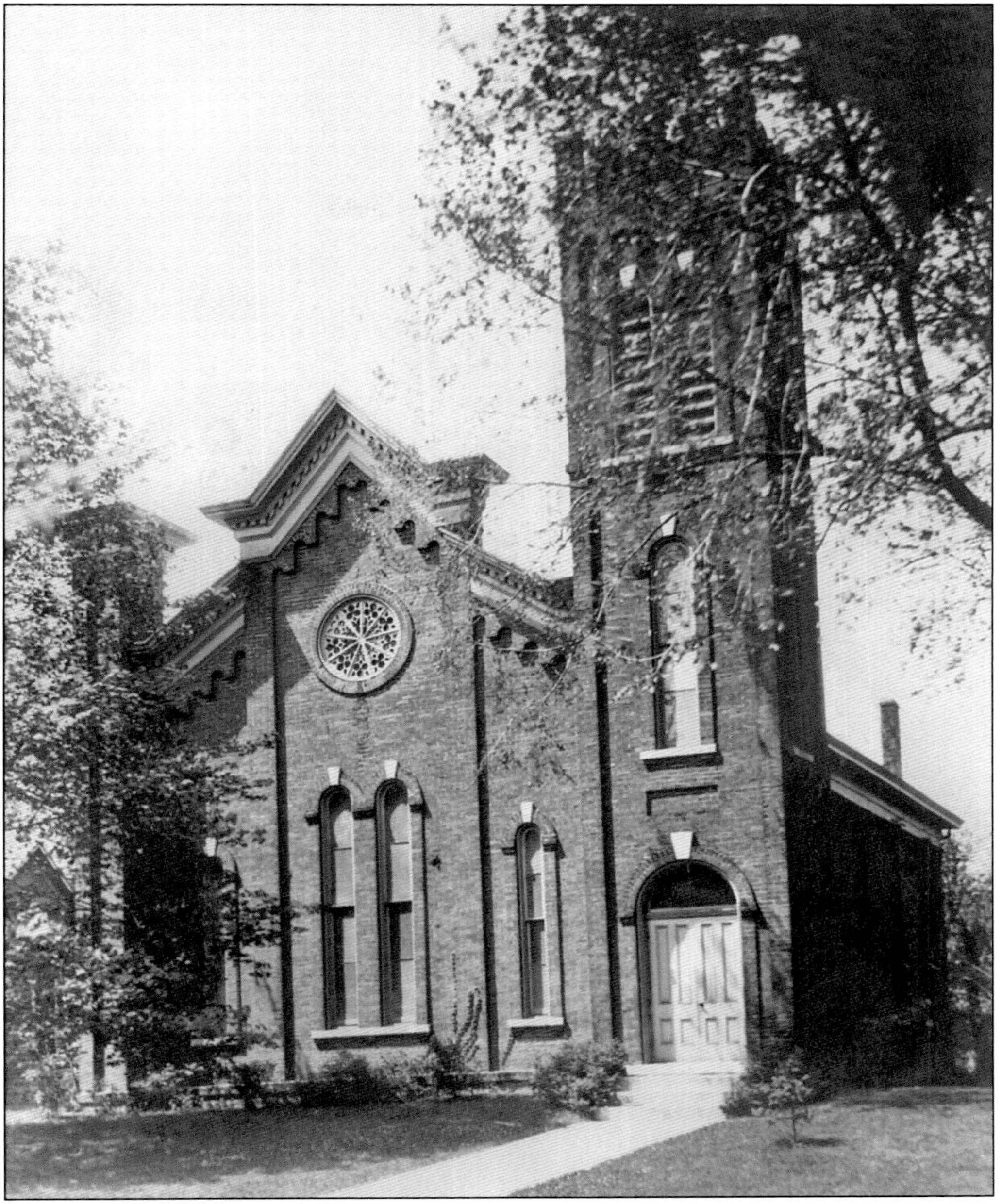

UNITARIAN CHURCH, 1876. On May 4, 1875, thirteen people met at the courthouse to form the Unitarian Church. The corner stone was laid November 21, 1875. The construction went quickly, and the church was dedicated on May 18, 1876. It was estimated to have cost $6,000. Jasper L. Douthit was the pastor. The "gingerbread" brickwork above the round window is very unique.

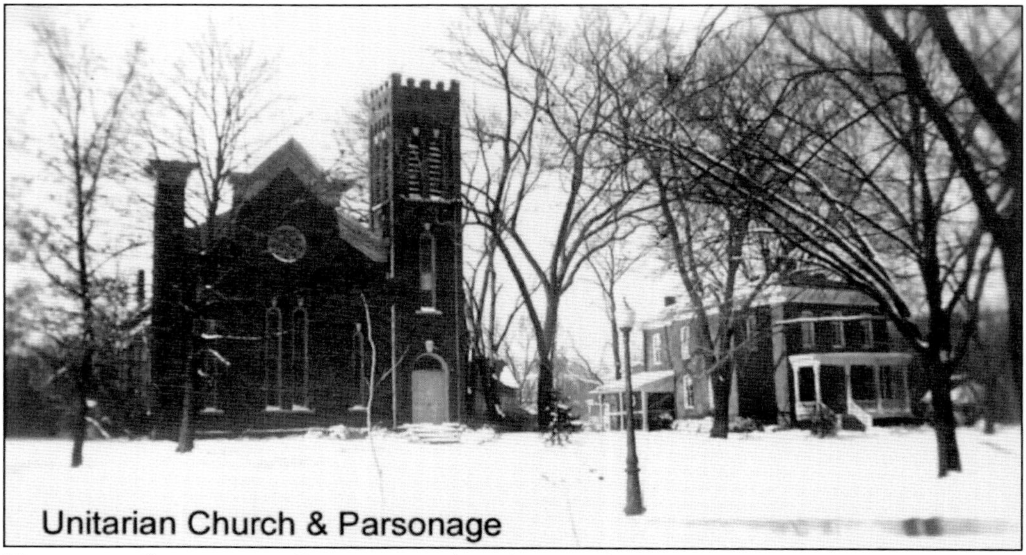

UNITARIAN CHURCH AND PARSONAGE. This photograph, taken in the 1900s, shows the large church parsonage. The Douthits entertained many guests of the church here as well as many performers from the Chautauqua at Lithia Springs. The parsonage was eventually split into an upstairs apartment and downstairs apartment.

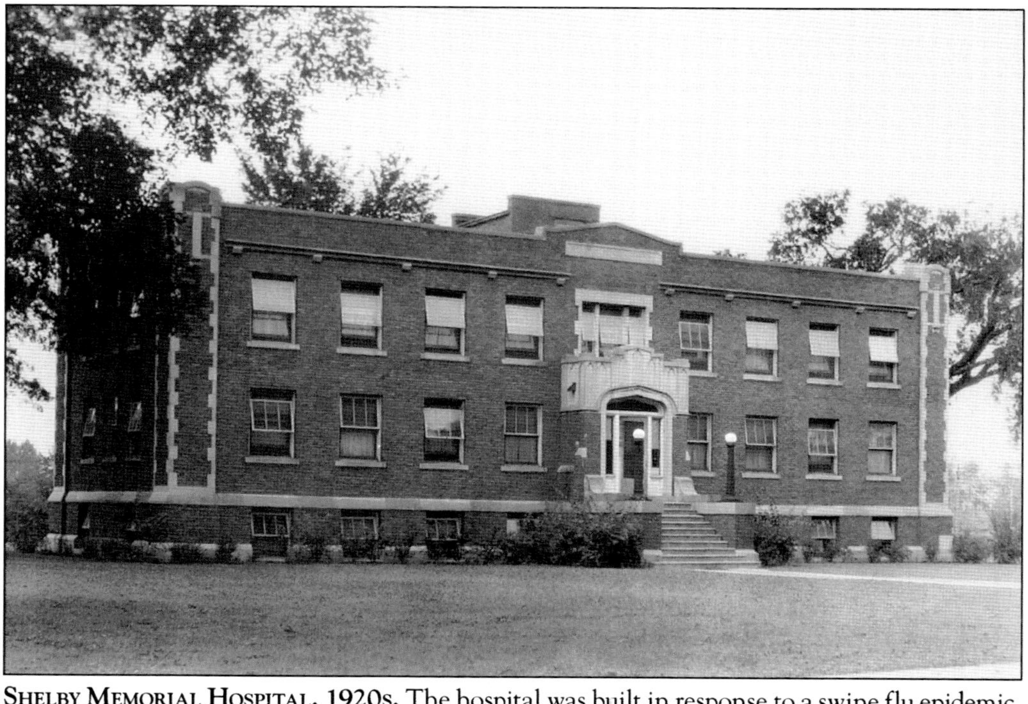

SHELBY MEMORIAL HOSPITAL, 1920S. The hospital was built in response to a swine flu epidemic. The people realized they needed a place for better medical care. In 1916 the citizens launched a five-day fund drive. Volunteers canvassed the county and raised $35,000. The building was dedicated in 1918. On August 5, O. C. Pancoast fell and became the first patient. The hospital was built on the vacated Lutheran cemetery.

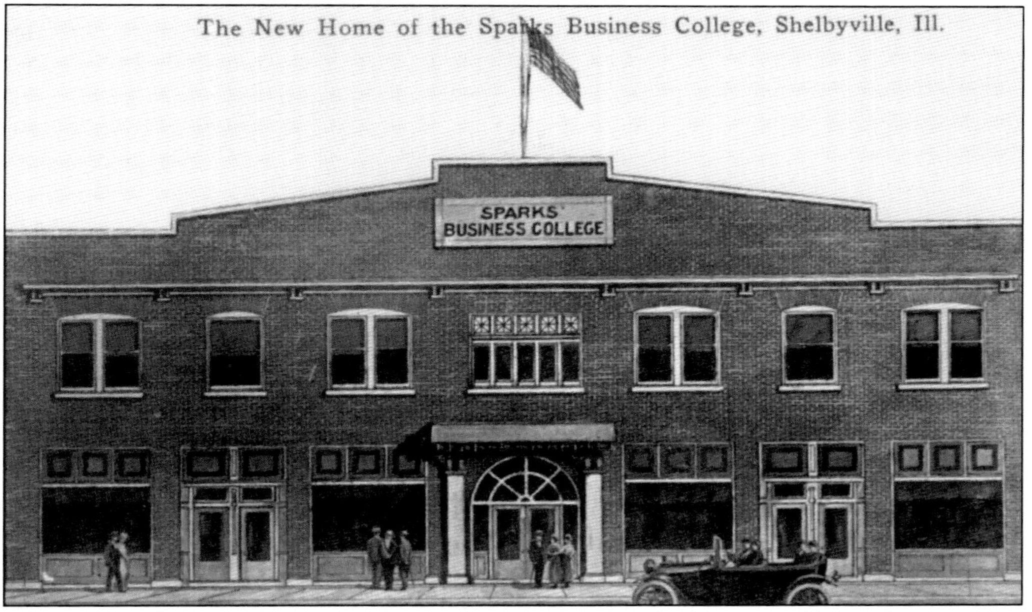

SPARKS BUSINESS COLLEGE, 1915. Henry Sparks had dreamed of opening a learning institution to train young people for business careers. In 1908 he resigned as principal of Madison High School in Indiana and relocated to Shelbyville. In the fall of 1908, thirteen students began their business educations. The college has been located on three different sites, the last from 1915 to the present.

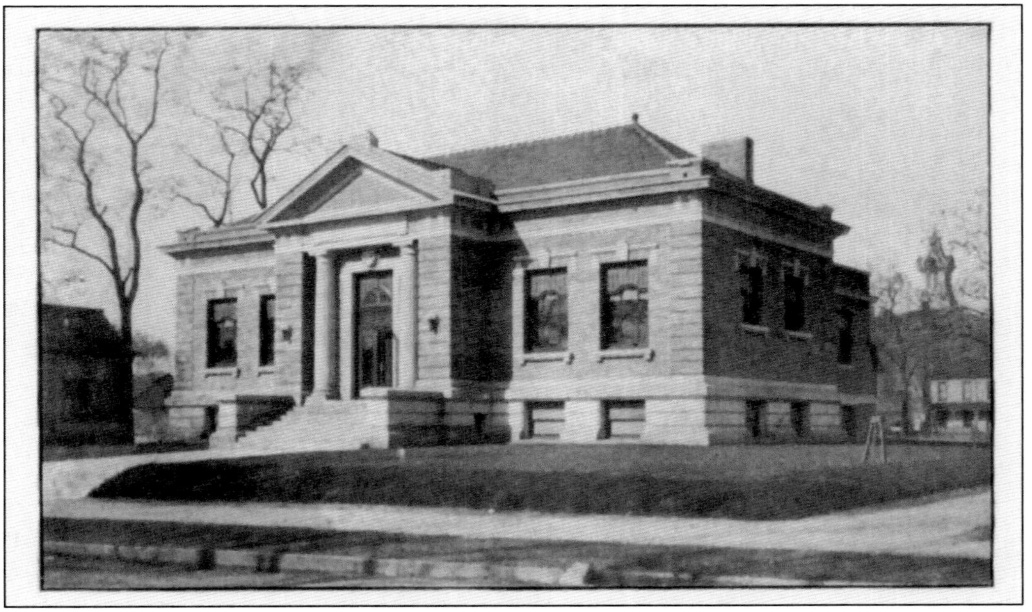

SHELBYVILLE PUBLIC LIBRARY. The Shelbyville Women's Club heard that Andrew Carnegie was giving towns money to help build libraries. They received $10,000 from Carnegie, the Board of Education donated the site, and the City of Shelbyville issued bonds and added a library tax. The dedication was held on May 3, 1905. The building is French Renaissance style with golden Roman brick and bedford sandstone.

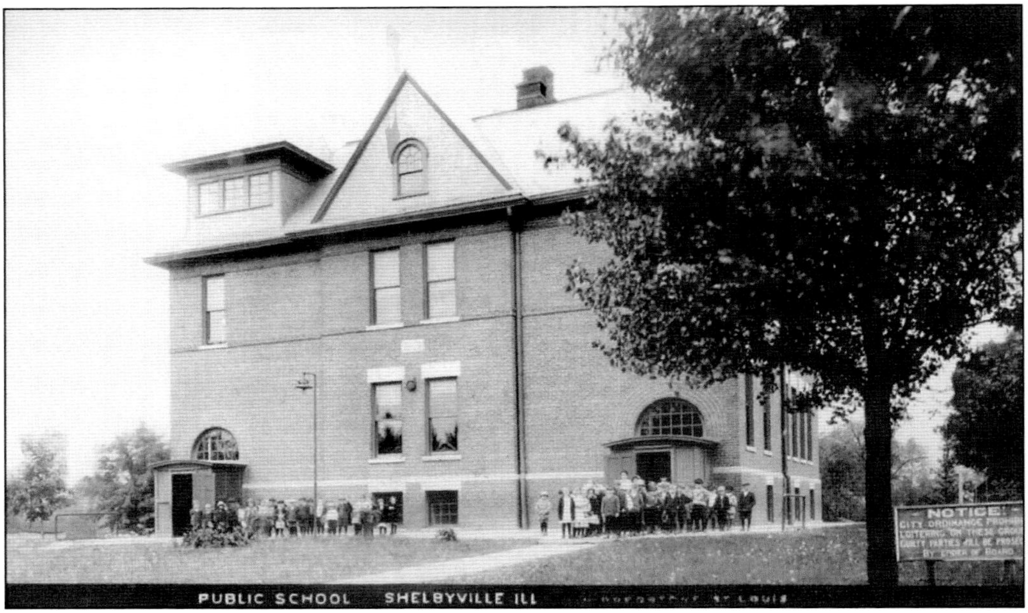

VINE STREET SCHOOL, 1900. Daniel and Cassandree Blackstone sold the lot their home was on to the City of Shelbyville for the school. Their house was moved by horses to 611 West South Second. The school was built in 1900 but was not open for students until September 1900. It was torn down after closing in 1990.

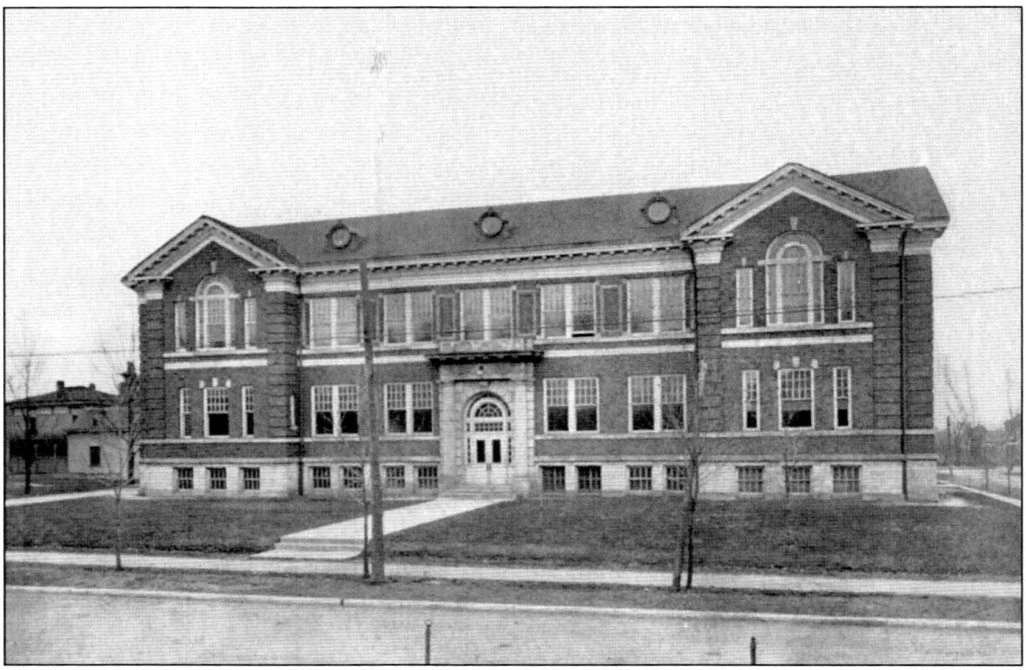

OLD SHELBYVILLE HIGH SCHOOL. On September 18, 1911, the old Shelbyville High School opened its doors. In 1957 it became the junior high school and was torn down in 1961. It was located just west of the library in what is now Leach-Wilson's car lot. The girls first wore caps and gowns in the graduating class of 1920.

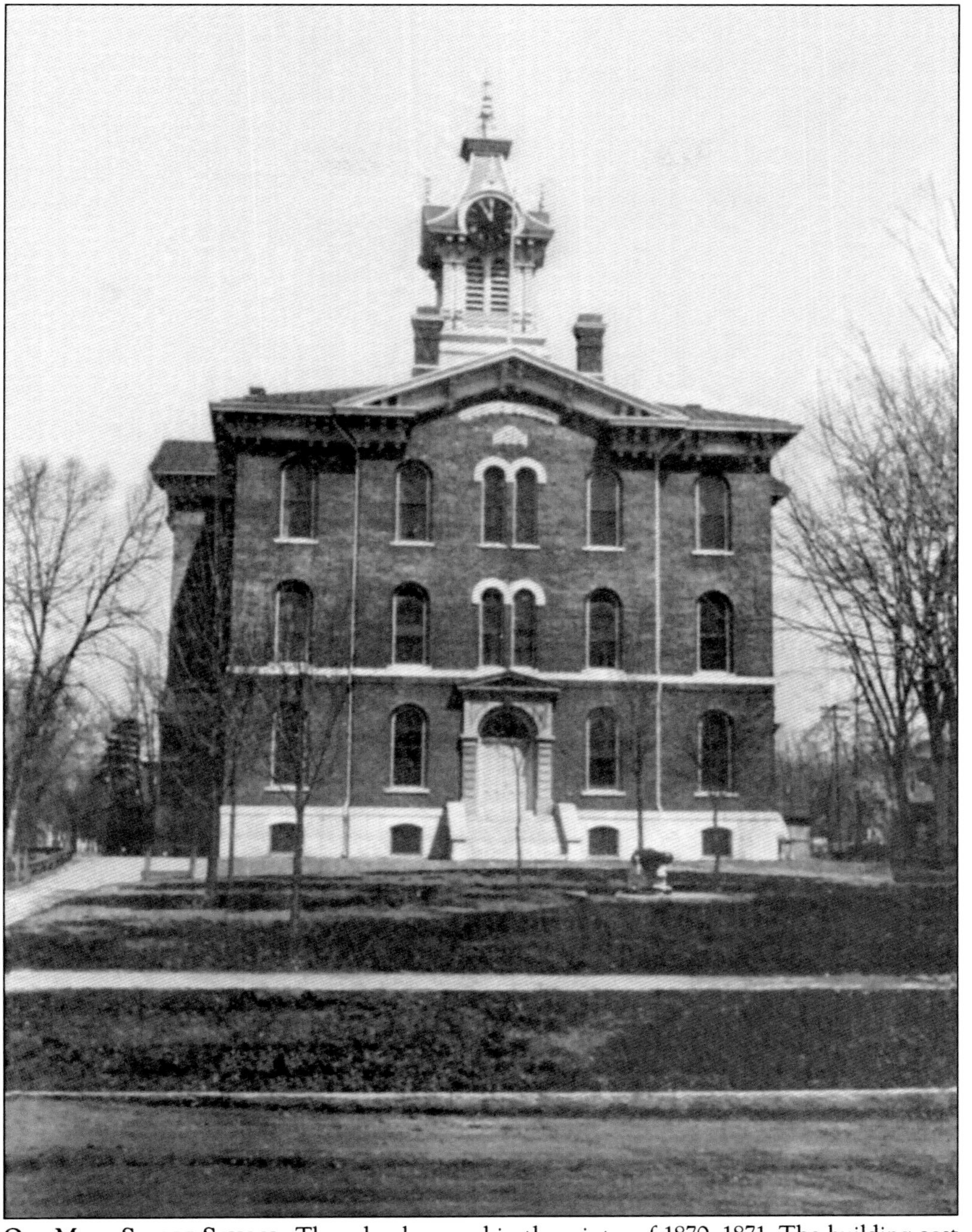

OLD MAIN STREET SCHOOL. The school opened in the winter of 1870–1871. The building cost $50,000. The new building could not accommodate all the children who arrived for school. The first superintendant, Jeptha Hobbs, reported 555 students. The school was torn down in 1925 to make way for the new school. It is located a little northwest of the old school. The clock was moved to the courthouse.

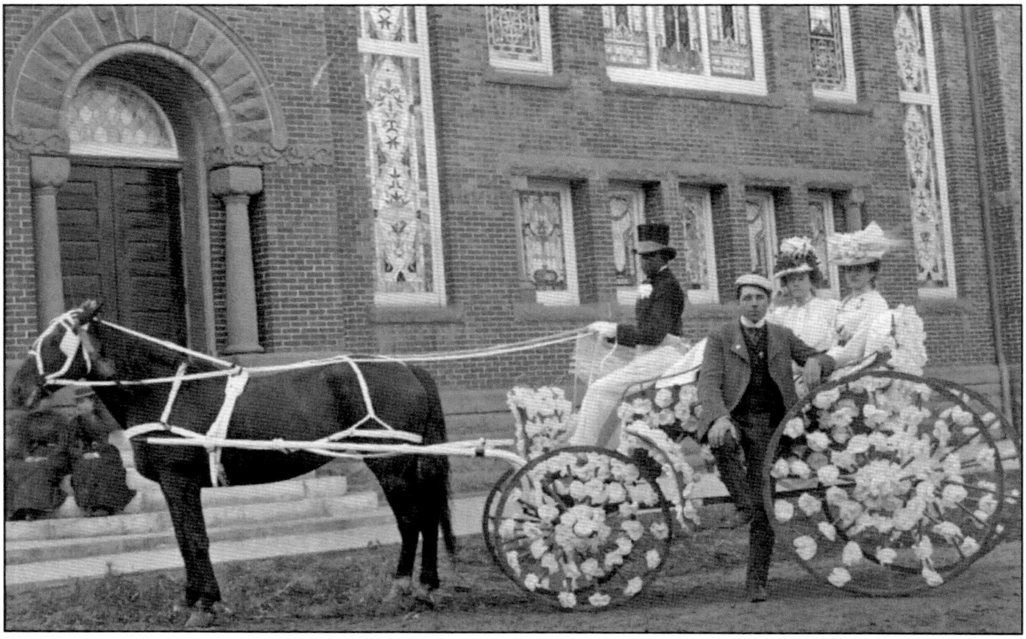

Decorated Carriage. Harry Baum, Mabel and Juanita Roberts, and coachman Jim Lee pose for a photograph in front of the First United Methodist Church. The occasion for the photograph is unknown but the white harness and flowers on the wheel spokes are dramatic. The streets are not bricked, which probably dates the occasion around 1900.

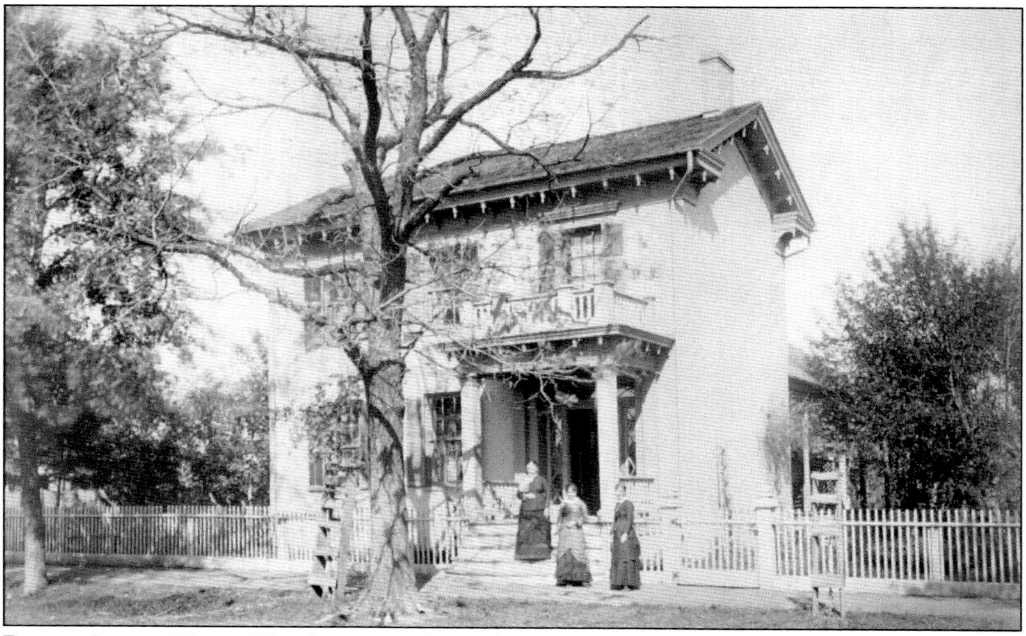

Phillip Lantz Home. This home was located at 215 West South First Street. The photograph must have been taken in the 1880s as Phillip had already died and passed the business on to his sons. The business began in 1855 with tinware and coppersmithing. Phillip also sold furniture when it was added to the store in 1868.

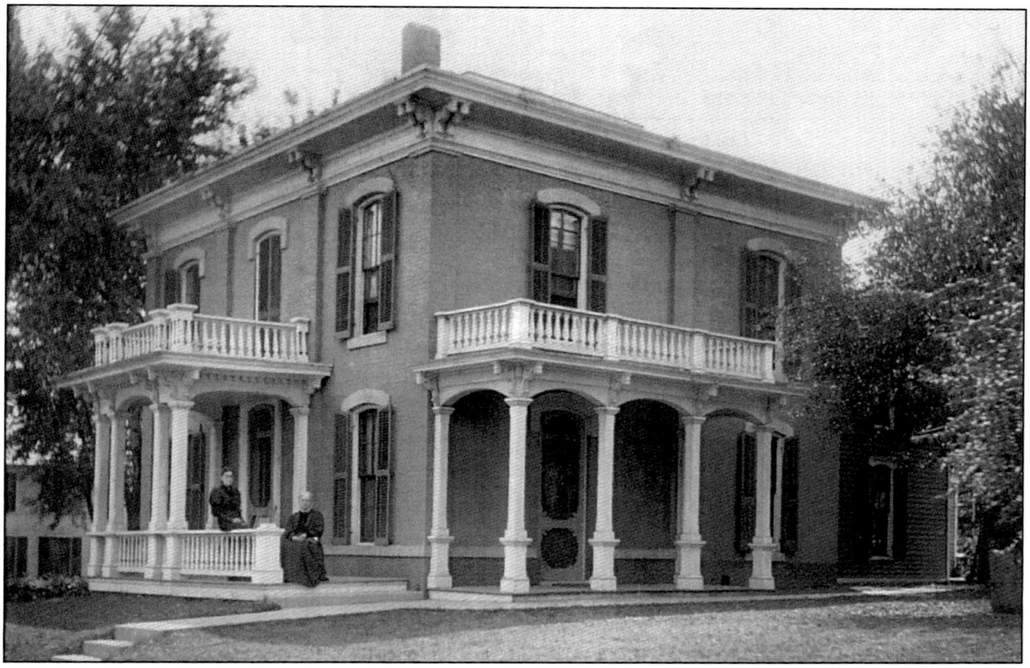

Enos Penwell Home. The Penwell house is located at 208 South Broadway. Dr. Penwell went to Indiana Medical College and then moved to Shelbyville to practice medicine in 1853. He practiced for almost 50 years, and the house also served as his office.

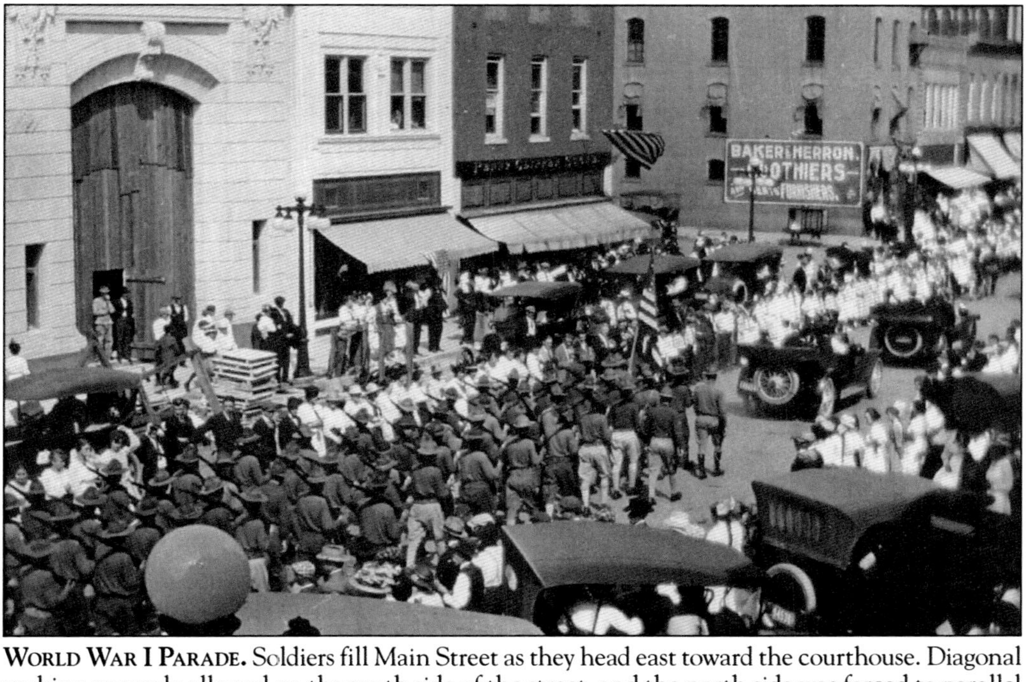

World War I Parade. Soldiers fill Main Street as they head east toward the courthouse. Diagonal parking was only allowed on the south side of the street, and the north side was forced to parallel park. The boarded-up Shelby County State Bank building was a result of the 1916 New Years Eve fire. Company H is returning home from France.

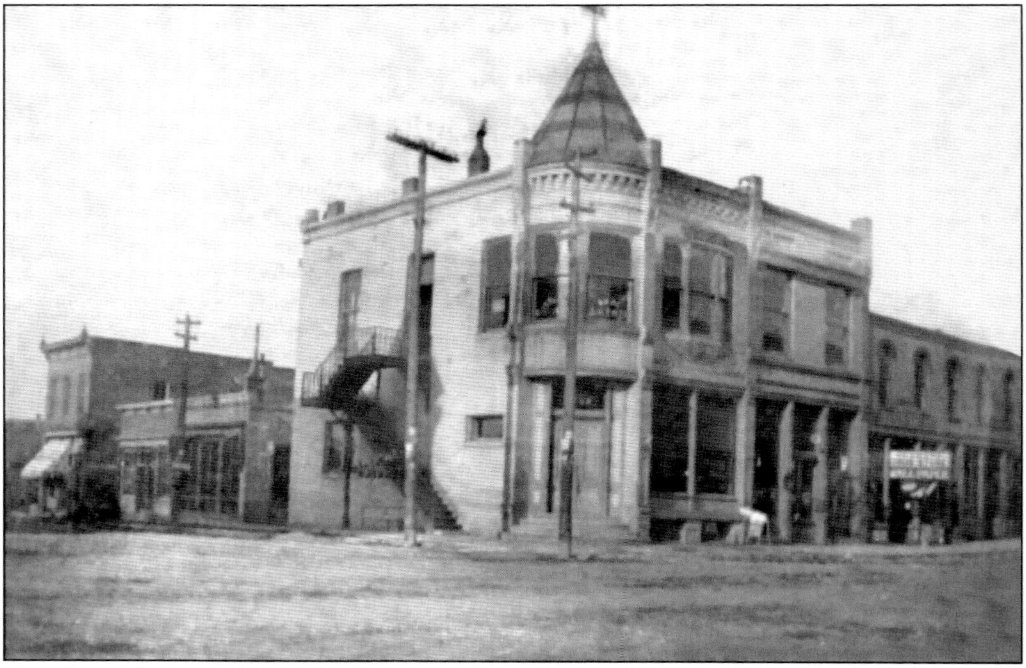

Old First National Bank. William Middlesworth founded the bank, located at the corner of Morgan and East Main Streets on the site of an old sawmill, in 1873. Pictured is the new brick building in 1916 that replaced an old frame structure. The Shelby Loan and Trust Company moved into the building and merged with the bank to form Shelby Loan and Trust.

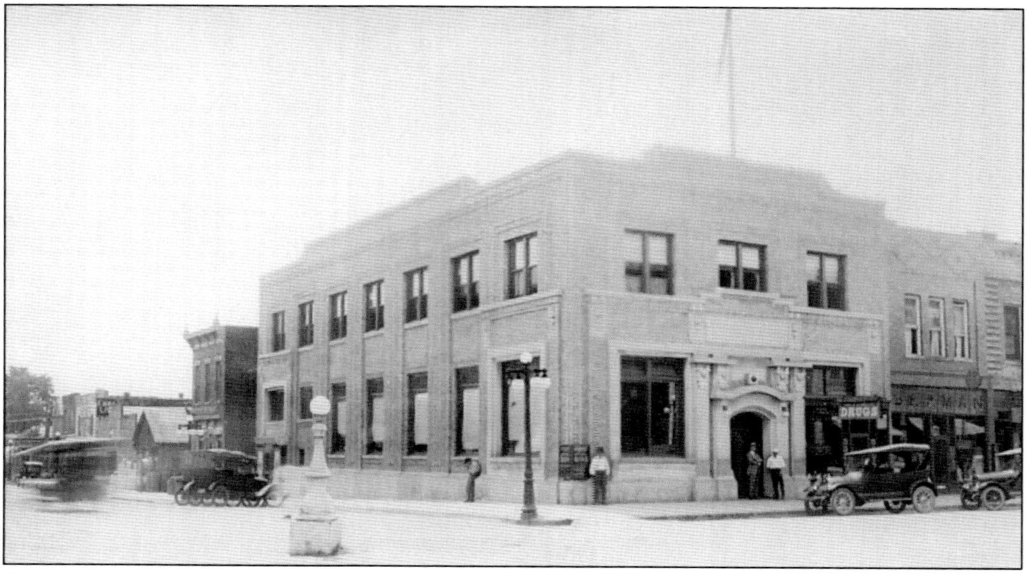

Shelby Loan and Trust. This photograph shows the expanded and remodeled building. The building behind the bank in the top photograph was torn down for the Shelby Loan and Trust expansion. When further expansion was no longer an option, a new building was built at 200 West Main Street. The old building is currently the Shelbyville City Hall.

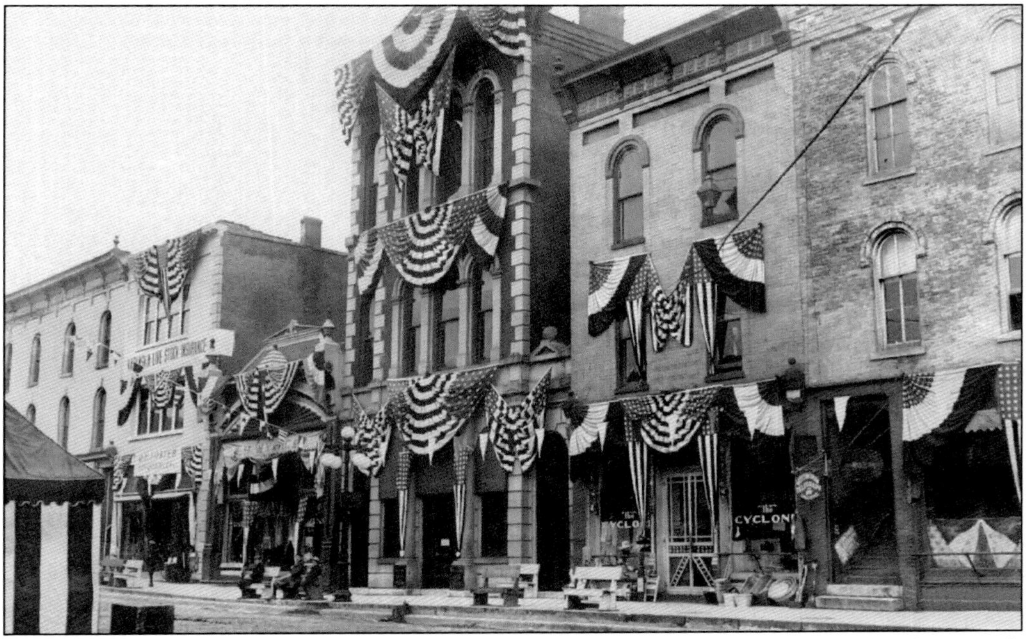

OLD SHELBY COUNTY STATE BANK. The town is ready for a carnival as pictured in this photograph taken before 1917. The State Bank is the tallest building in the photograph. The oldest bank in Shelby County opened on May 11, 1895. This first bank building was occupied by the W. F. Thornton and Son Bank that closed after the grain depression.

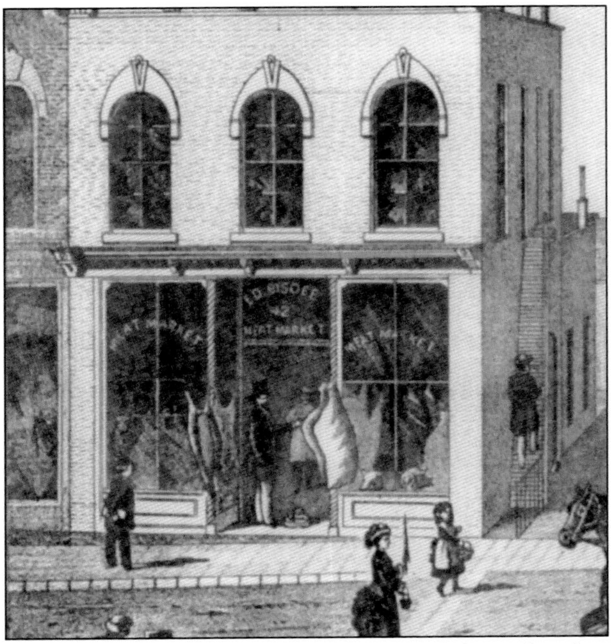

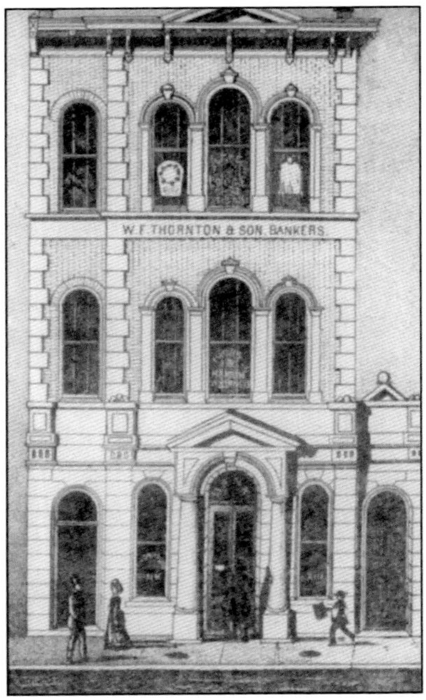

BISDEE'S MEAT AND THORNTON BANK. These sketches show two prominent businesses. The Thornton Bank opened in 1876 and closed in the 1890s. A lawyer's office and lodge occupied the upper two stories. The Bisdee brothers from England moved to Shelbyville in 1867 and opened a butcher shop.

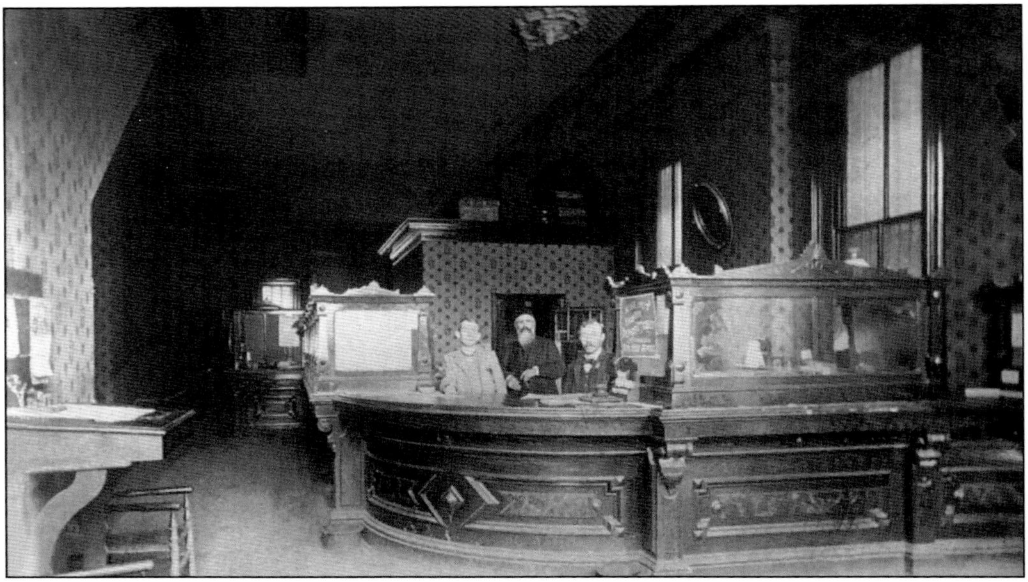

Inside Thornton Bank. In 1859, Gen. W. F. Thornton established a bank located on the square. In 1876, the bank moved to the north side of Main Street. The first "greenbacks" brought to Shelbyville came to this bank in 1887. Greenbacks were the first paper money issued from 1862–1971, the bill size was much larger before 1929. Seventy-five-thousand dollars worth of greenbacks came off the train in Moulton and were hidden in a sack of oats for "safe" transport to the bank.

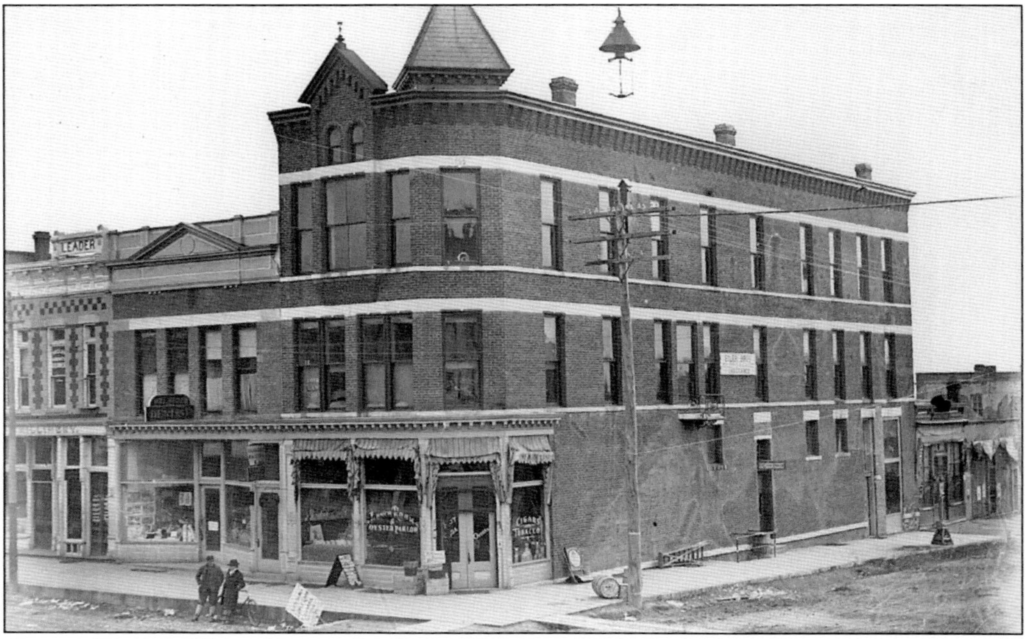

Oyster Parlor. This photograph along Main Street is from the late 1800s. *The Leader* was a newspaper that began in 1863 and occupied the top floor. The Lunchroom and Oyster Parlor on the corner also sold cigars, tobacco, and "hot soda." During the winter, soda fountains offered hot versions of summer drinks to attract customers. In the late 1800s, there was a national Oyster craze. Oyster bars opened all across the country, but it died out after 1900.

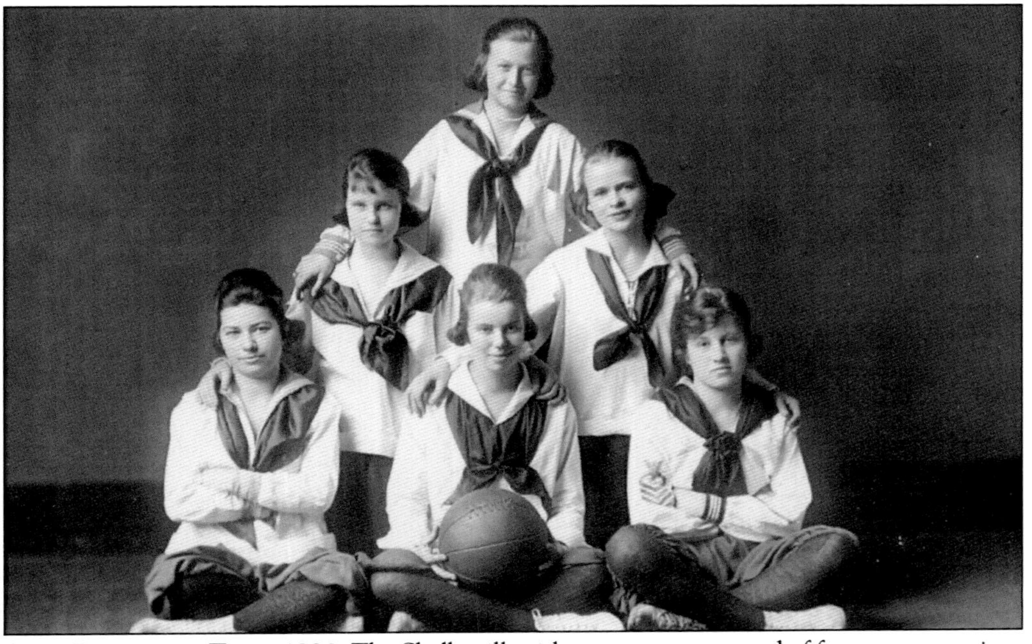

GIRLS BASKETBALL TEAM, 1920. The Shelbyville girls team was composed of four groups: seniors, freshman, reds, and blues. The group shown here are the seniors. The girls are, from left to right, (first row) Florence Gallagher, Helen Seaman, and Mildred Lamb; (second row) Zula Beem and Pearl Pate; (third row) Mabel Miller. The girls' uniforms are very different from the styles worn today.

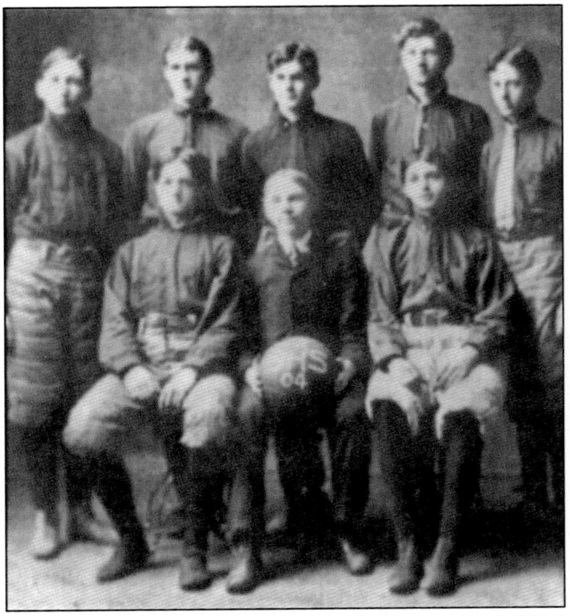

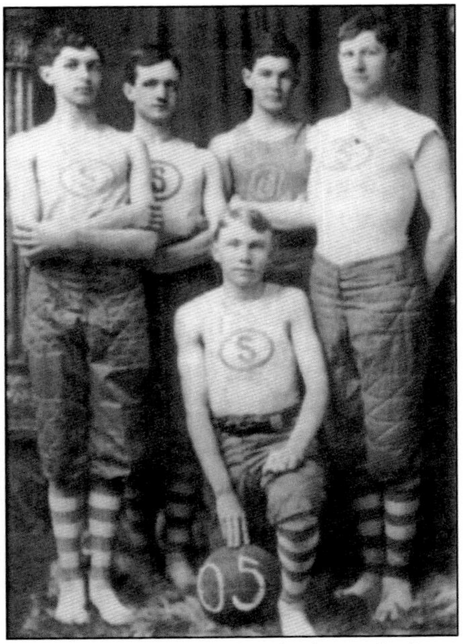

SHELBYVILLE'S FIRST BASKETBALL TEAM, 1904. With the approval of the school, the eight boys on the left became the first high school basketball team. They bought their own uniforms, which were blue flannel shirts, Spaulding pants, and black stockings. They hired a coach, paid for equipment, and rented the armory to practice. The 1905 team on the right changed their uniforms to "athletic" shirts and purple and white stockings.

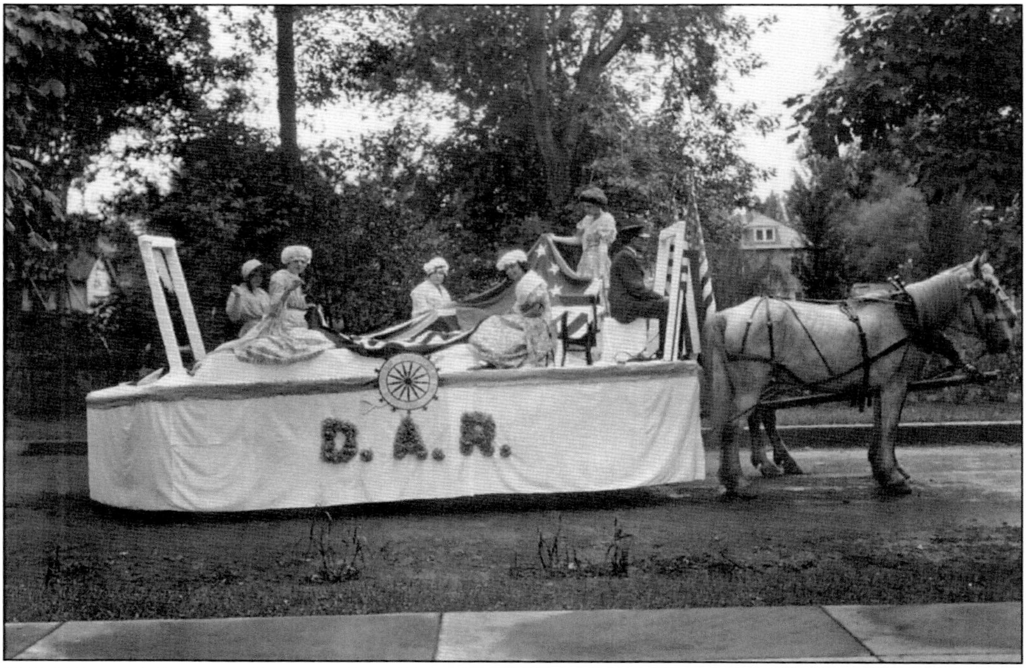

DAR FLOAT WINNER. Organized in 1922, the Kuilka Chapter of the Daughters of the American Revolution entered their float in the Defense Day Parade in September 1924. The historical event commemorated Betsy Ross and her companions, who constructed the first flag. The float won first place.

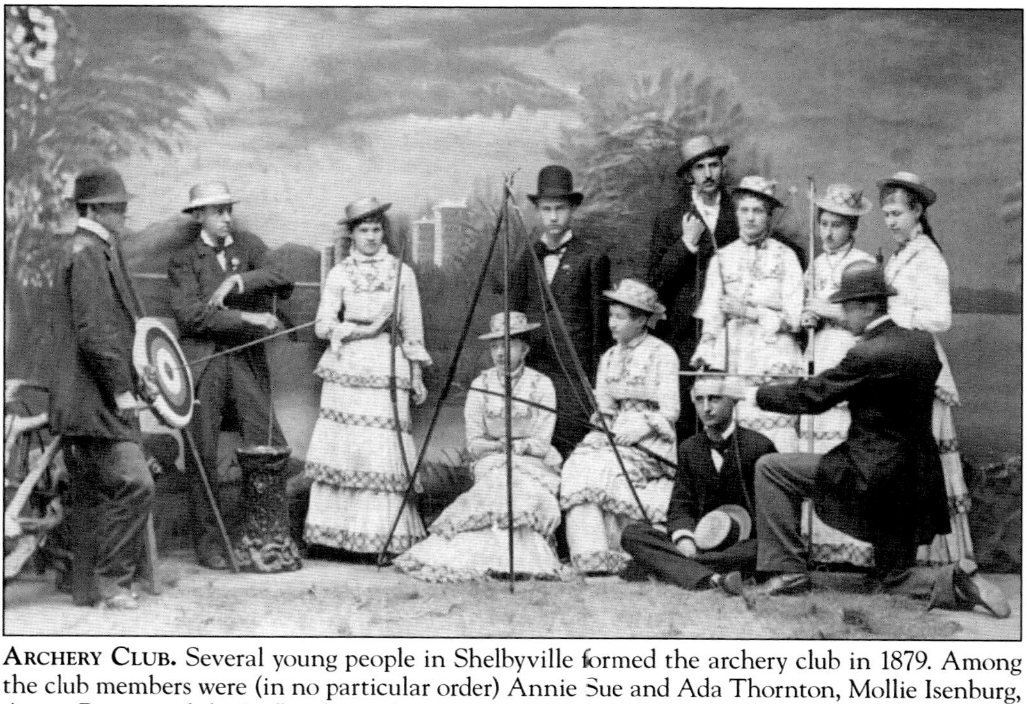

ARCHERY CLUB. Several young people in Shelbyville formed the archery club in 1879. Among the club members were (in no particular order) Annie Sue and Ada Thornton, Mollie Isenburg, Annie Basye, and the Lufkin boys who were relatives of the Chaffees.

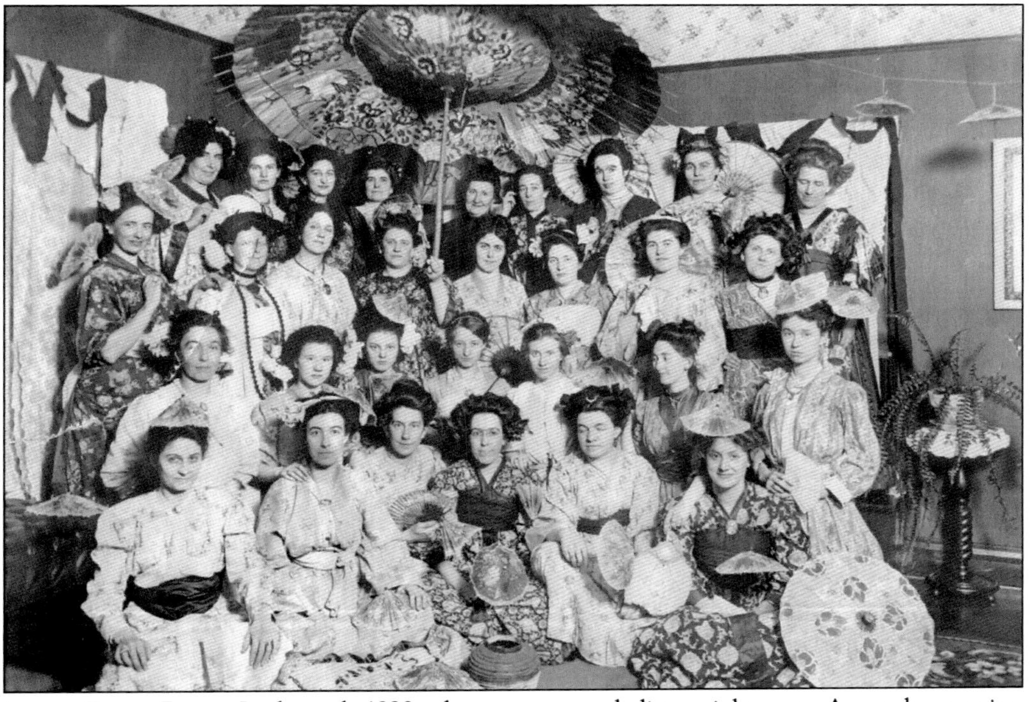

LADIES THEME PARTY. In the early 1920s, there were many ladies social groups. A popular meeting theme was to come in costume and be photographed. This meeting had a Japanese theme.

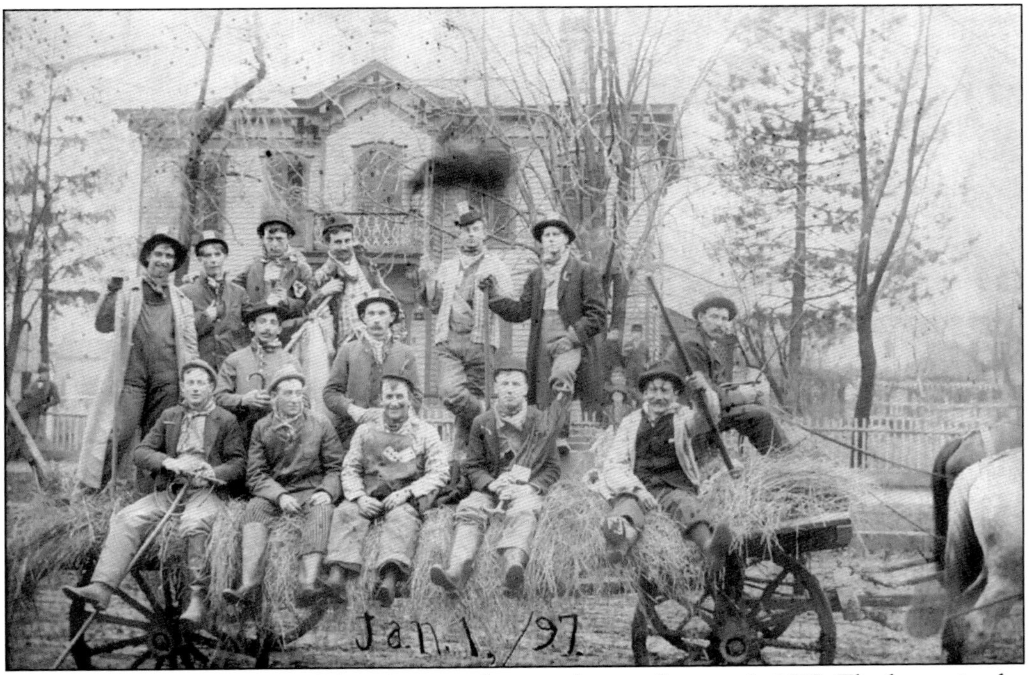

MEN WITH PLAYING CARDS. This photograph was taken on January 1, 1897. The house in the background is 814 North Broadway. It was identified as the former A. L. Ward home. The occasion is unknown, but the entertainment was card games.

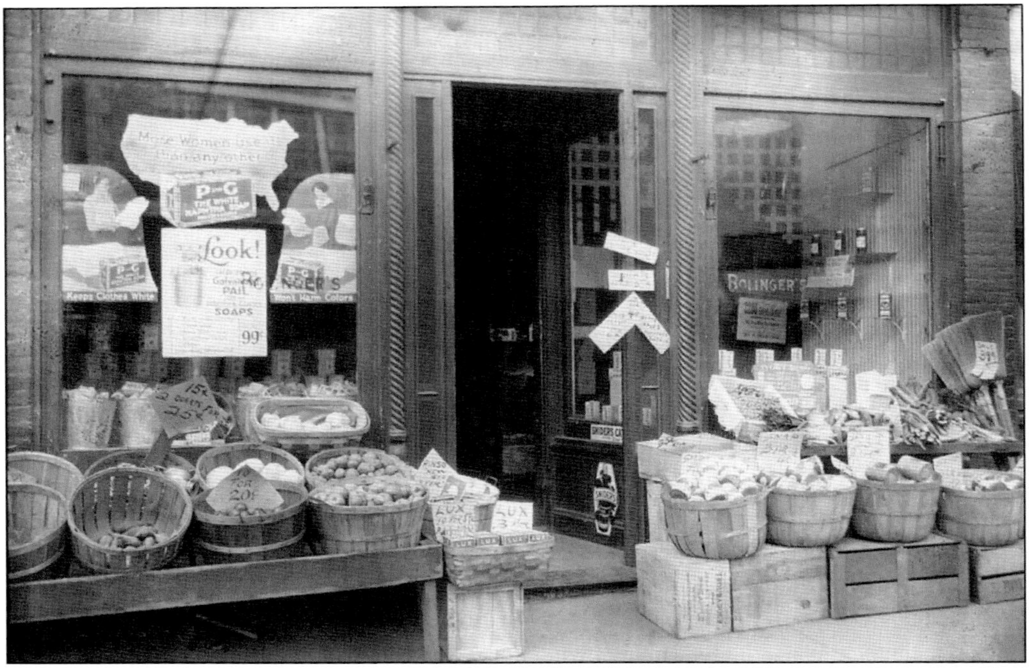

Bolingers Stores. George Bolinger moved to Shelbyville in 1885 and entered into partnership with F. J. Fraker in a general merchandise store. In 1888, Bolinger and his four sons opened a dry goods and clothing store. By the 1900s the Bolingers operated four stores on Main Street. One was the grocery store pictured in the top photograph, which was managed by Frank Bolinger. Another one of the stores is pictured in the bottom photograph. It carried carpets, cloaks, and ladies suits. The other two stores sold clothing and dry goods.

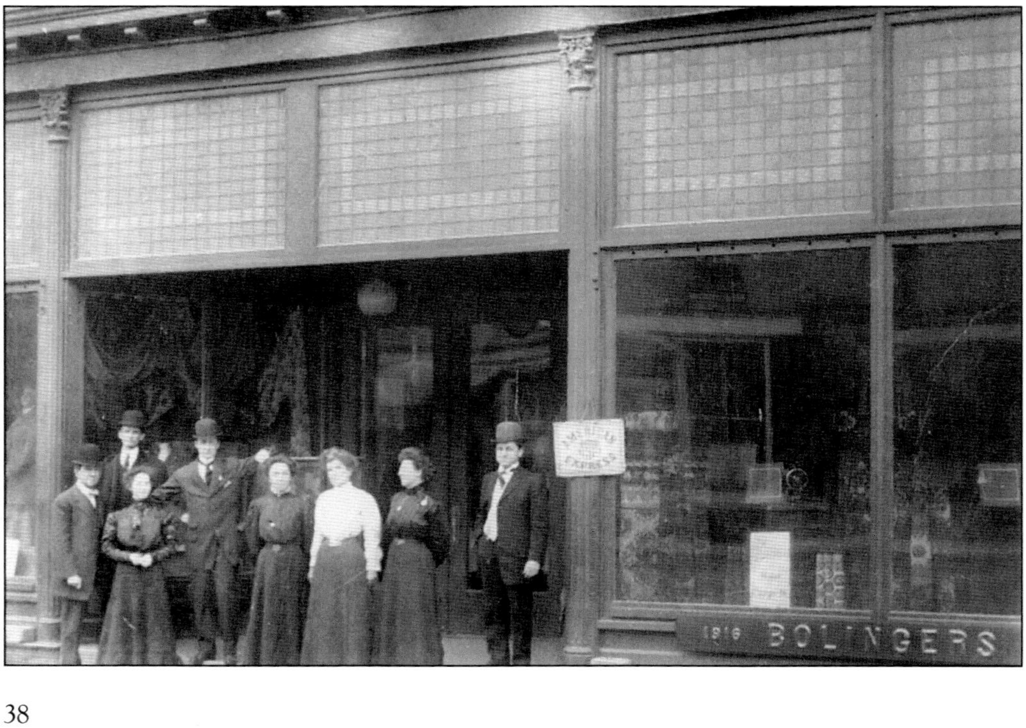

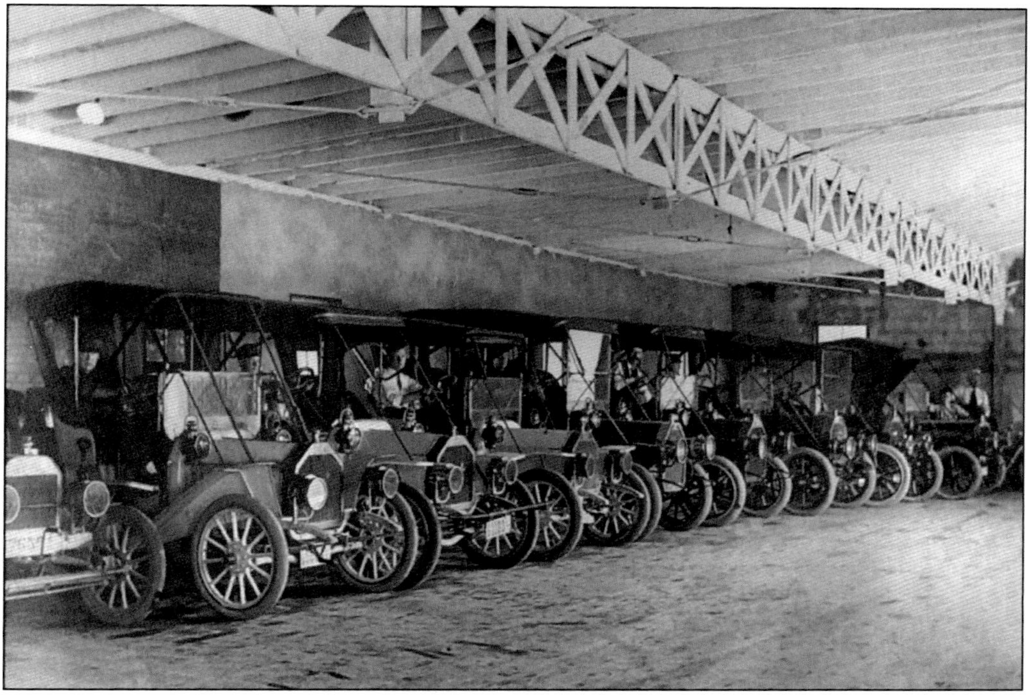

Buicks on Display. The Tallman brothers owned a Buick garage that was located east of the old C&EI Depot. The photograph was taken around 1910.

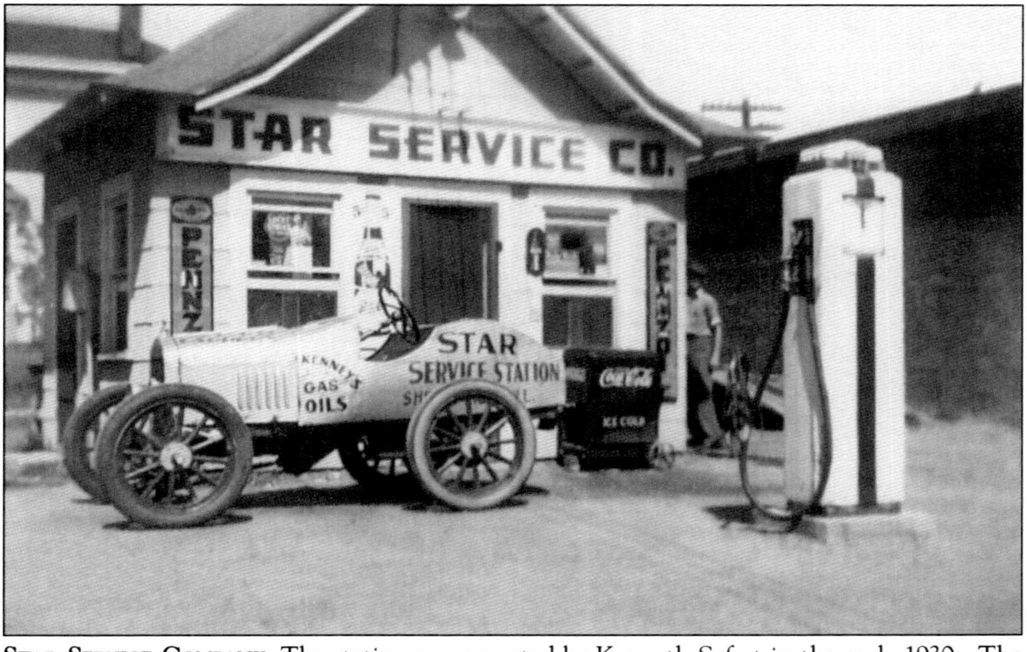

Star Service Company. The station was operated by Kenneth Syfert in the early 1930s. The station, along with a large warehouse to the north, was demolished to make way for the new post office. The post office was built in 1940. The service station would have been located where the post office workers park, south of the building.

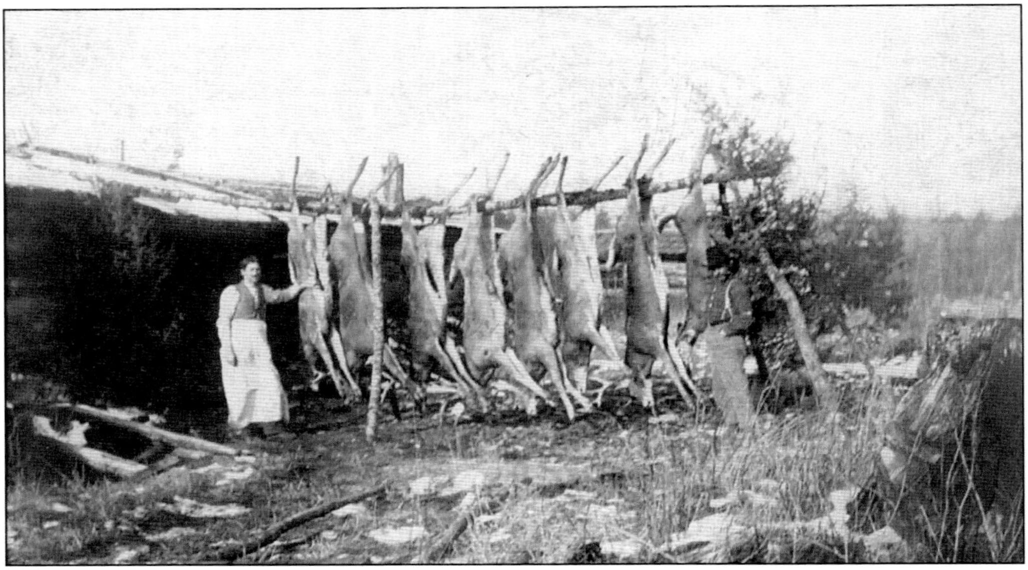

Butchering Deer. Pictured is John Sturgis in the 1920s. Sturgis and his brothers took over their father's implement business. Not butchers by trade, the deer probably came from a family hunt. Their father W. B. invented the walking cultivator in 1871. In 1903 he manufactured the "New Western Scoop Board" and was quite successful.

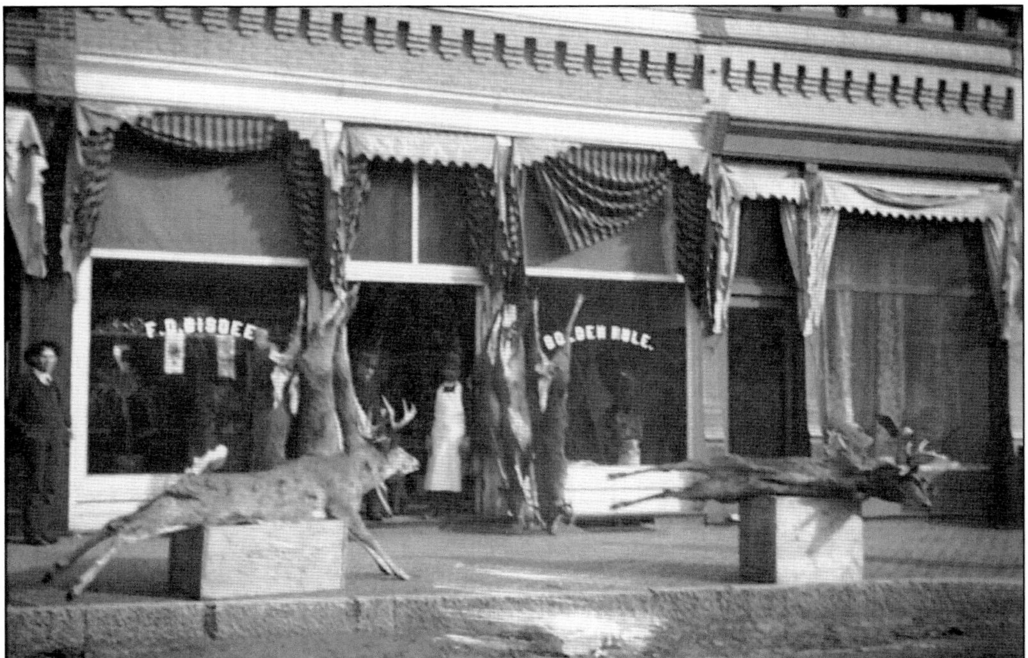

Bisdee Brothers Butchers. Edward and William moved from England to Shelbyville in 1867 and opened a meat market. It was located on the south side of Main Street. The slaughterhouse was located north of Ninth Street. Numerous deer are pictured here. They also sold bear meat for Thanksgiving and Christmas. This photograph was taken after 1907, because Frank and Charles had already taken over the business.

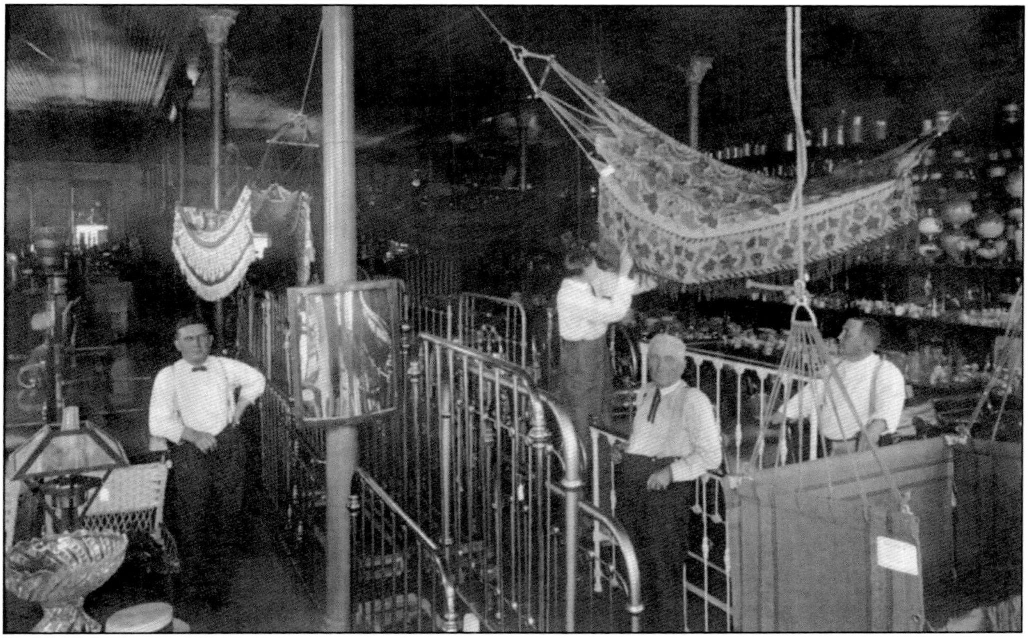

Lantz Brothers. Philip Lantz and his sons started their first business in September 1855. In 1868, undertaking was added to the business and son Isaac became the first funeral director in Shelbyville. Charles was in charge of sales, and William was the tinner and coppersmith like his father. Furniture was added in 1868. The old building in the bottom photograph was torn down for the new store in 1893. The top photograph is a view inside the store showing the variety of items that could be purchased. By 1941 the brothers were dead and their heirs closed the businesses. Fred Boettcher had become a partner in the mortuary business. They sold the mortuary business to Lockart Funeral Home, now Lockart-Green Funeral Home.

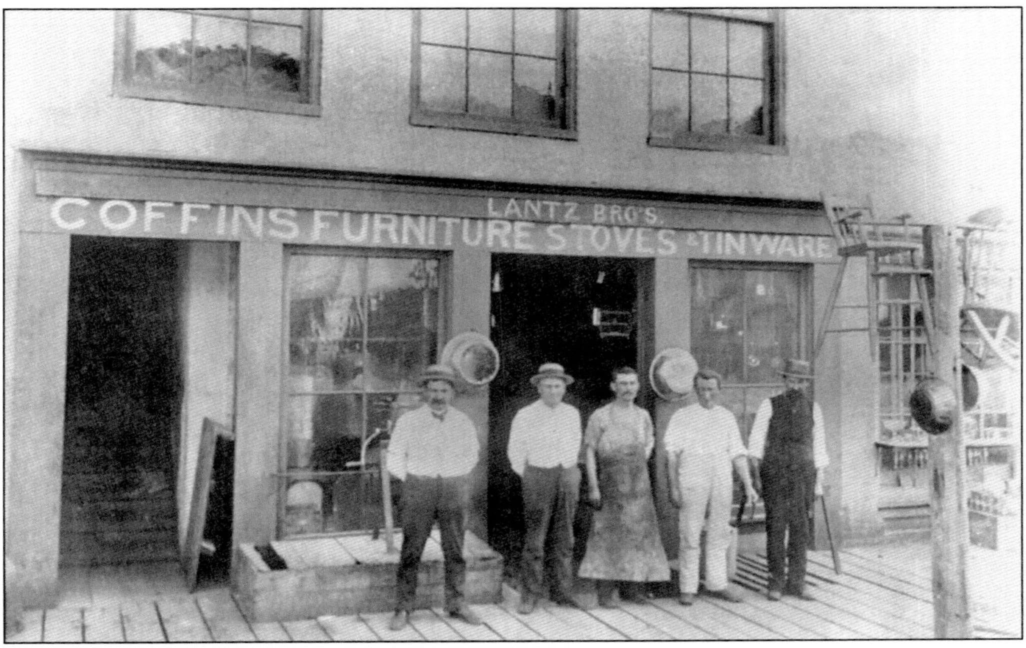

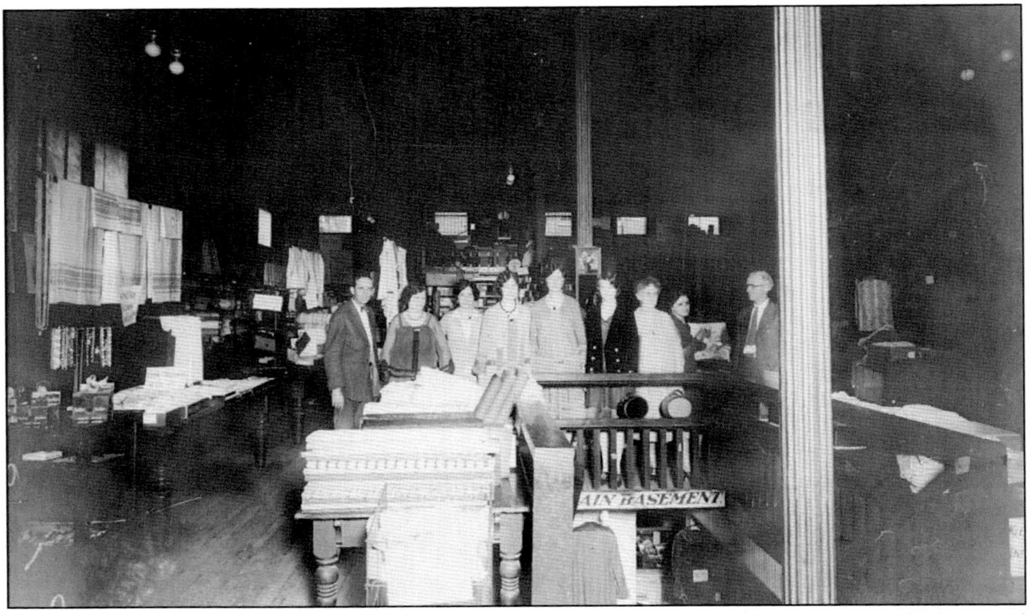

Herron's Department Store. The store was located on the northeast corner of Main and Broadway, the current location of the Shelbyville Connection. Those identified in the 1920s photograph are Raymond Syfert, Vida Seaman, Mrs. Richardson, Eva Fox, and Ed Herron. After Herron passed away in 1933, Mrs. Herron and her daughter Edna Merrill managed the store. In 1978 the building was put on the National Register of Historic Places.

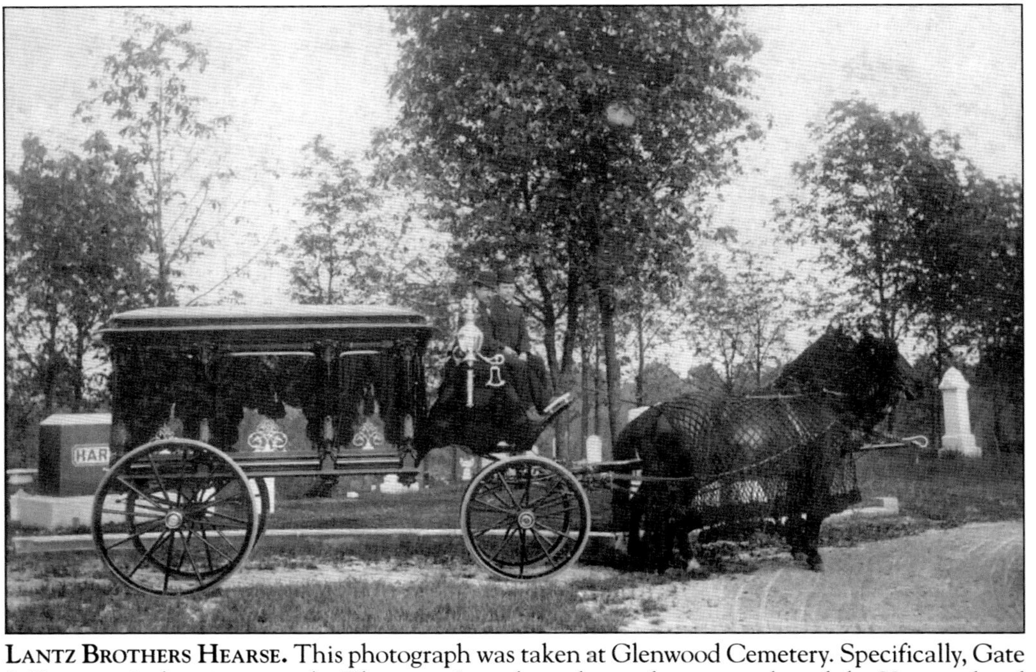

Lantz Brothers Hearse. This photograph was taken at Glenwood Cemetery. Specifically, Gate 3, Division 4, then just past the Thornton Lot where the road turns south and the Harwood and Coplin stones can currently be seen on the east side of the drive. Please note the fine decorations on the hearse and the fly nets on the horses.

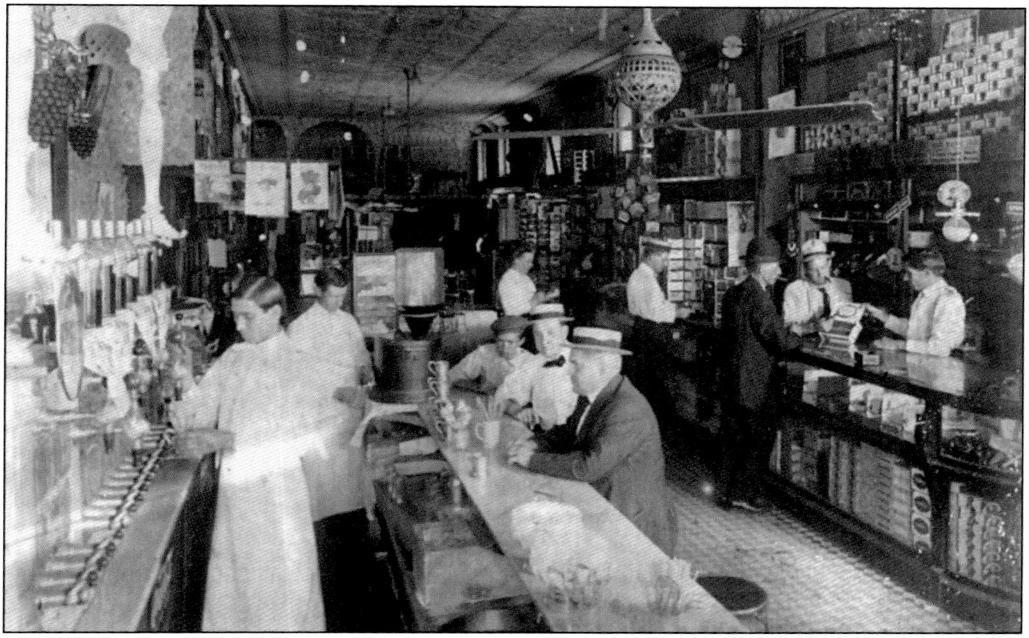

Interior Beetle's Confectionery. In 1901 Charles Beetle was operating a book and stationery store. His stock included Eastman Kodak cameras and supplies, Victor and Edison talking machines, postcards, periodicals, sporting goods, and papers. Later a soda fountain was added and was quite popular.

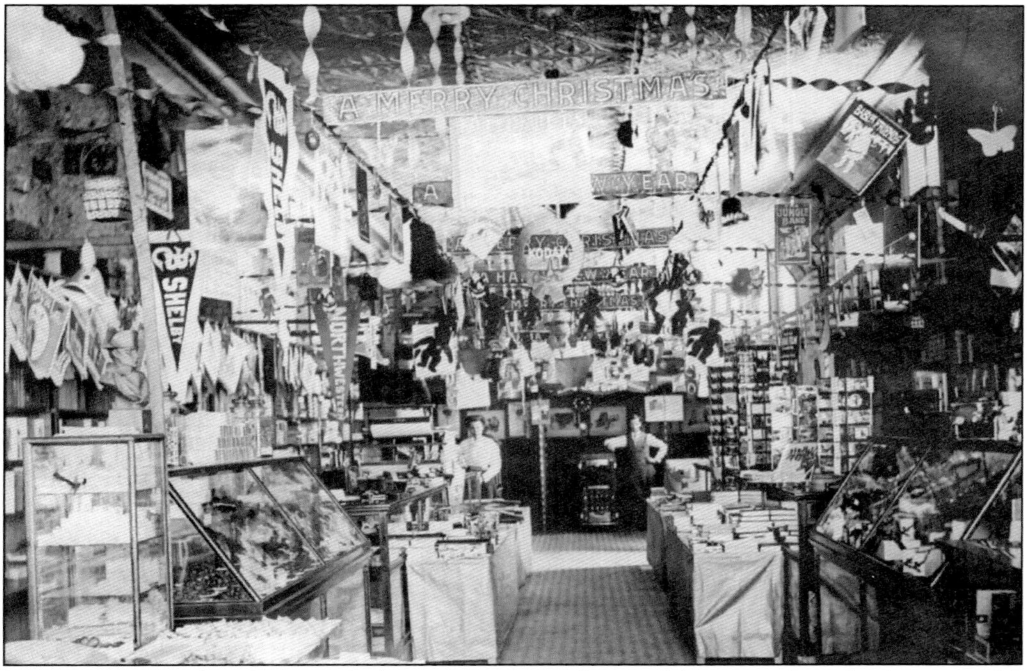

Beetles, 1908. This photograph shows an interior of part of the store where books were sold. Banners for Christmas and New Years are shown in abundance. Tables of books, racks of postcards, and lots of flags are some of the numerous articles for sale.

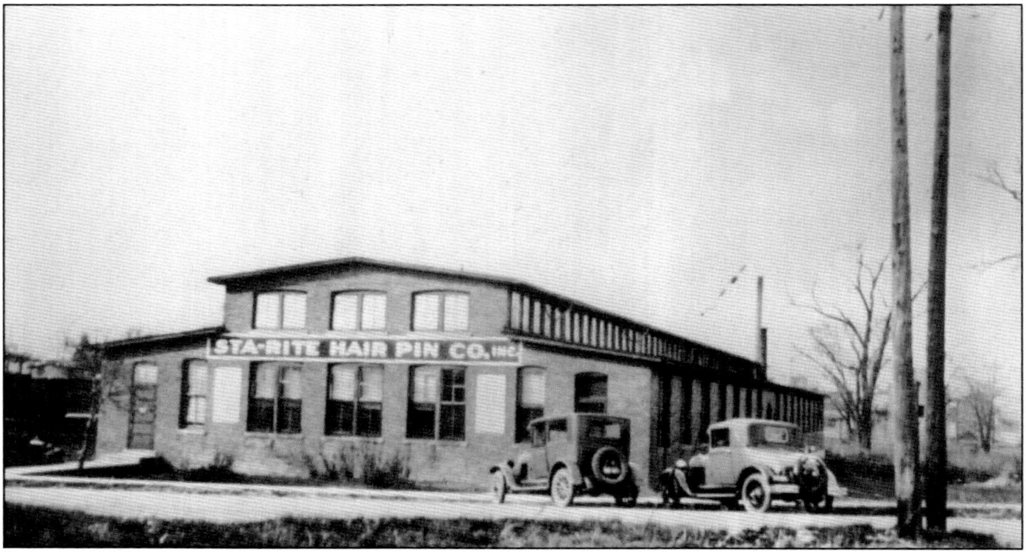

STA-RITE Hair Pin Company. S. E. Creech of Sullivan, Illinois developed the hairpin in 1917 and chose Shelbyville for his factory. George C. Bolinger later managed the factory. The name STA-RITE was chosen because women in Chicago said Bolingers hairpins stayed in place better. In 1928 they began making bobby pins, which became a nationwide craze. In 1942, to help the World War II effort, this bobby pin factory made pins for bombs.

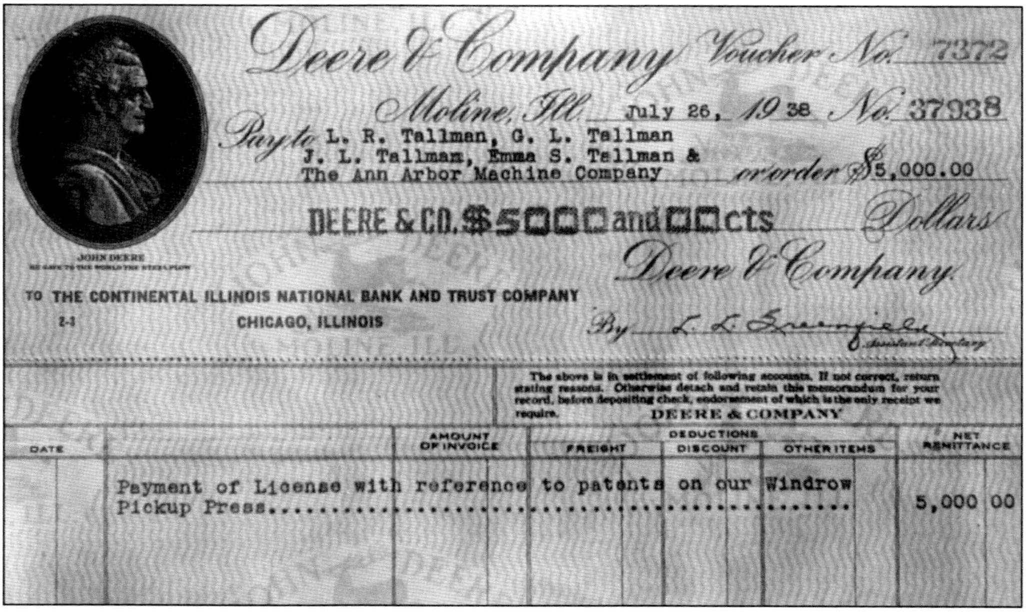

Deere & Company Voucher No. 7372

Moline, Ill. July 26, 1928 No. 37938

Pay to L. R. Tallman, G. L. Tallman
J. L. Tallmam, Emma S. Tallman &
The Ann Arbor Machine Company or order $5,000.00

DEERE & CO. $5000 and 00 cts Dollars

Deere & Company

JOHN DEERE

TO THE CONTINENTAL ILLINOIS NATIONAL BANK AND TRUST COMPANY
2-1 CHICAGO, ILLINOIS

By L. L. Greenfield
Assistant Secretary

The above is in settlement of following accounts. If not correct, return stating reasons. Otherwise detach and retain this memorandum for your record, before depositing check, endorsement of which is the only receipt we require.
DEERE & COMPANY

DATE		AMOUNT OF INVOICE	DEDUCTIONS FREIGHT	DEDUCTIONS DISCOUNT	DEDUCTIONS OTHER ITEMS	NET REMITTANCE
	Payment of License with reference to patents on our Windrow Pickup Press					5,000 00

Windrow Pickup Press. In July 1928, the John Deer Company bought the Windrow Pickup Press patent from the owners of the Ann Arbor Machine Company. The company had gone into bankruptcy, and all the machinery and materials were shipped to Shelbyville. In 1928, the company also began producing hay balers and it was a success. Later the company was sold to Oliver Corporation.

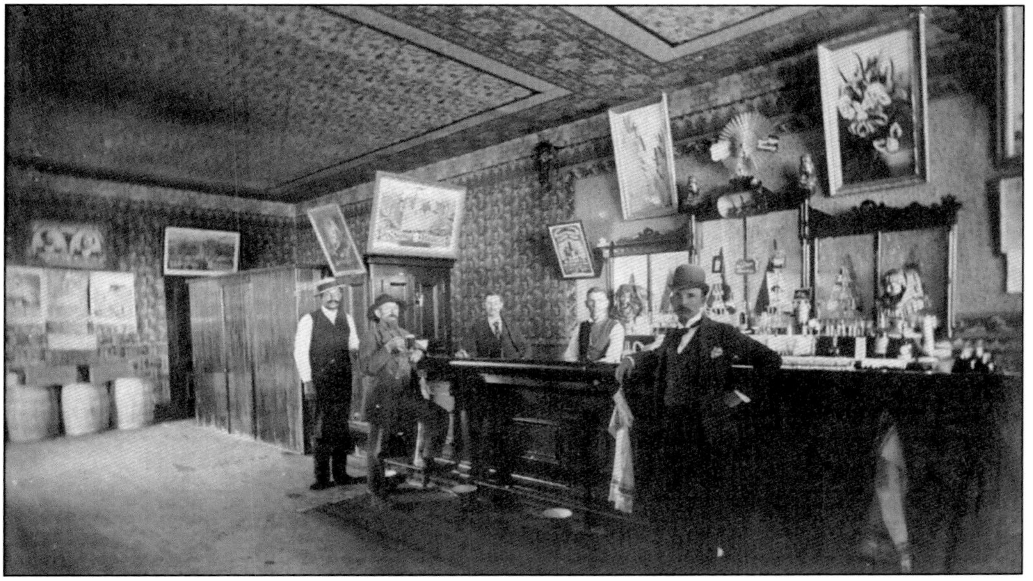

Kensil Saloon. Clint Kensil operated a saloon on the corner of North Morgan and Main Streets. There are a lot of paintings for saloon decoration. Genealogical records show a Clinton Kensil that was a lifelong Shelbyville resident that made a living playing in a band. However, it is unknown if these are the same men.

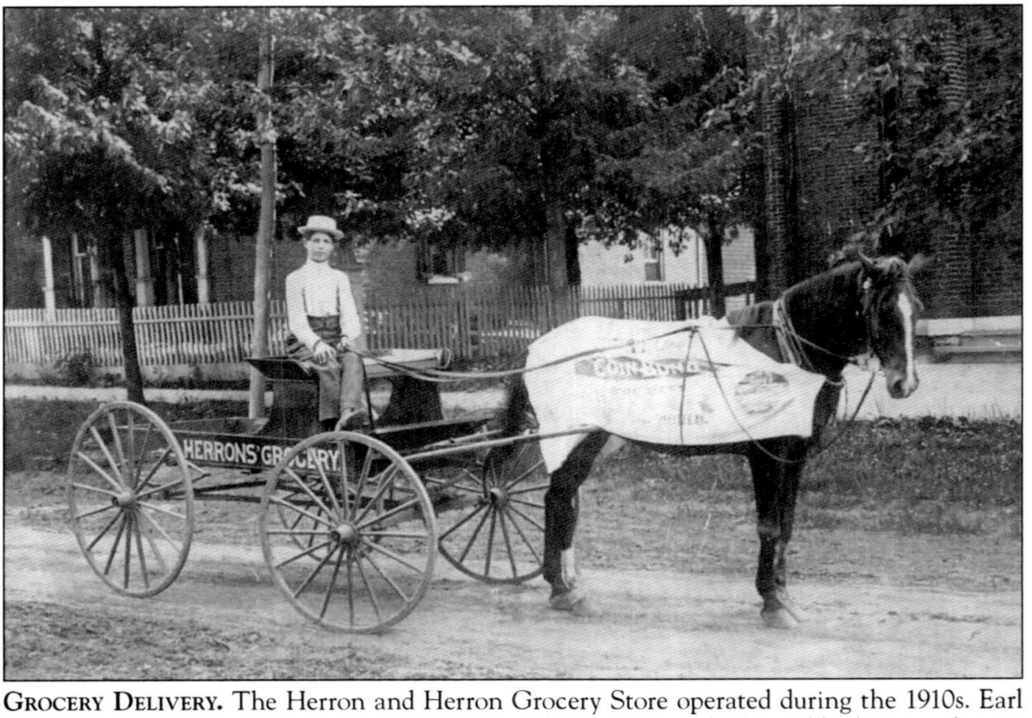

Grocery Delivery. The Herron and Herron Grocery Store operated during the 1910s. Earl Blacker is shown here at the corner of Morgan and First Street. The horse blanket even has an advertisement.

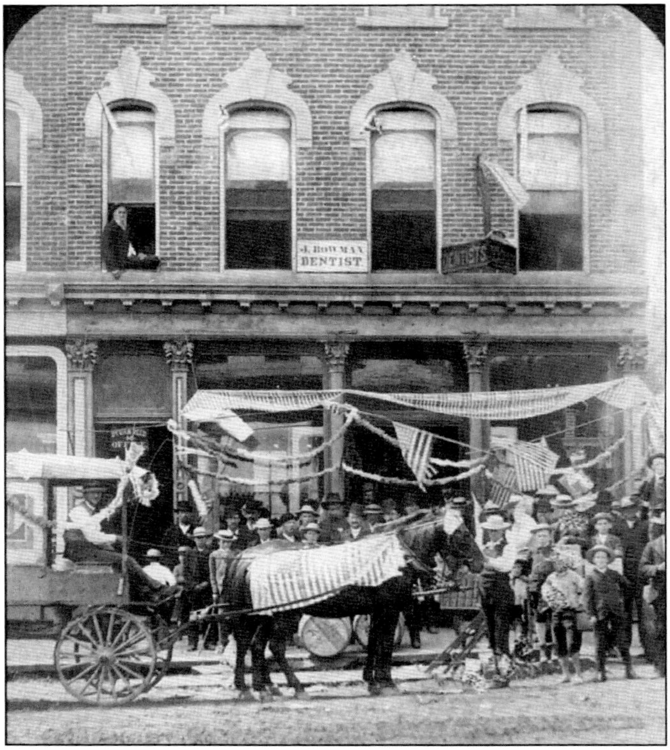

PORTERS GROCERY. This building was located on the southeast corner of Main and Broadway. On the first floor Billie Porter operated one of the many small groceries that were downtown. The dentist, J. Bowman, occupied the second floor. He was a dentist in Shelbyville in the 1880s and 1890s. A patriotic event is the occasion for the photograph.

PLAYING BILLIARDS. Two unidentified men are shown playing billiards at one of the tables. Early records from the City of Shelbyville show there were numerous billiard parlors. A license was required to operate a parlor in the city. The ceiling and wallpaper are distinctive but the exact location is unknown.

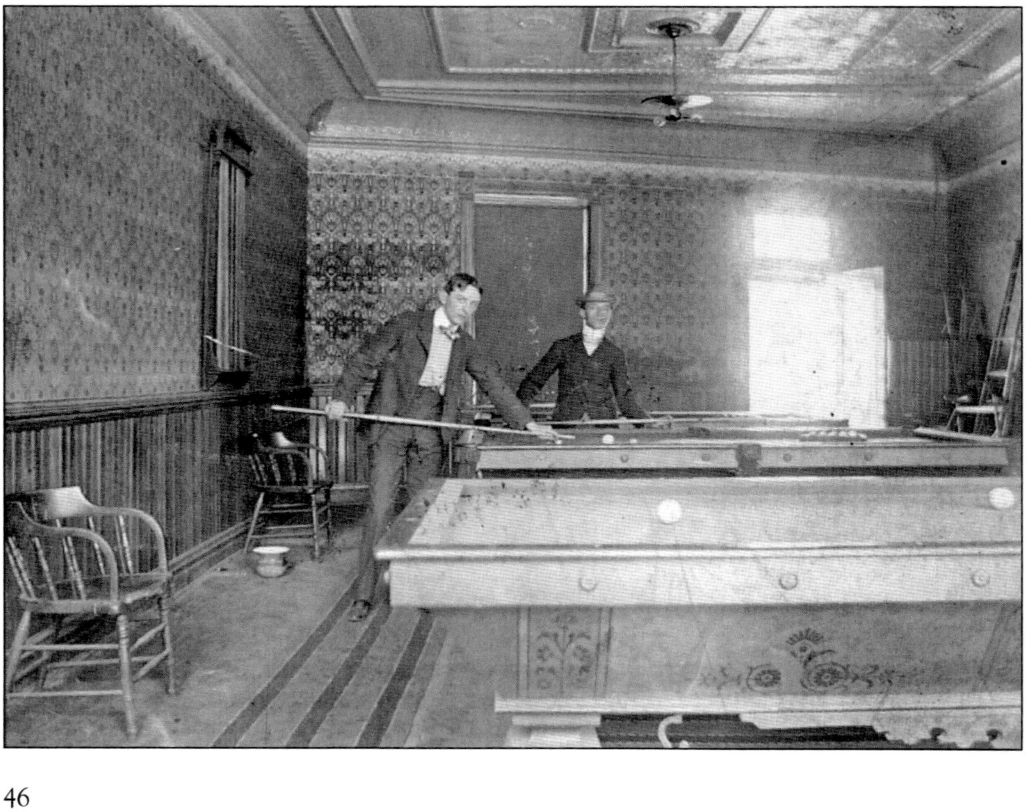

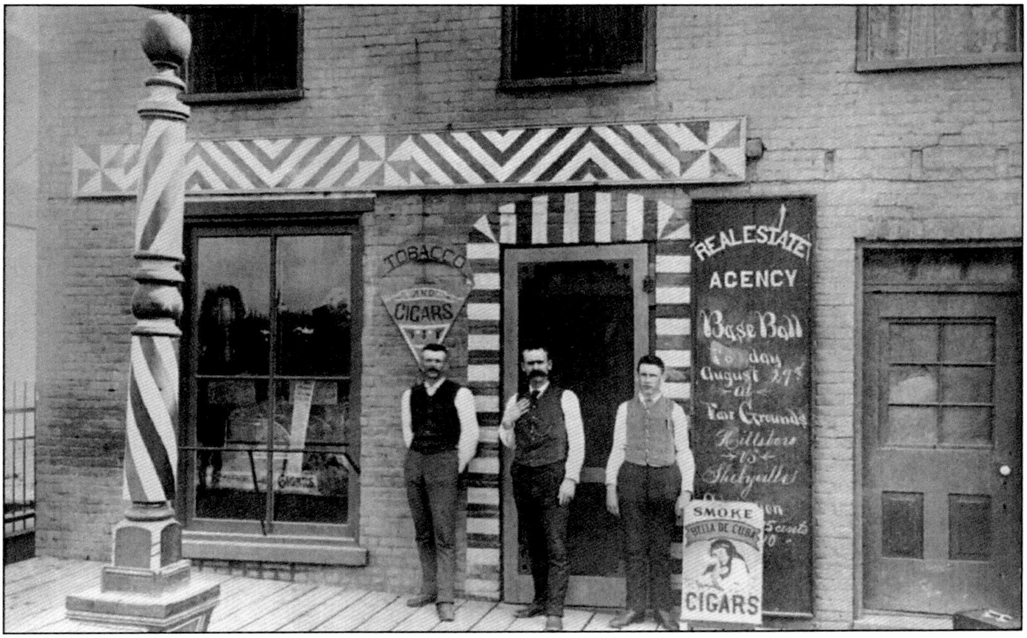

HENDERSON'S BARBER SHOP. In early Shelbyville, the barbershop was one-stop shopping for men. The new wooden sidewalk would place this photograph in the early 1880s. The painting definitely identifies it as a barbershop. Cigars were sold here, and it was also a real estate agency that provided information on the baseball games at the fairgrounds.

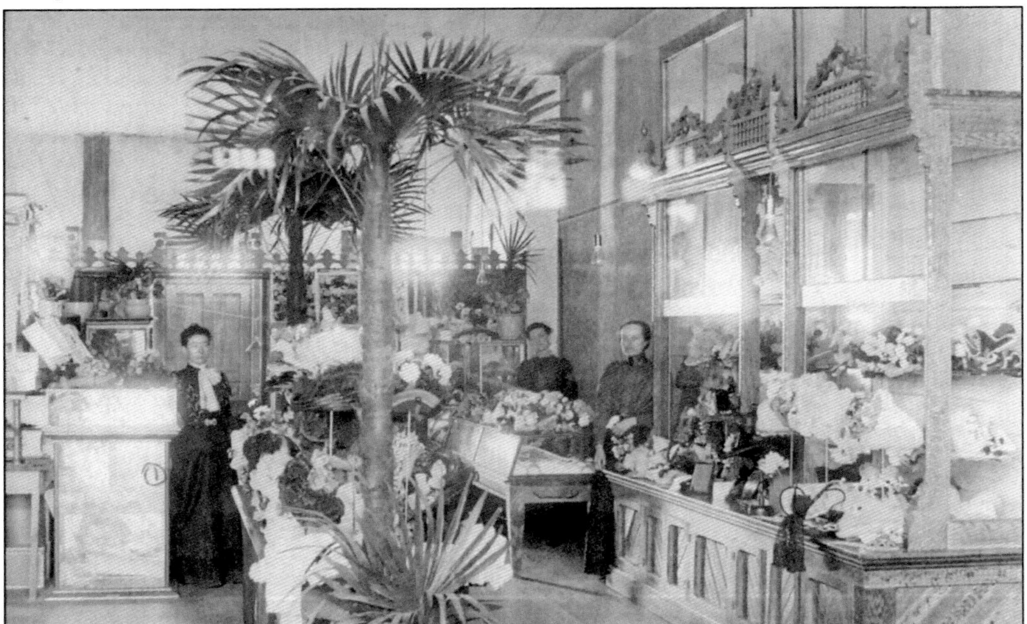

CAMPBELLS MILLINERY SHOP. This shop was located on the south side of Main Street near the Lantz building. Mrs. Pollard ran the shop in the 1890s. Mrs. Campbell took over the shop and ran it into the 1900s. It was also noted on the back of the photograph that it showed Mrs. Campbell and the "trimmers" in the shop.

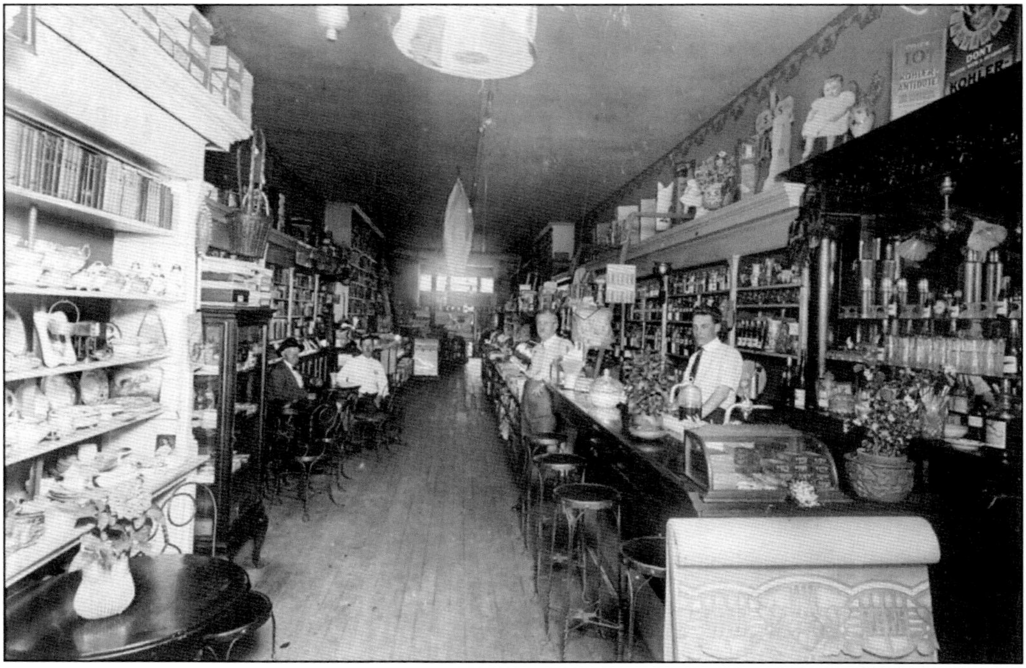

Hopkins Drugstore Interior. E. M. Hopkins established the drugstore in 1877. It was located at 136 East Main. Adolph Reiss worked for Hopkins as a pharmacist. When Hopkins died in 1933, Reiss purchased the store and renamed it Reiss's Drugstore.

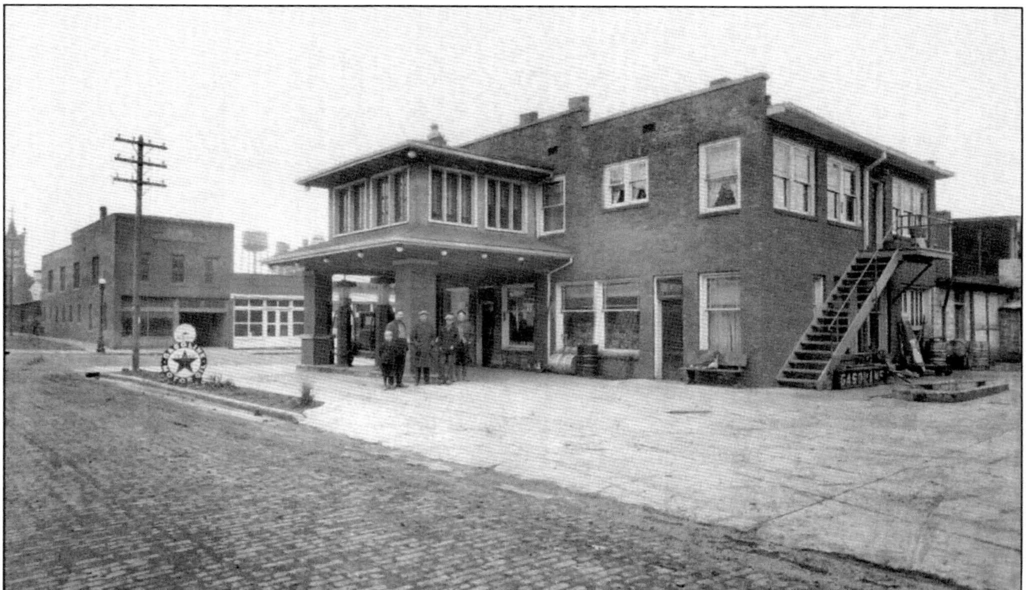

Finks Filling Station, 1924. M. O. Finks operated a livery stable just south of the building at the corner of North First and Morgan Streets. With the changes in transportation, he tore down the livery stable and built a garage. The first gas pump was installed here in 1910. Expansion from 1922–1924 resulted in the building pictured in the photograph. This business continued until it was sold in 1933.

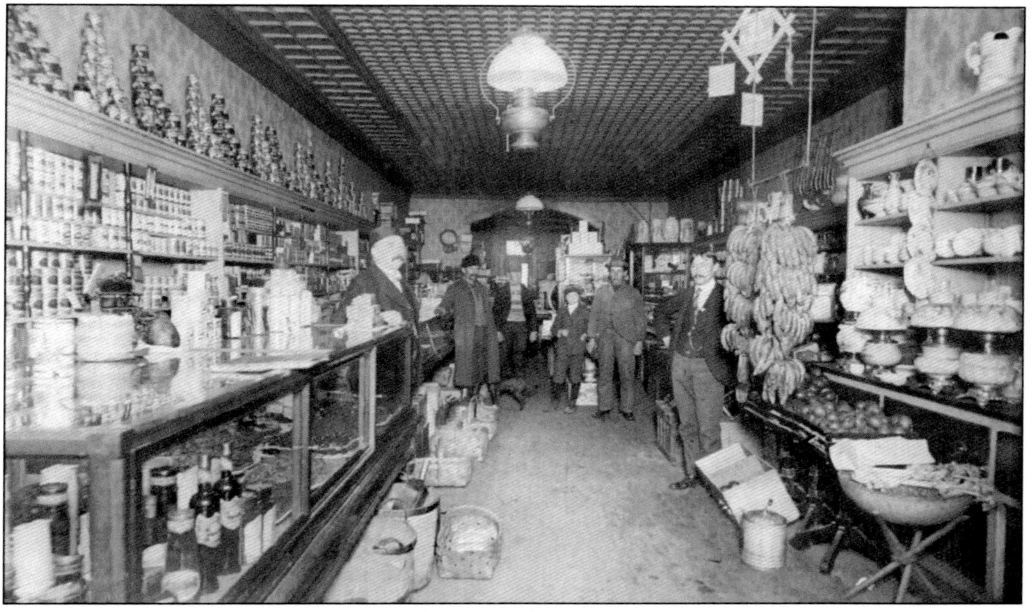

Isenburg Grocery Interior. J. B. Isenburg ran this grocery store from the 1890s until the early 1900s. Bunches of bananas can be seen in the store.

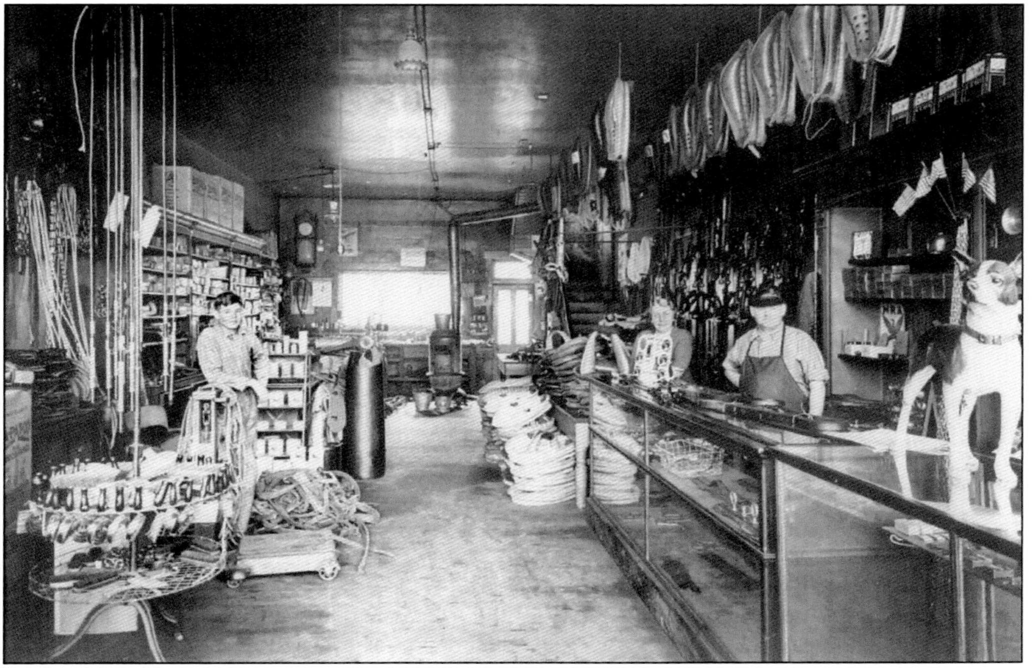

Klausers Harness Shop. G. C. started a harness manufacturing shop in 1882. When his brother August joined the partnership, it became Klauser Brothers. August worked the public side of the business, and G. C. stayed upstairs in the shop making harnesses. The business stayed in the family but changed to focus on combine canvasses in the 1940s. Early combines like those made by Allis Chalmers used canvas for conveyors, apparently they wore out frequently before designs were improved to use belts.

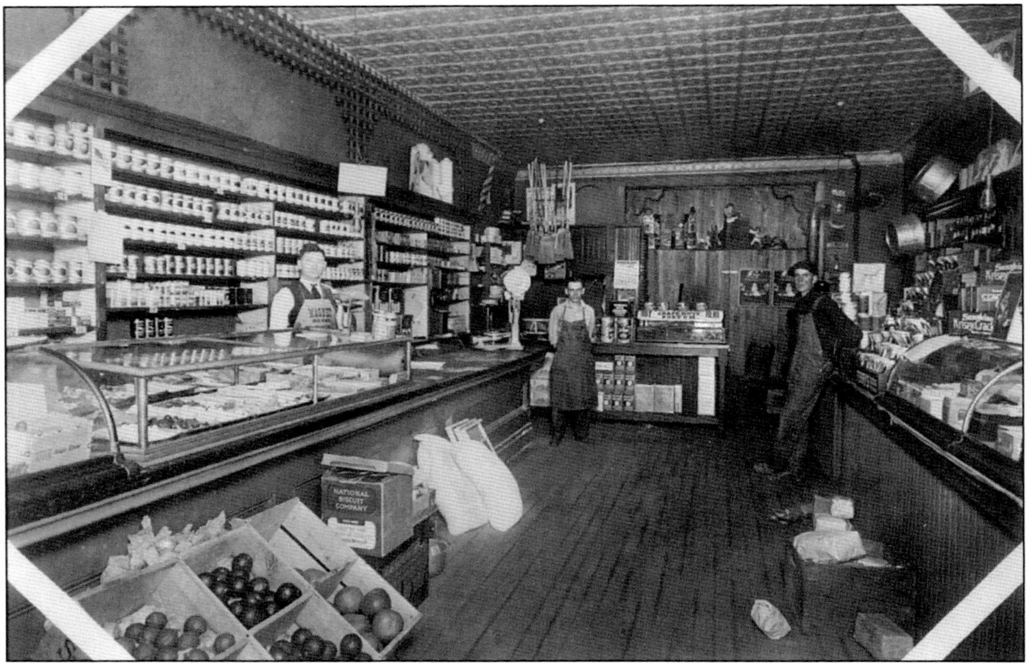

HENDERSON'S GROCERY STORE INTERIOR. Henderson and Zimmer ran a grocery store in the 1910s. By the 1920s the store was only run by H. M. Henderson. A Grape-Nuts display can be seen in the center of the photograph.

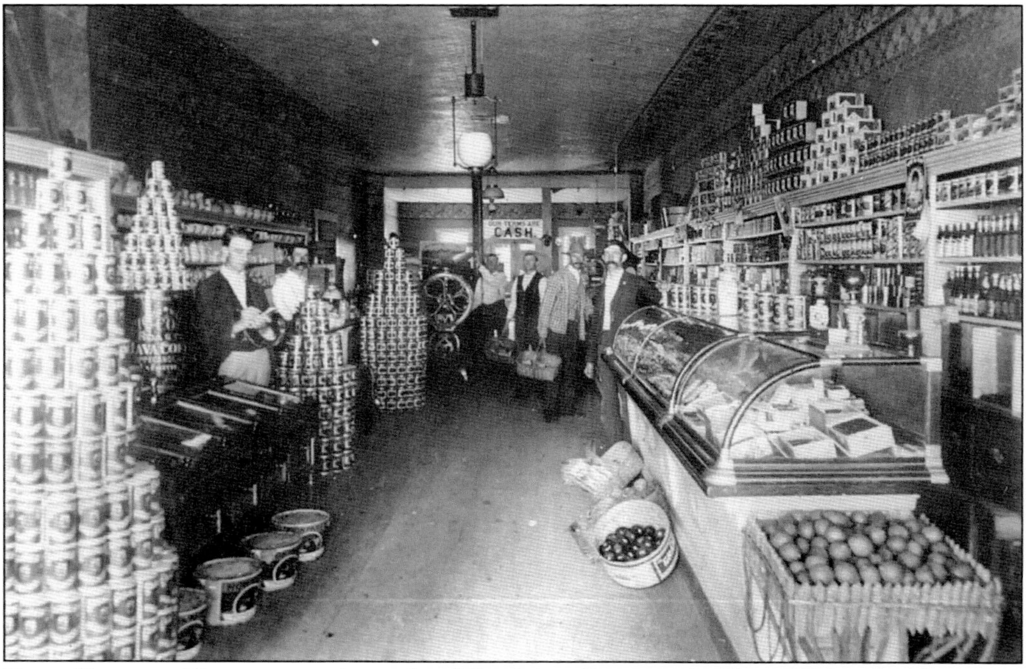

DAVIS GROCERY. This store was located on West Main Street in the Elmer Walton building. J. M. Davis opened his store in the 1890s, but it did not last into the 1910s. It is obvious by the sign that their terms were "cash." The photograph shows a well-stocked store with numerous canned goods.

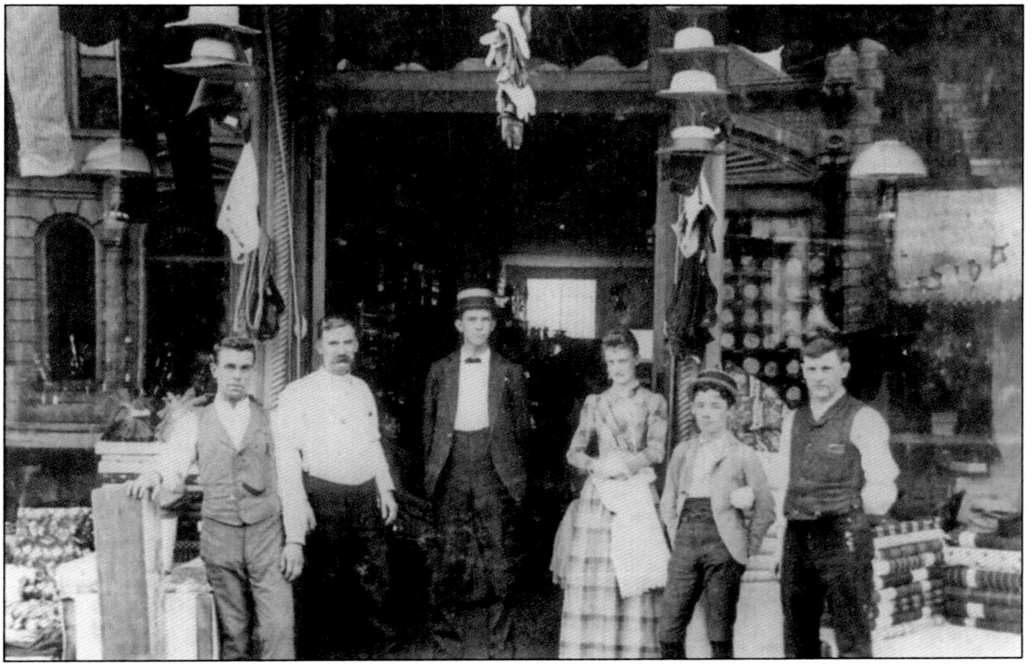

Ballards Clothing Store. In 1885 J. N. Ballard and Jesse Levering opened a dry goods store, Levering and Ballards. Ballard took over the business, but he died in 1910. In 1915 C. W. Waggoner purchased the store. Two of the men in the photograph are Levering and Ballard.

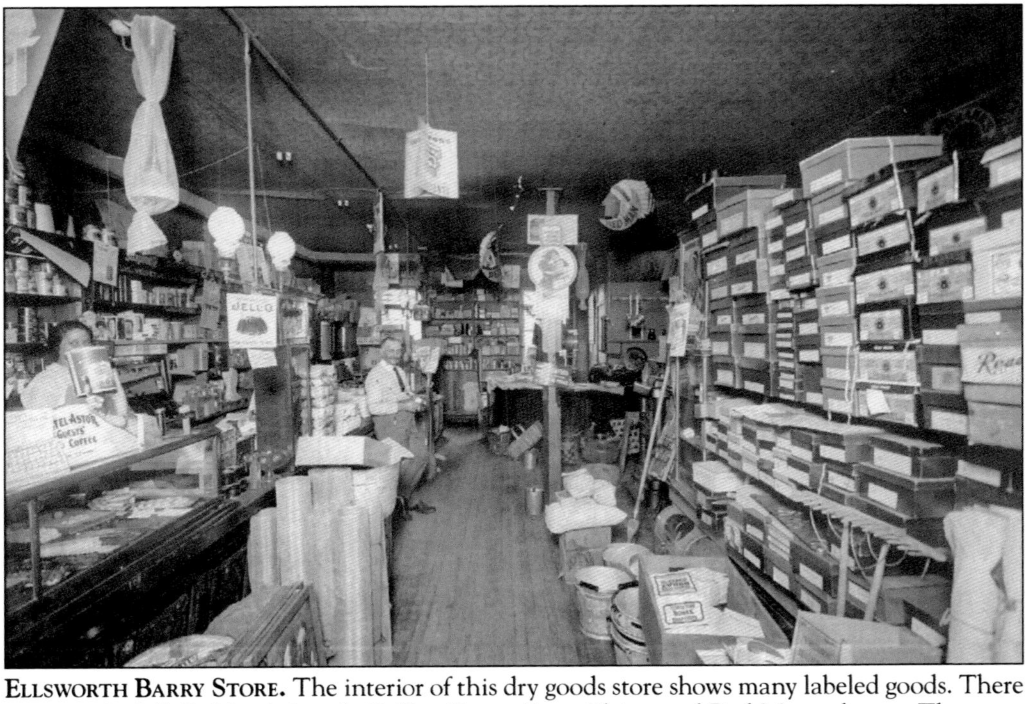

Ellsworth Barry Store. The interior of this dry goods store shows many labeled goods. There is a sign for Jell-O, Hotel Astor's Coffee, Borax Soap Chips, and Red Man tobacco. There are also rakes, buckets, paintings, baskets, and more.

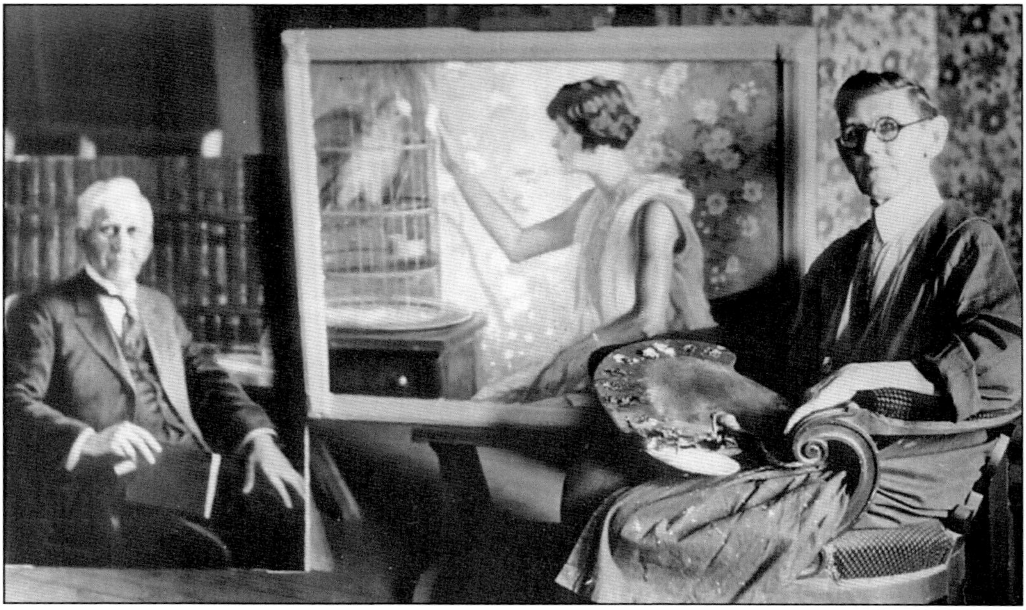

ROBERT MARSHALL ROOT, 1863–1937. Root, a local Shelbyville artist noted for landscapes and portraits, is shown here with two of his paintings. He painted the Lincoln-Douglas debate that hangs in the Springfield State House and the Lincoln-Thornton debate in the Shelby County Courthouse. The portrait of Livingston C. Lord that hangs in Old Main at Eastern Illinois University is one of his most notable portraits. Root also designed the Soldiers and Sailors Monument.

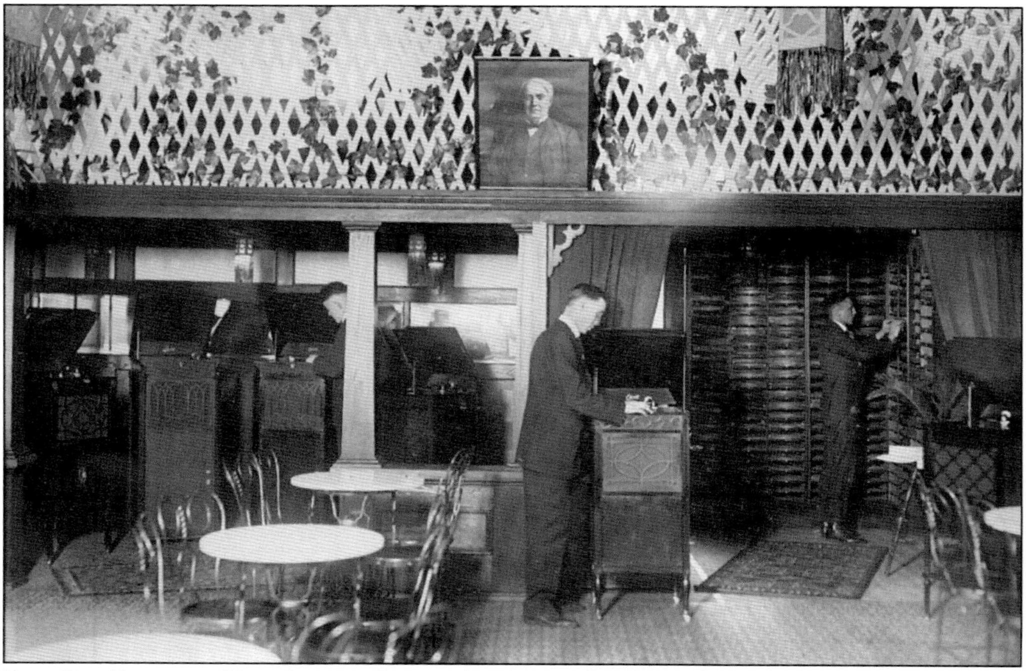

BUSY BEE COMPANY. This photograph was taken on April 1, 1918. This view shows the phonograph section of the store. A portrait of Thomas Edison is prominently displayed. The store also sold stationery and books. Busy Bee was open from 1910–1920.

Irma Tackett, 1880–1967. Tackett was the daughter of John A. Tackett. In the 1870s he was listed as a "capitalist" and in the 1890s he became vice president and later president of the Shelby County State Bank. Irma married Dr. H. E. Monroe, and they had two children, Henry and Florence Rachel. The family home was at 220 North Broadway.

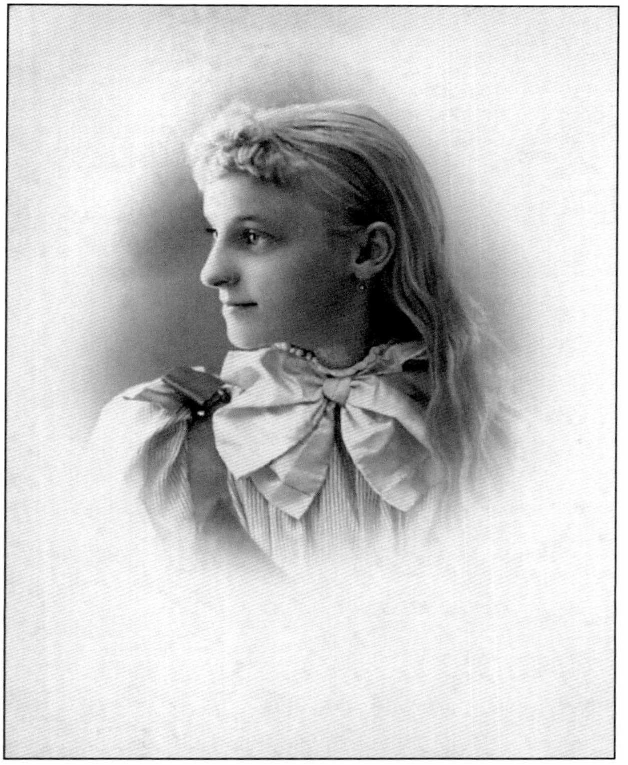

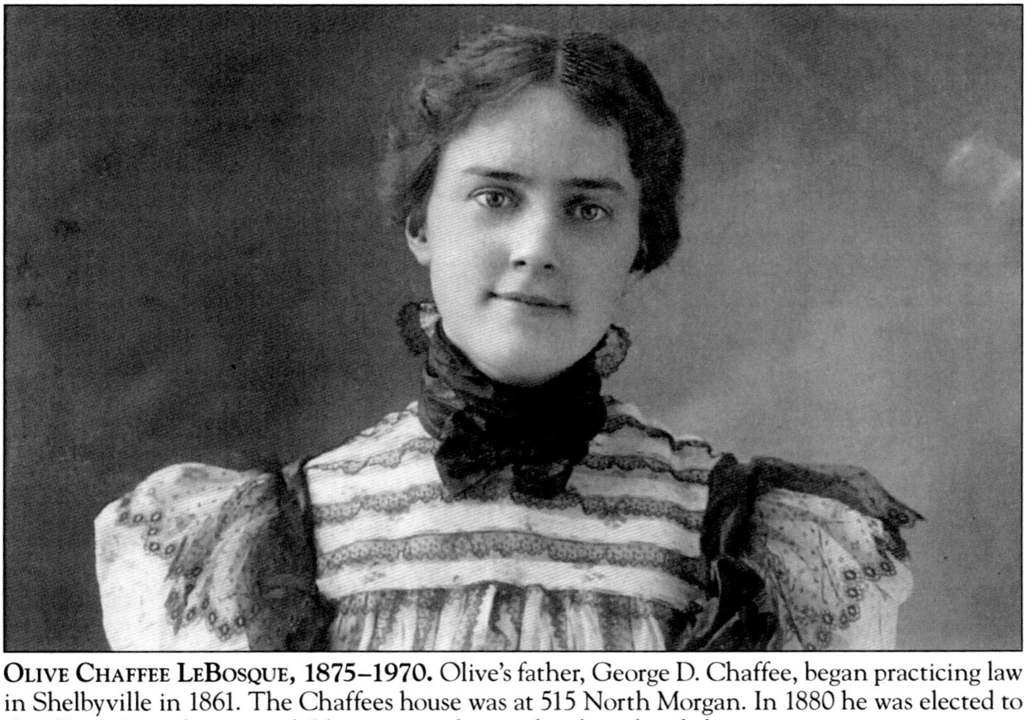

Olive Chaffee LeBosque, 1875–1970. Olive's father, George D. Chaffee, began practicing law in Shelbyville in 1861. The Chaffees house was at 515 North Morgan. In 1880 he was elected to the Illinois Legislature, and Olive wrote a biography about her father.

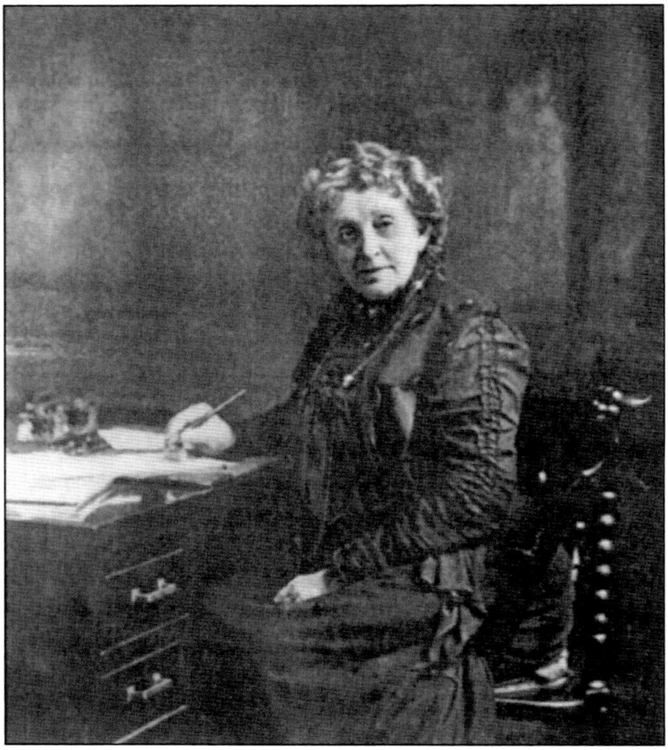

DISHWASHER INVENTOR. Josephine Cochran frequently gave formal dinners but the dishwasher broke lots of dishes. Cochran designed a machine in her woodshed that had individual compartment for plates, saucers, and cups. These sat inside a copper boiler while hot, soapy water cleaned the dinnerware. Cochran patented the dishwasher in 1886. Hotels and restaurants were the biggest customers. Cochran's company merged with an Ohio firm to produce KitchenAid dishwashers.

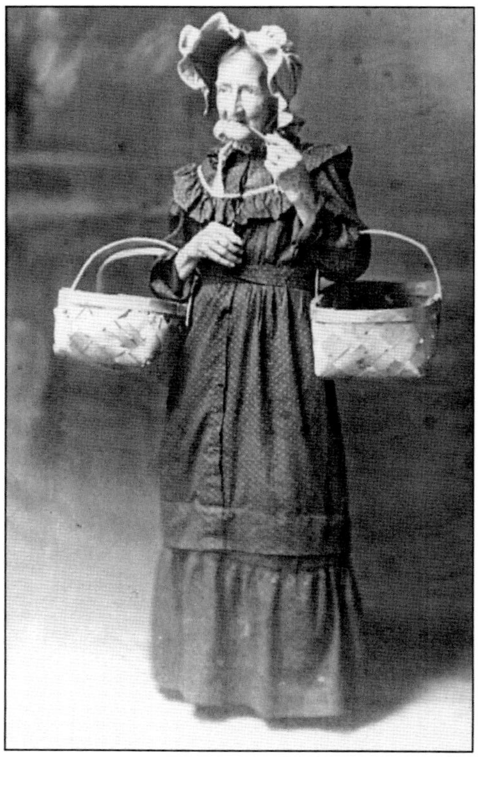

GRANNY KELLER. Parlesa Ann Keller was born in 1812 and lived to be 100. She smoked a pipe like many women did in that time. Her home was near "Dugout," a coal mining ravine southeast of the old part of town. Keller's baskets contained vegetables that she sold or gave to friends.

SAMUEL MOULTON. Moulton came to Shelbyville in 1850. Moulton was elected to the legislature in 1853 and served three terms, and introduced the Free Public School Bill in Illinois. He wanted to make education available to all. Moulton was one of the original trustees of the State Board of Education, and served as its president for 16 years. In 1864, he was elected to congress from the state of Illinois at large.

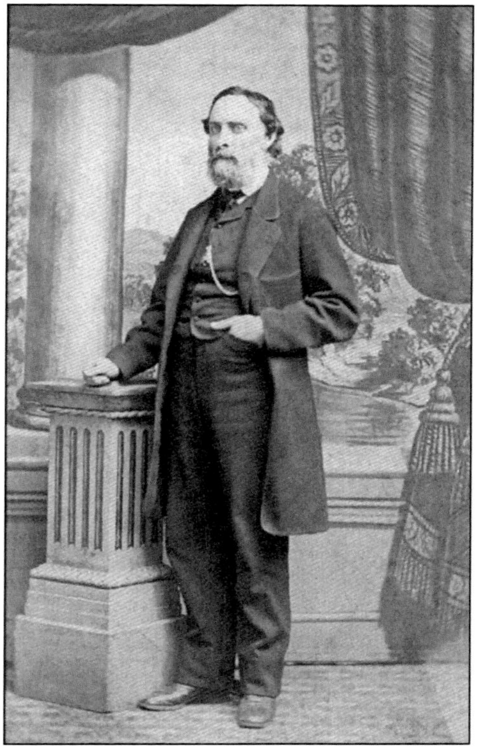

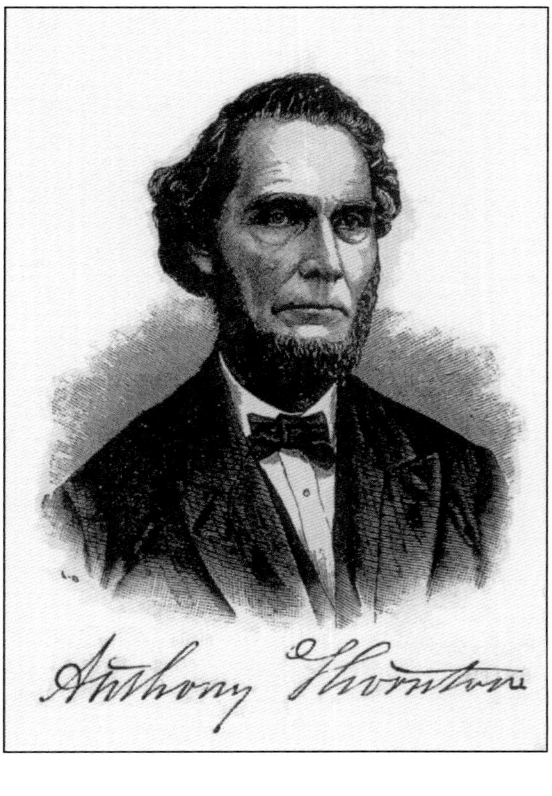

ANTHONY THORNTON. On his way to Missouri in 1836, Thornton stopped to visit relatives in Shelbyville and stayed. He opened a law office and rode the circuit with Abraham Lincoln. In 1850, Thornton was a Whig, but by 1862 he considered himself a "War-Democrat." He supported the effort to put down the "rebellion" and preserve the Union. He served in the Illinois Supreme Court from 1870 to 1873.

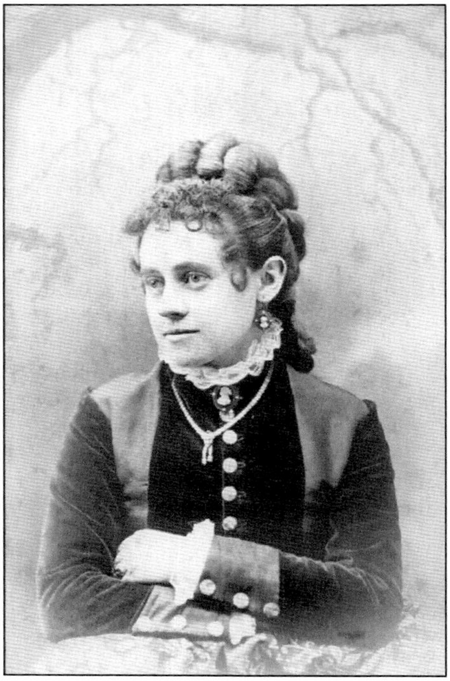

VIOLA KEELER, 1855–1940. Keeler was the daughter of George and Elizabeth. Her father was the postmaster during the Civil War. Viola was a second and third grade teacher. This photograph portrays young women's fashions during the Civil War.

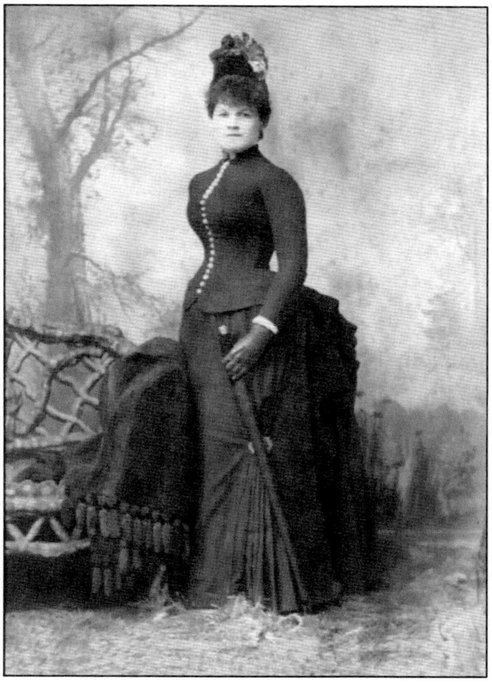

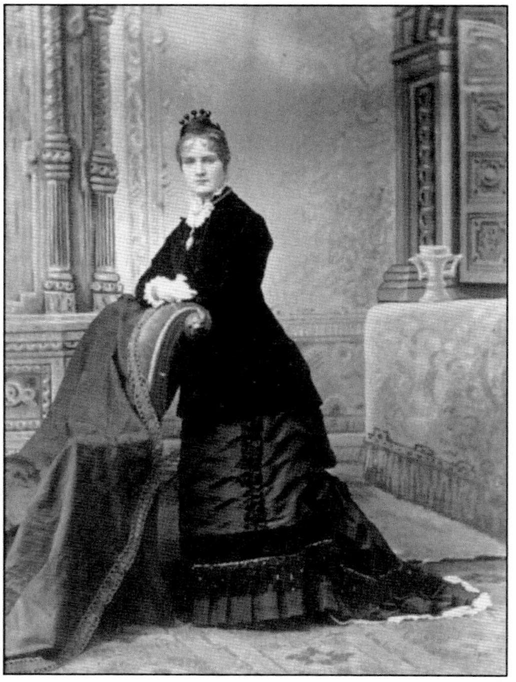

VICTORIAN LADIES. Mary Trower Ballet is pictured on the left, and the lady on the right is unidentified. Both women wear Victorian Age–style clothing, as demonstrated by excessive use of buttons. Mary Trower Ballet is buried just south of the location of the Lantz Brothers Hearse photograph (page 42). Her tombstone in the Ballet-Gehm family plot reads, was born "Sept" X, MDCCCLX (September 10, 1860) and died "Feby" I, MCMXX (February 1, 1920).

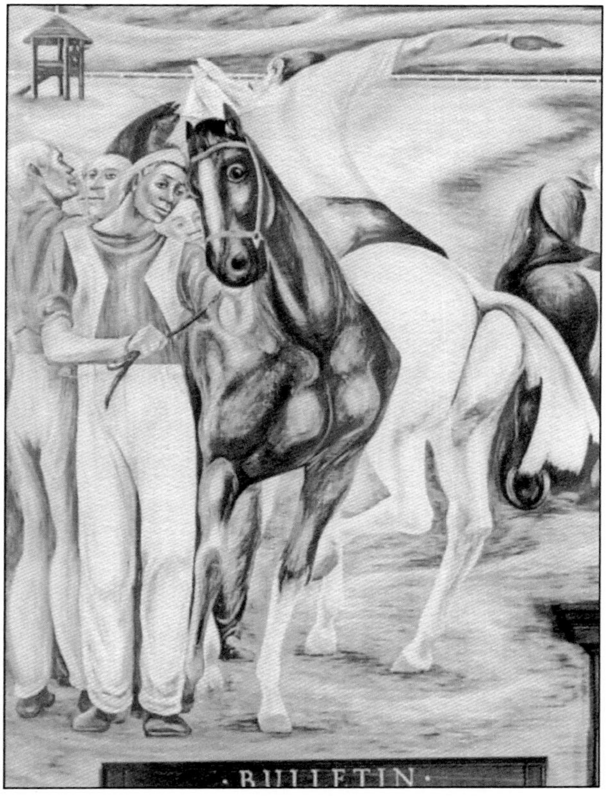

DETAIL OF THE "SHELBY COUNTY FAIR" BY LUCIA WILEY. A noted mural painter, Wiley won the WPA competition for the Shelbyville Post Office. The WPA was building post offices and the art project employed artists to create art for the people. Her theme was the 1900 Shelby County Fair. The Chautauqua Auditorium is included in the full painting. James Lee, a local horse breeder and the grandfather of Garfield Willis, was the inspiration for one of the men in the painting. The mural was dedicated in 1941.

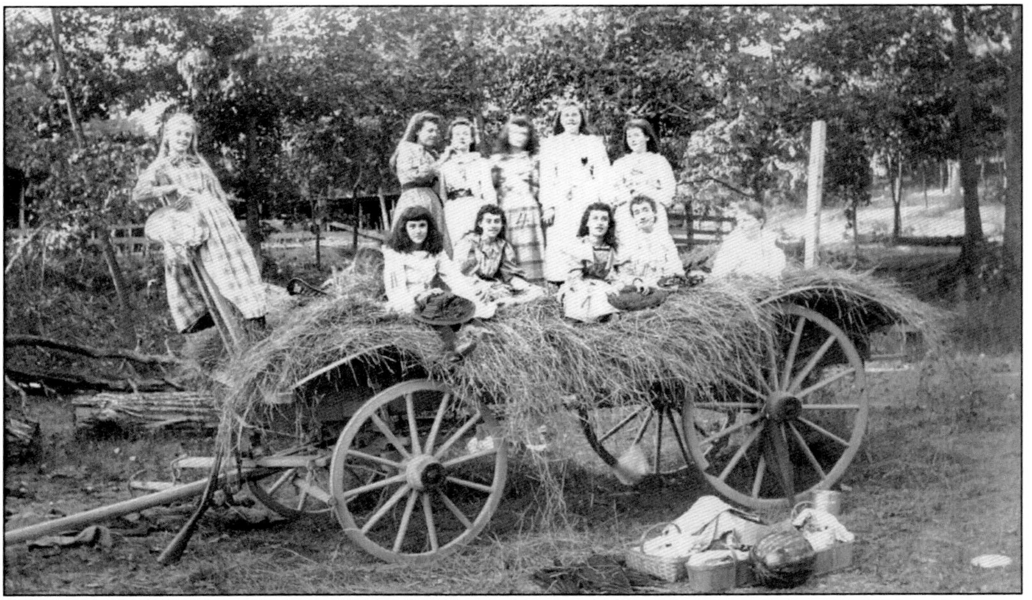

HAYRIDE AND PICNIC. Irma Tackett is at the front of the wagon on the left. Jess Moore is at the rear on the right. Three of the other girls are Bess Besden, Kitt Roberts, and Mary Hoxsey. Their lunches are packed, and they have a watermelon. Note there is also a gun at the front of the wagon.

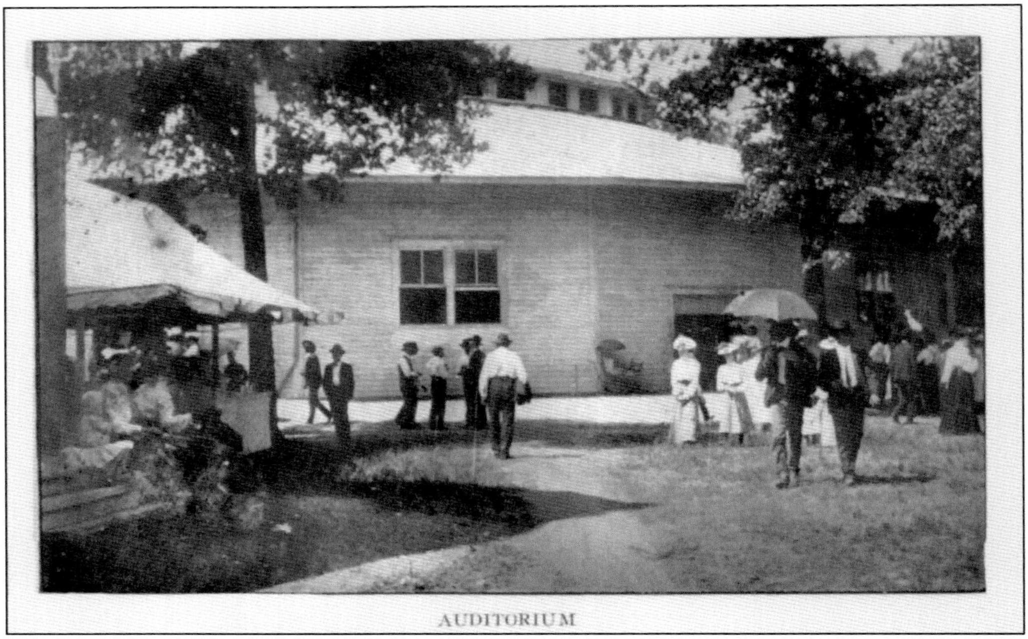

Chautauqua Auditorium. This photograph shows the popularity of the Chautauqua. Large groups of people came for the entertainment and education. The *Shelbyville Democrat* reported in July 1901 that for 25¢ you could be entertained all day or $1.50 for the 11-day season.

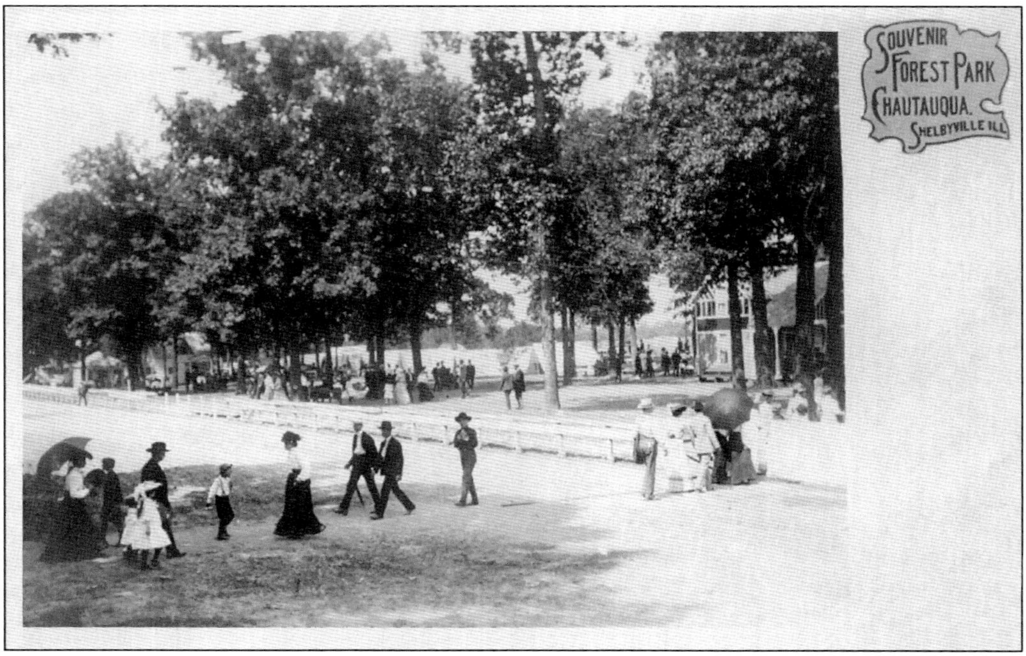

Ticket Entrance and Tents. Just to the right of the photograph is the ticket entrance. Permanent cottages can be seen as well as numerous rows of tents. If the performance was good everyone gave the "Chautauqua Salute." For the salute, people stood and waved their handkerchiefs.

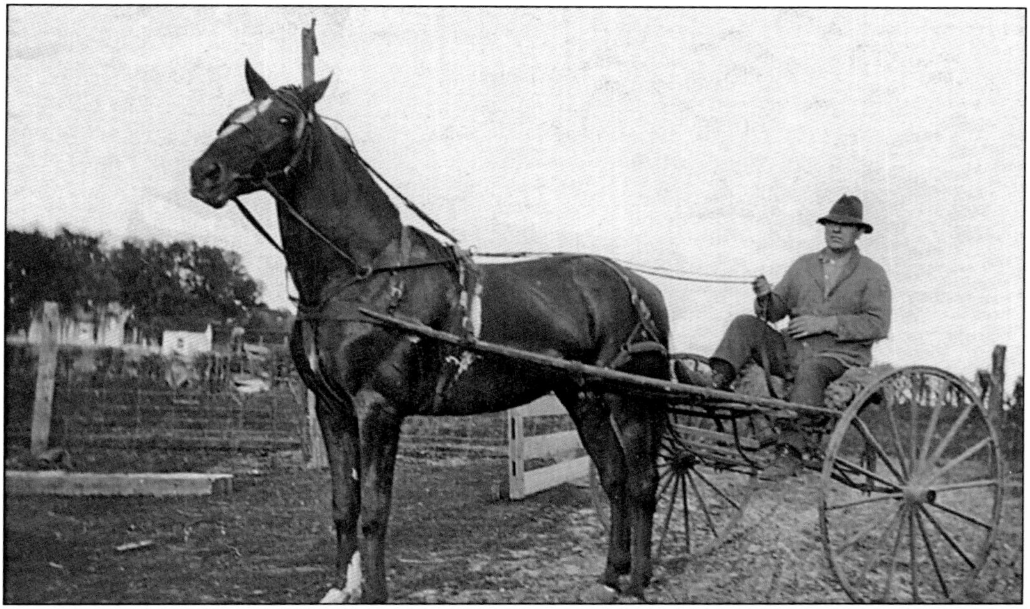

READY TO RACE. Before Forest Park was created, it was known as the Shelby County Fairgrounds. There was a racetrack and grandstands. The mural in the Shelbyville Post Office gives the best view of what the fairgrounds looked like. Carl Rittgers is shown here with his horse and racing cart.

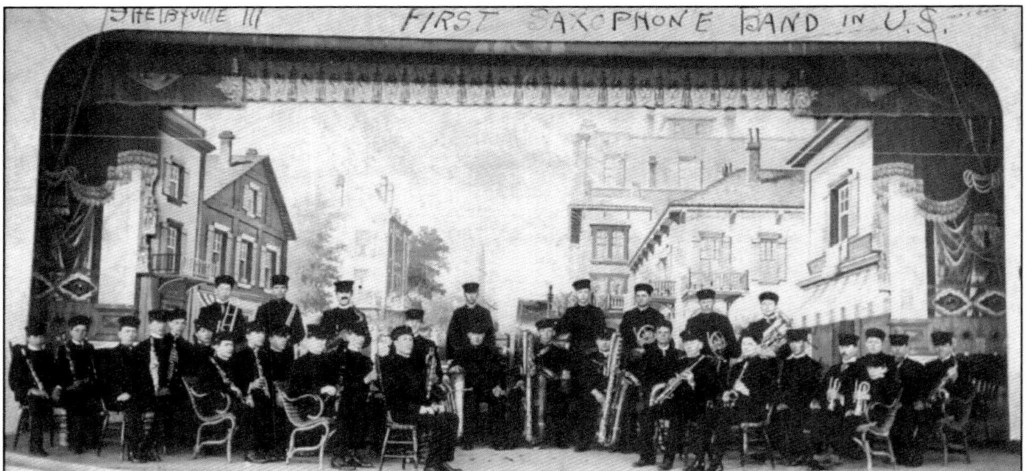

SAXOPHONE BAND. Shelbyville had already organized a cornet band in 1853 and another in 1888. This band, thought to be the first of its kind in the U.S., was probably organized in the late 1800s. The band is on stage at the Chautauqua Auditorium. The backdrop is spectacular, possibly one of the many backdrops that Robert Root painted.

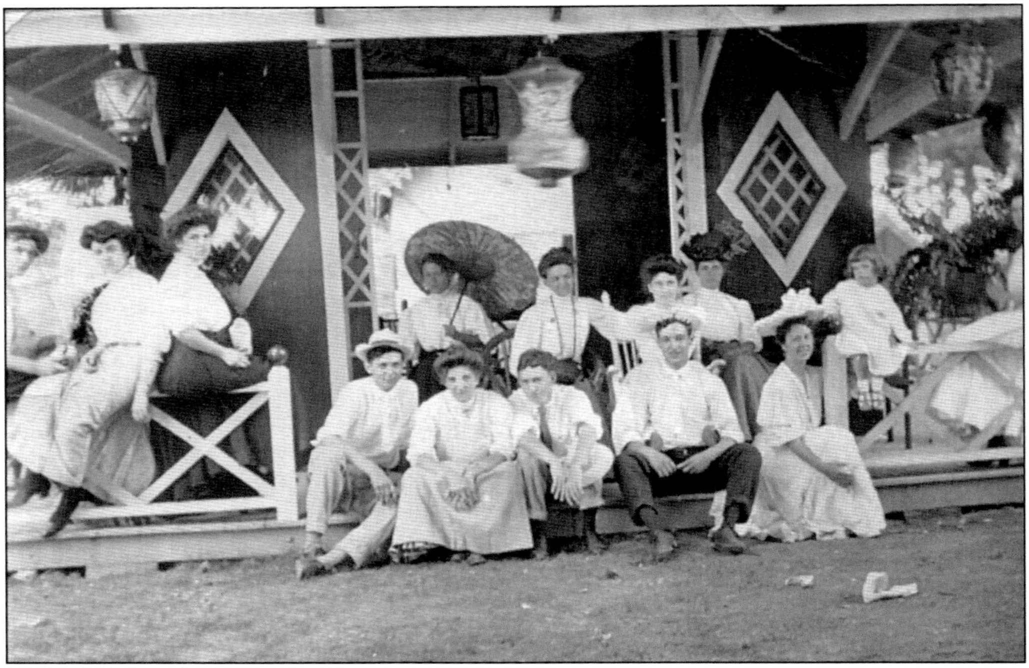

MIDDLESWORTH COTTAGE. Pictured is one of the larger and more ornate permanent cottages in Forest Park. They were built specifically for use at the Chautauqua, but some owners used them for the entire summer. Most of these cottages were removed by the end of the 1930s.

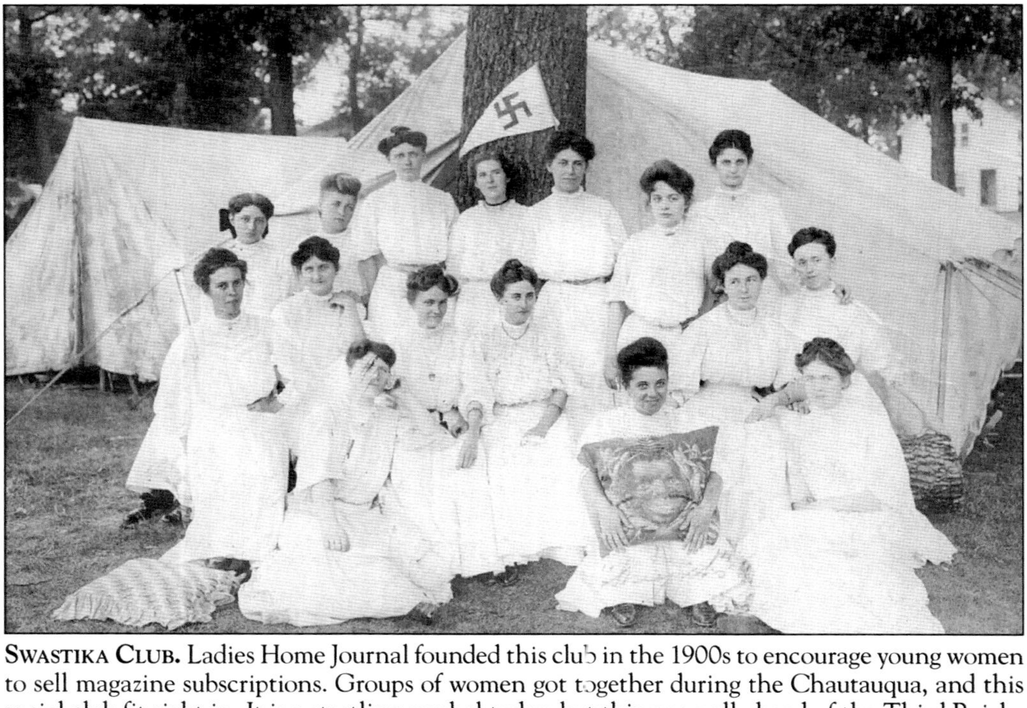

SWASTIKA CLUB. Ladies Home Journal founded this club in the 1900s to encourage young women to sell magazine subscriptions. Groups of women got together during the Chautauqua, and this social club fit right in. It is a startling symbol today, but this was well ahead of the Third Reichs adoption of the symbol in 1933.

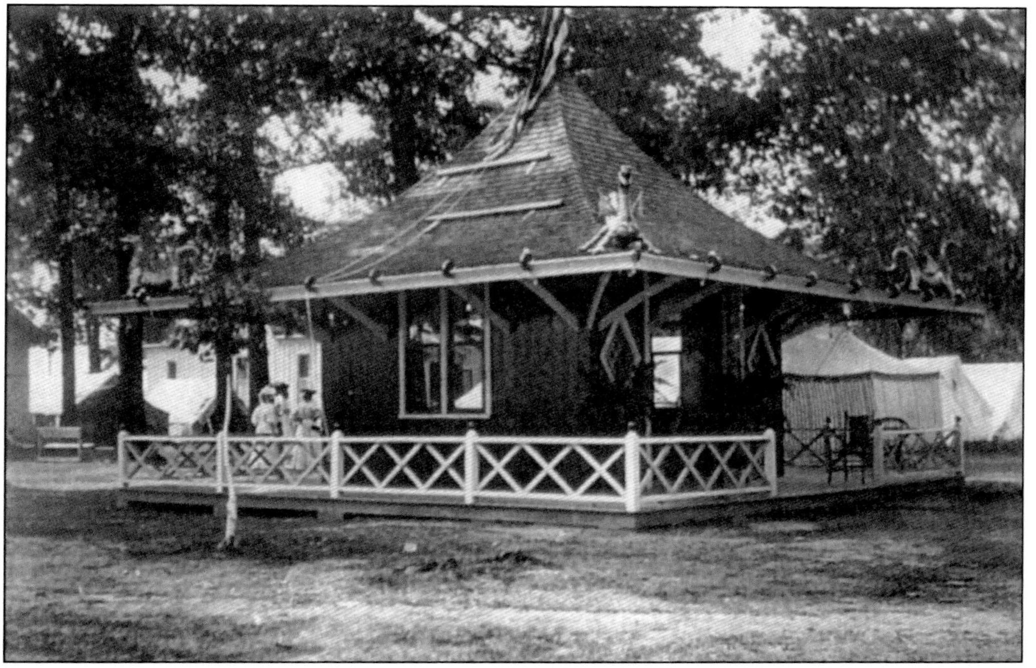

DRAGON COTTAGE. This was a very unique Chautauqua Cottage. Each corner of the cottage roof has a large dragon decoration. The complete wraparound porch lent itself to the outdoor times at the Chautauqua.

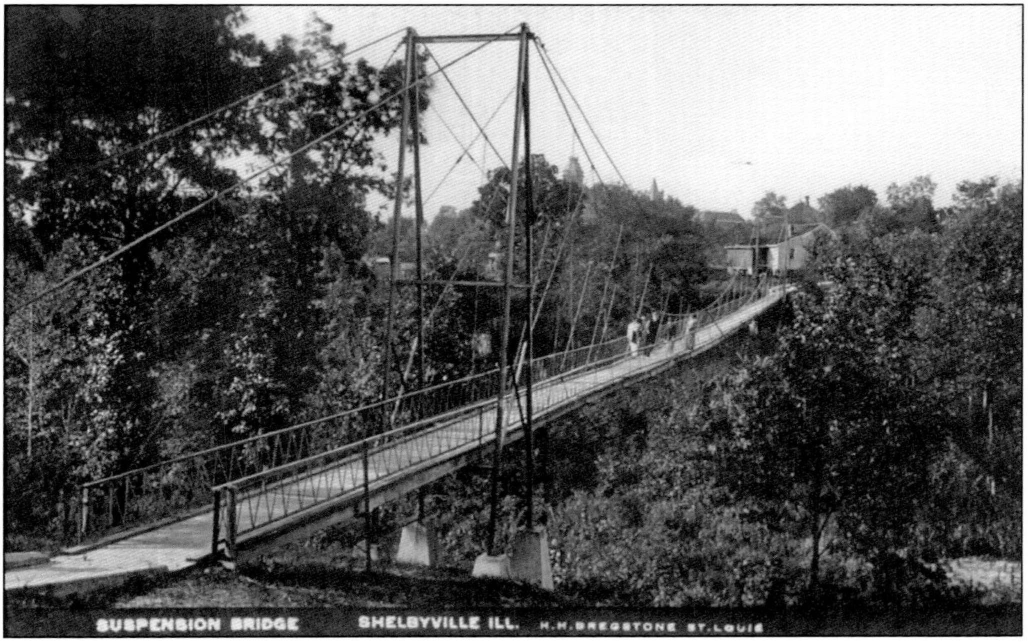

SUSPENSION BRIDGE. In the early 1900s this bridge connected the southeast corner of Glenwood Cemetery to the railroad tracks at the east side of town. L. E. Fish Bridge Company built the 100-foot bridge. It became dangerous and was torn down in 1929. Concrete footings for the bridge in the cemetery are the only evidence of its location.

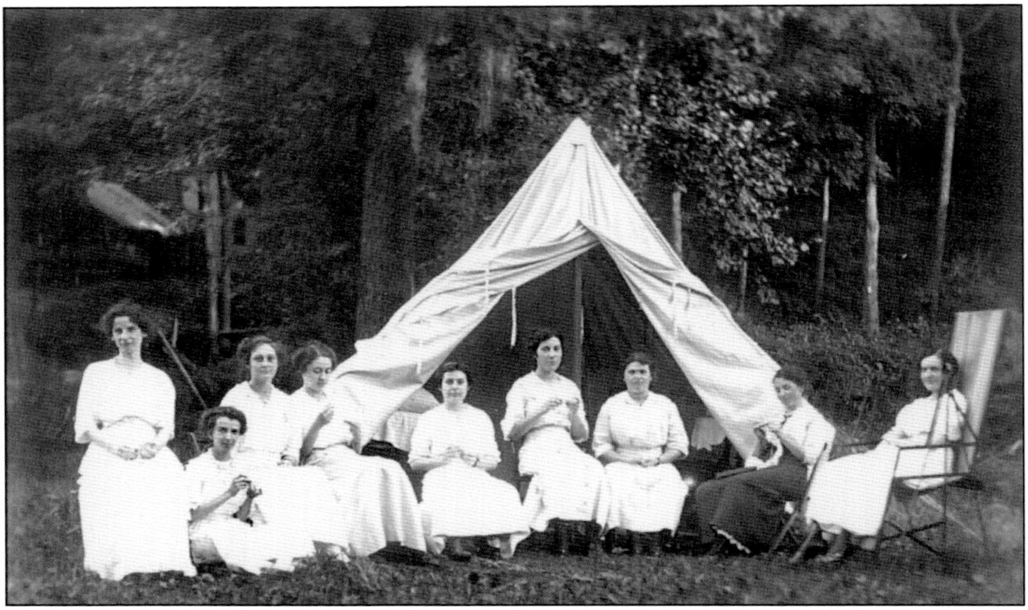

LADIES AT SHELBYVILLE CHAUTAUQUA. These ladies are working on crafts while being photographed. It could be crocheting or tatting. Chautauqua also included instructions in various types of crafts and household chores. There was an educational component for *Bible* study, poetry, and literature. Entertainment was also a large part of the Chautauqua experience.

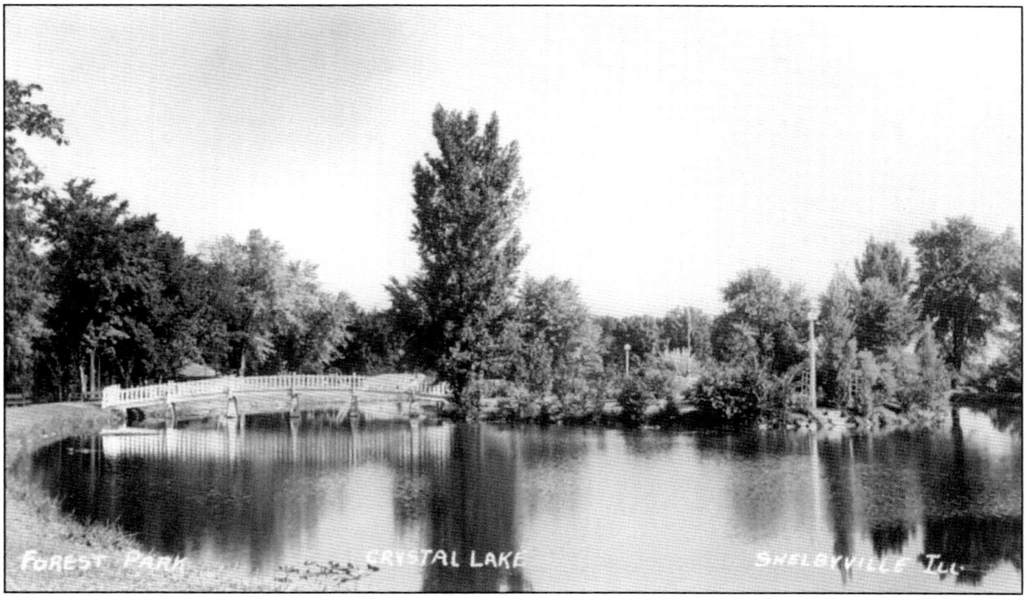

CRYSTAL LAKE. This lagoon was built about the same time as the auditorium and the swimming pool. A bridge over the lagoon connects the shore to the center island. During the Chautauqua, small boats were used on the lake. Water sports were also played on the lake.

Two

Rural Area around Shelbyville

The city of Shelbyville dominates the center of the county. Few villages or towns sprung up within a 5-mile radius. Central Place Theory determines the market area for various types of goods and services. Obviously those that could be provided by a village were ignored within this area around Shelbyville because people would travel to Shelbyville. If the distance was too far from Shelbyville, other small towns like Moweaqua, Tower Hill, and Stewardson provided goods and services. The people shopped in the small towns and did not go to Shelbyville. This is an example of Distance Decay Theory for retail activities. For example, if you lived in Shelbyville Township, half way between Shelbyville and Clarksburg, you would head to Shelbyville for most of your needs. You would not head to the Village of Clarksburg, although this is a good place for a small village and it would have been even better before the faster and more readily available transportation.

The south half of Shelbyville Township, including all of Rose Township and the southeast quarter of Ridge Township, fell into the aforementioned situations. However, there were lots of farms and people in these rural areas that were not associated with a small village and not considered a true part of Shelbyville. The images in this chapter are from these predominately rural areas.

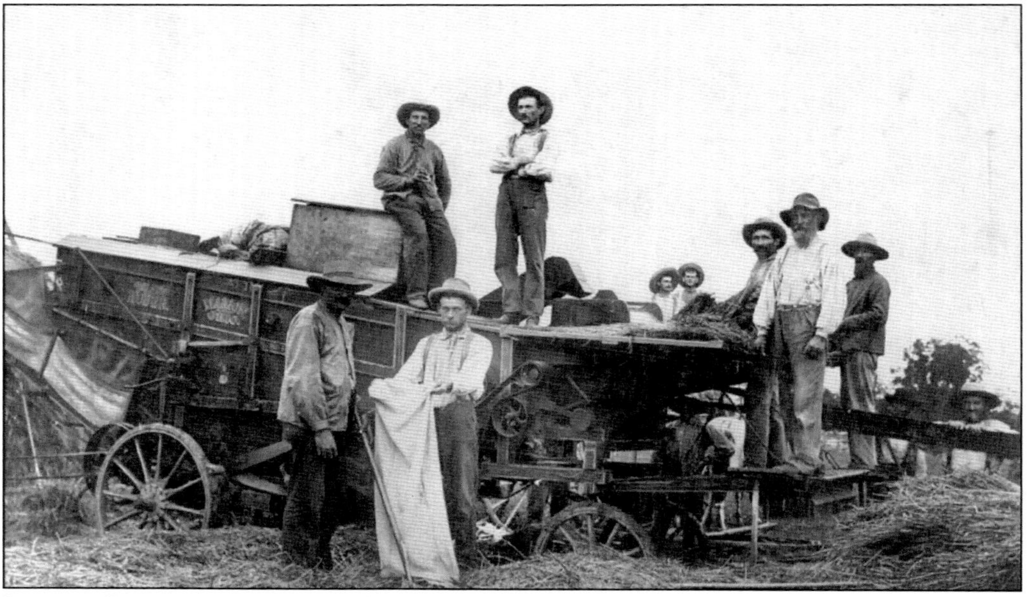

Largent Brothers Separator. The Largent brothers of rural Shelbyville Township are threshing near Herborn. Work has stopped to show off the separator belt of the threshing machine. It took a relatively large group of men to run the operation. Ten men are in this photograph. The front of the machine reads, "Made in Ohio." (Courtesy of Robert Largent Family.)

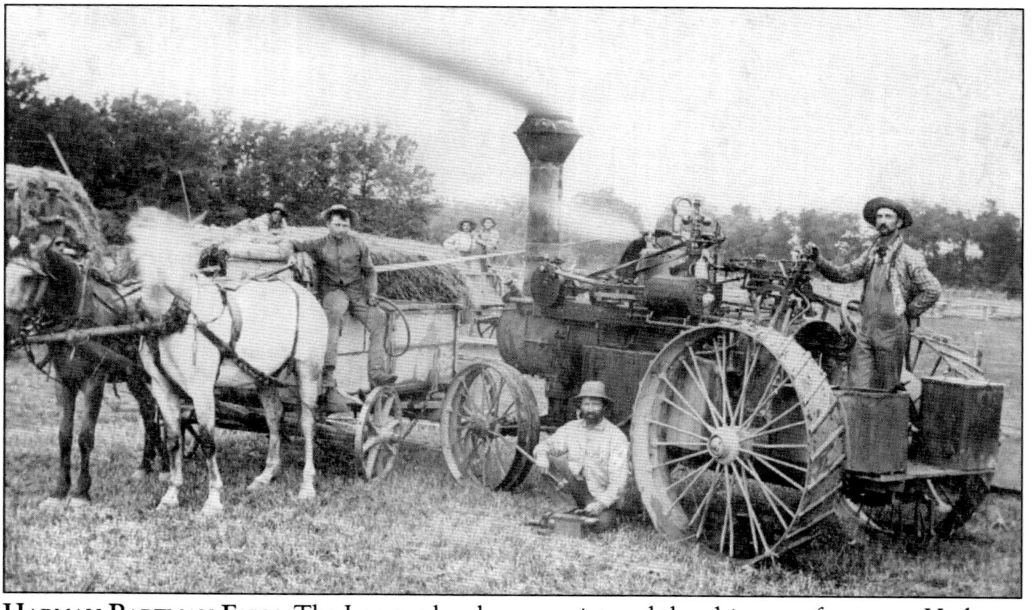

Harman Bartman Farm. The Largent brothers are pictured threshing at a farm near Herborn. The photograph was taken in the early 1900s. Dan Largent is identified as the man standing on the engine. The other two men in the foreground are "Tins" (left) and "Body" Wade. (Courtesy of Robert Largent family.)

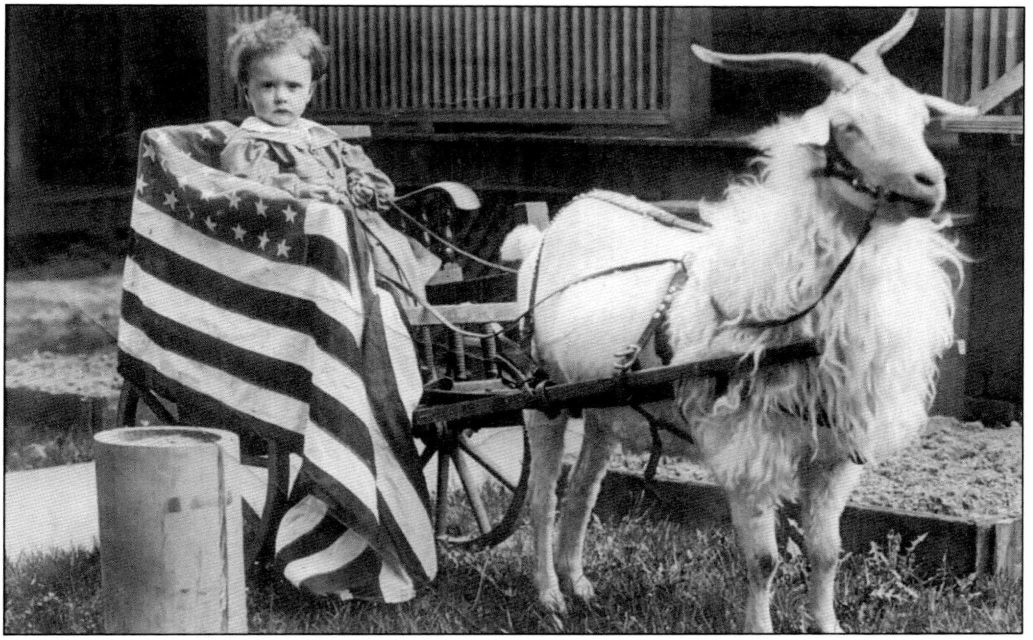

PATRIOTIC CART. Goat carts were a popular form of entertainment for children around 1900. The goat pictured is well groomed, and the cart is very detailed. This may have been part of a Fourth of July celebration. Although the child has hold of the reins, it may just be for the camera. (Courtesy of Robert Largent Family.)

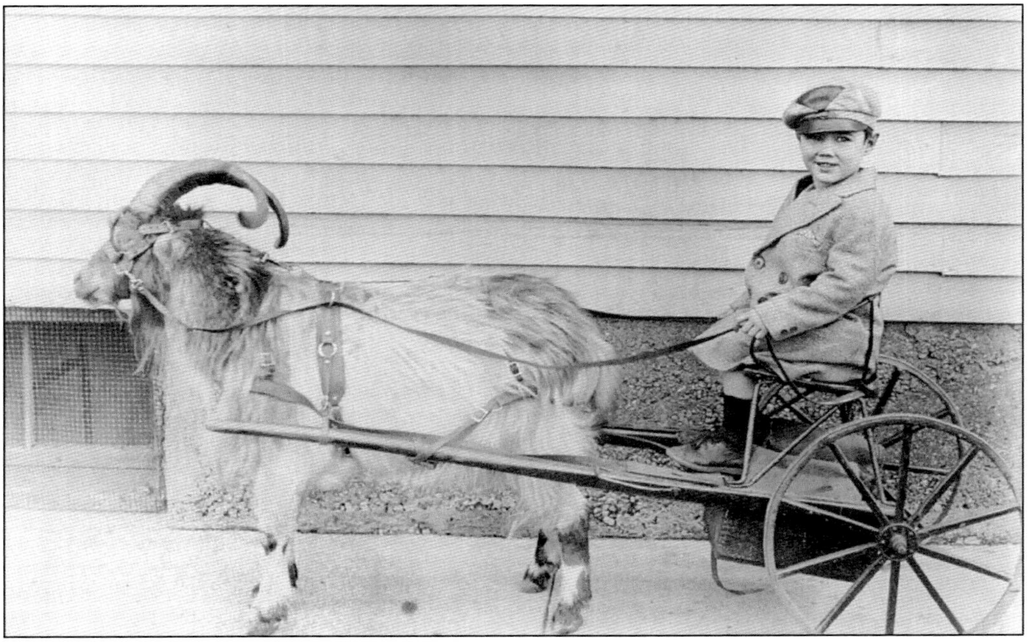

BOY WITH GOAT CART. Goat carts were a popular way to get to school. This little boy's cart looks practical. Many children travelled long distances to school, and the goat cart was an efficient way to get to school. The carts were smaller and cheaper. The goat was not as expensive as a horse and could be handled by a child.

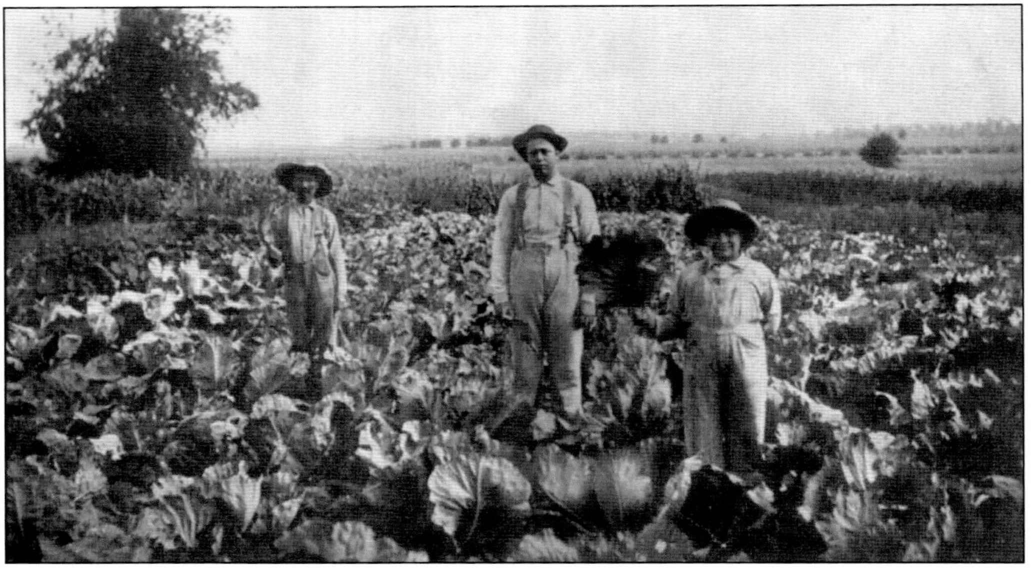

Poor Farm. The Shelby County residents realized there was a need for a place where the poor residents could live. Beulah Gordon noted that the residents were those who no one wanted because of their mental challenges, not because they were poor. The "Poor Farm" was located in rural Rose Township. Pictured is J. L. Heinz, superintendant of the farm. Standing to his left is assistant George Heinz, and to his right is assistant Ora Heinz.

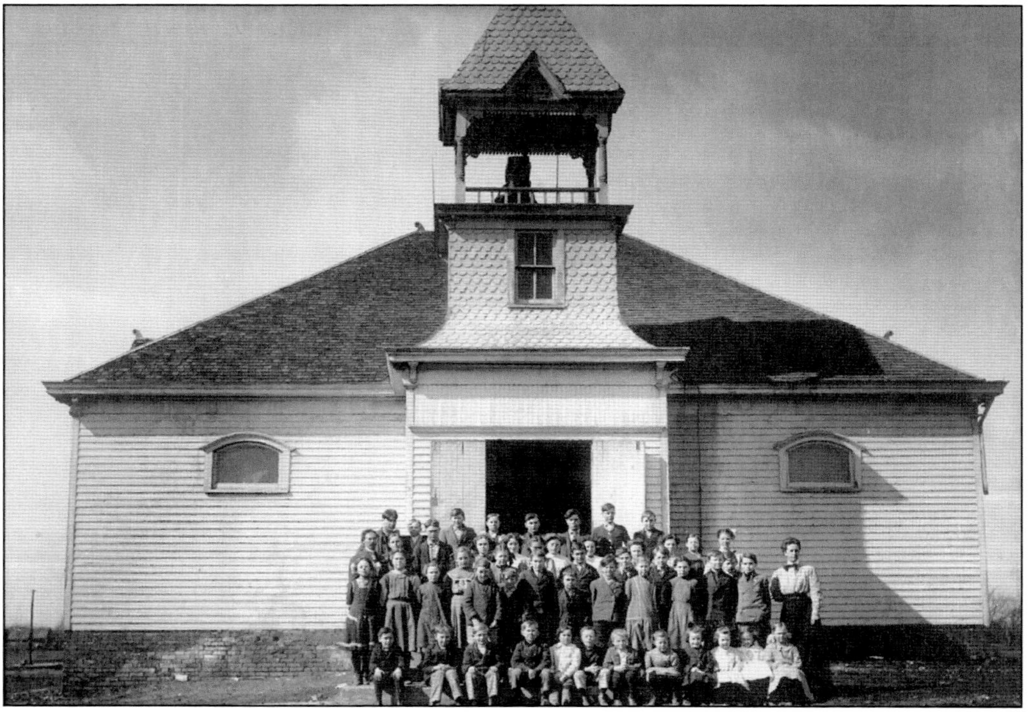

Ward School. This school was also known as Cussac's School. The school was located in rural Shelbyville Township. This photograph was probably taken in the 1800s. The school was relatively large for the number of students pictured.

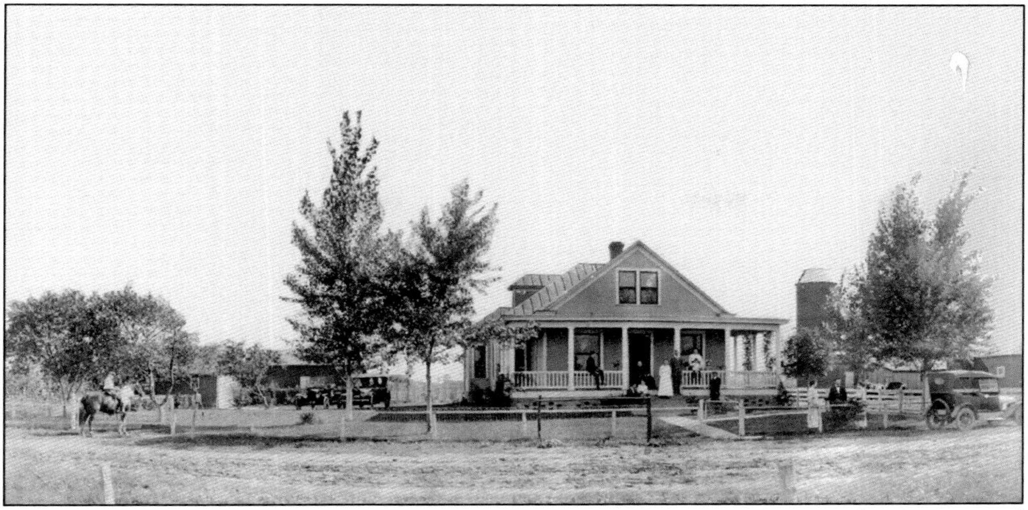

Wilson Farmstead. This is the middle section of a large panoramic photograph taken around 1910 at the A. J. Wilson farm in Rose Township. The little boy on the pony at the left side is Howard Wilson. The occasion for the photograph is unknown as several generations are pictured. (Courtesy of Clark Furr family.)

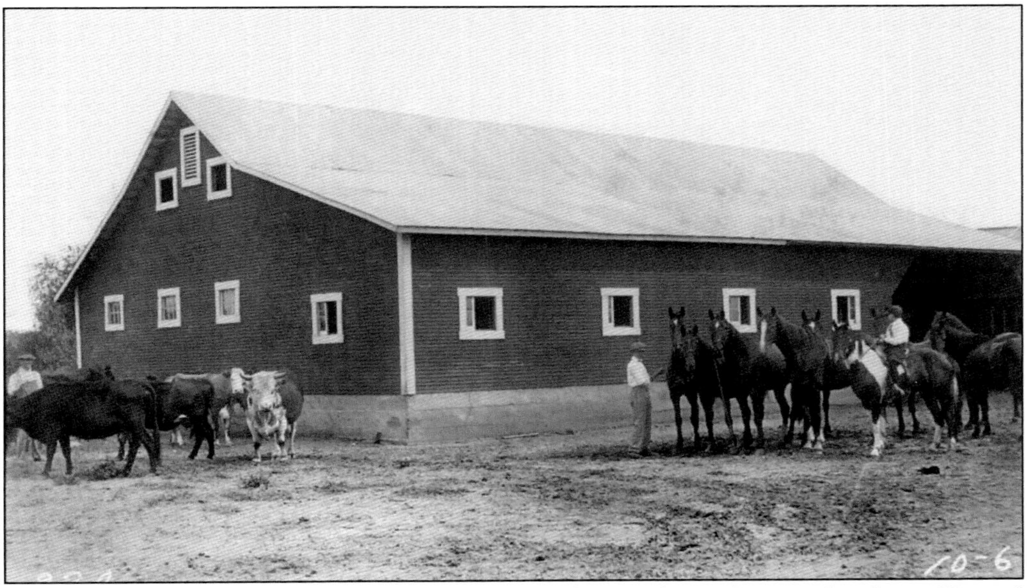

A. J. Wilson Barn. This photograph, taken around 1910, shows the complete barn. Howard Wilson is seated on his pony on the right. Horses and cattle are in the barnyard along with two unidentified men. (Courtesy of Clark Furr family.)

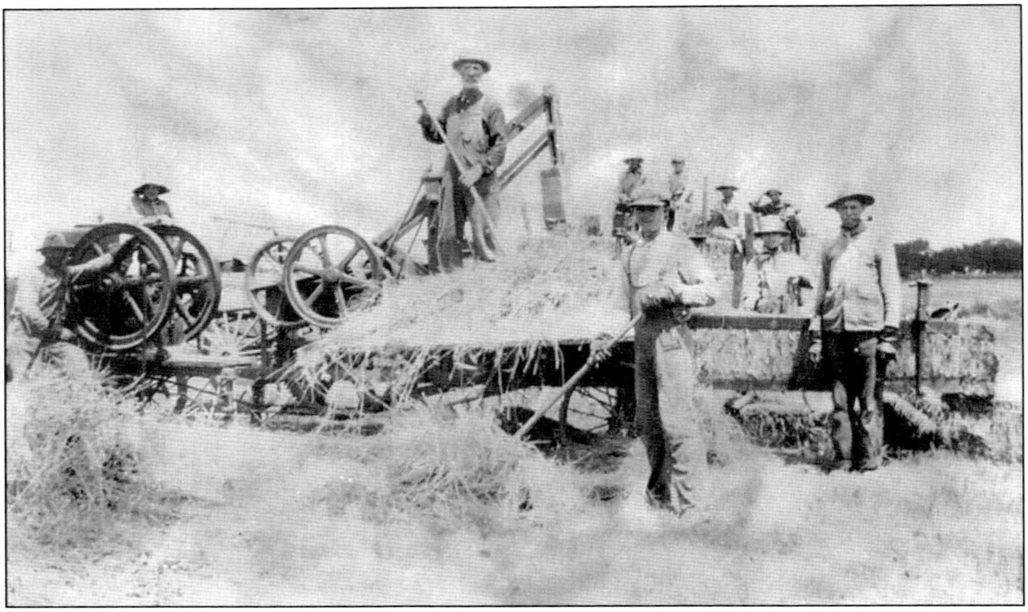

Stationary Baler. These Shelbyville Township men took a moment to be photographed. The men are loading hay, and the beats of hay can be seen behind two of the men. Hay would be manually fed into the baler and then the beats would be wired together to form a bale. These balers were used before the 1930s. (Courtesy of Robert Largent family.)

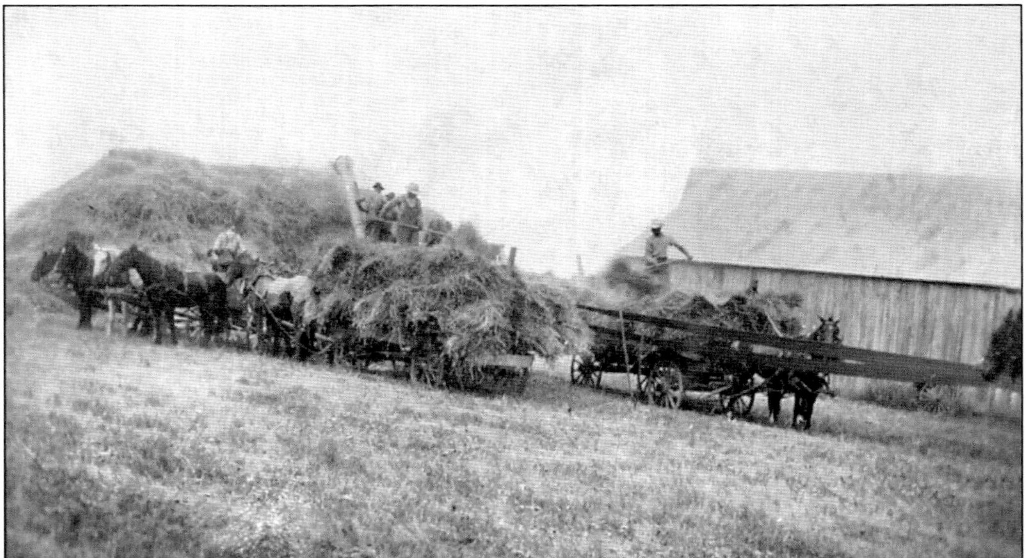

Threshing. This photograph was taken at a distance and shows the men in action. The engine belt can be seen along with the wagon and men unloading the wheat. Horse teams are also pictured. This view is almost opposite to the view of the other threshing photographs. (Courtesy of the Robert Largent family.)

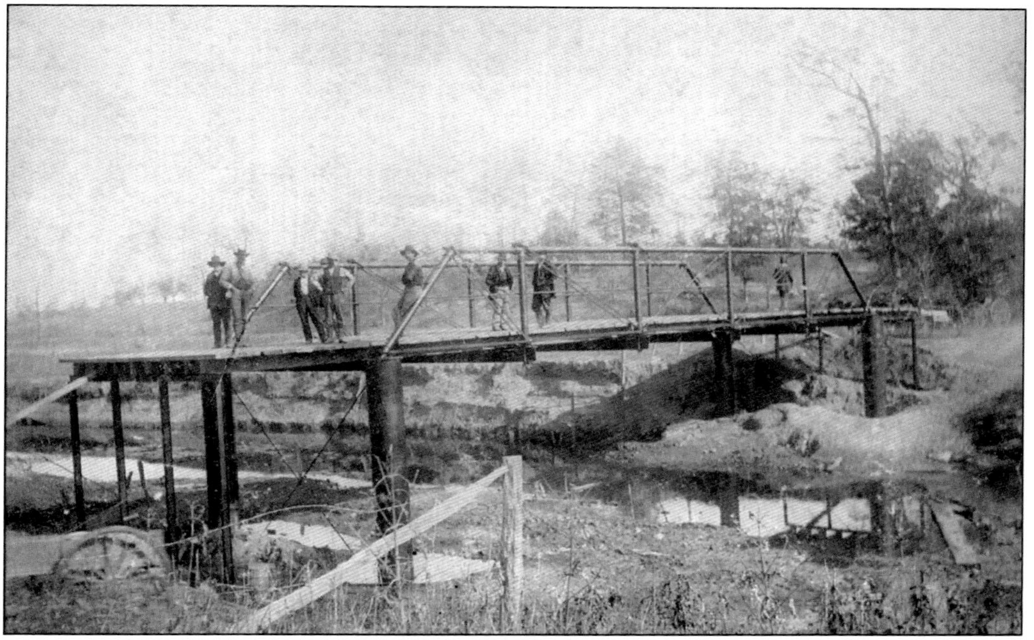

ROBINSON CREEK BRIDGE. This was a tubular iron bridge with a 120-foot span built over Robinson Creek. The bridge was built by the Trout Brothers, who operated a construction company from the 1890s. H. B. Trout was the builder of the Chautauqua Auditorium in Shelbyville. (Courtesy of Robert Largent family.)

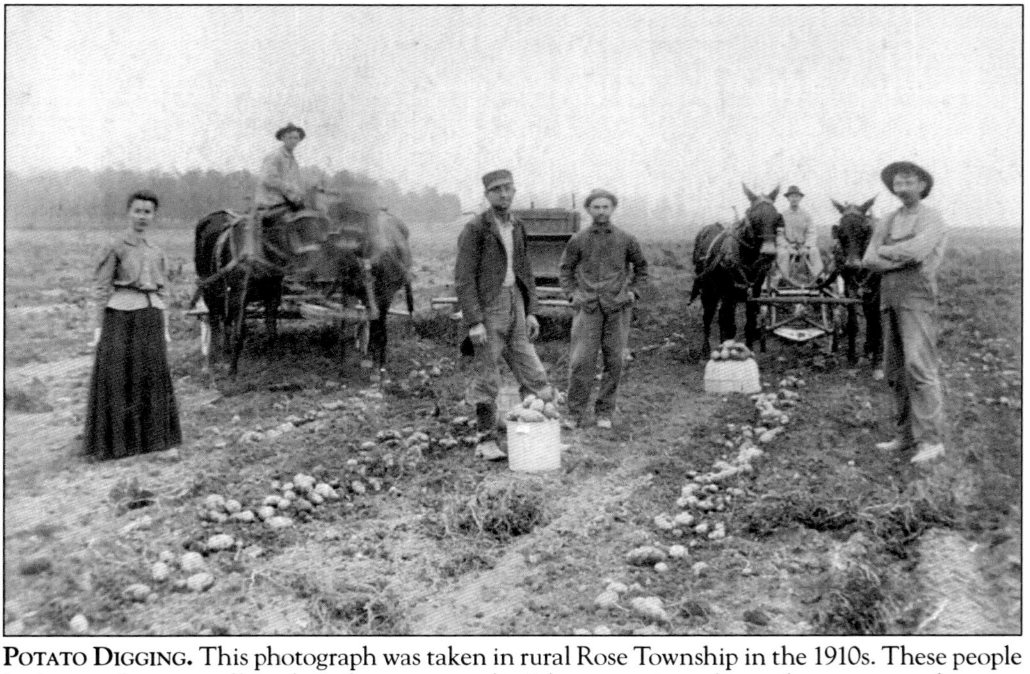

POTATO DIGGING. This photograph was taken in rural Rose Township in the 1910s. These people had more than a small garden of potatoes to dig. They are using a horse drawn potato digger to harvest their crop, spread over large acreage. The potatoes look very nice. (Courtesy of Clark Furr family.)

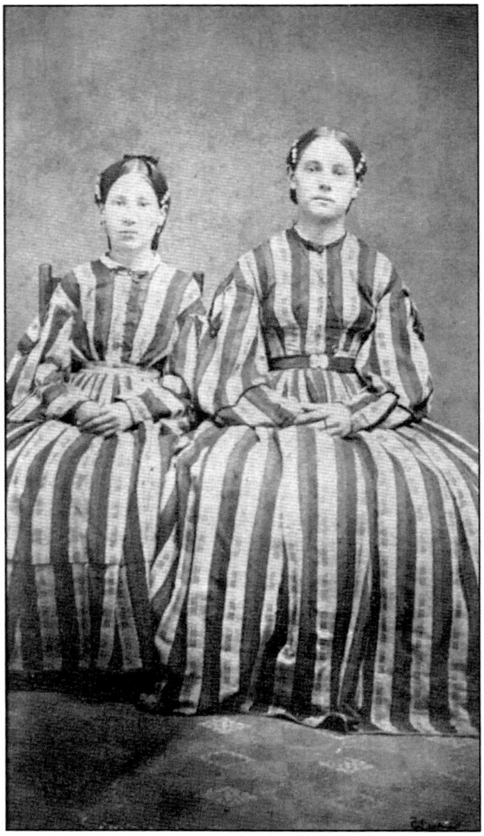

MATCHING DRESSES. These two girls pose for a photograph in their almost identical dresses. The older one has a belt and a slightly different colored collar. Their hairstyles and hair clips at the side are the same. This was probably taken in the 1920s. The striping effect of the dresses must have been time consuming. (Courtesy of Clark Furr family.)

SHOW HORSE. Clarence Dagen of rural Shelbyville poses with one of the Donnel families' show horses. This photograph was taken in the 1930s. The horse is a Percheron, the most popular breed of draft horse in the United States, and it also has some Arabian ancestry. Breeding stock was imported from the La Perche region of France. The number of Percherons began to dwindle with the increasing mechanization of agriculture. (Courtesy of Clark Furr family.)

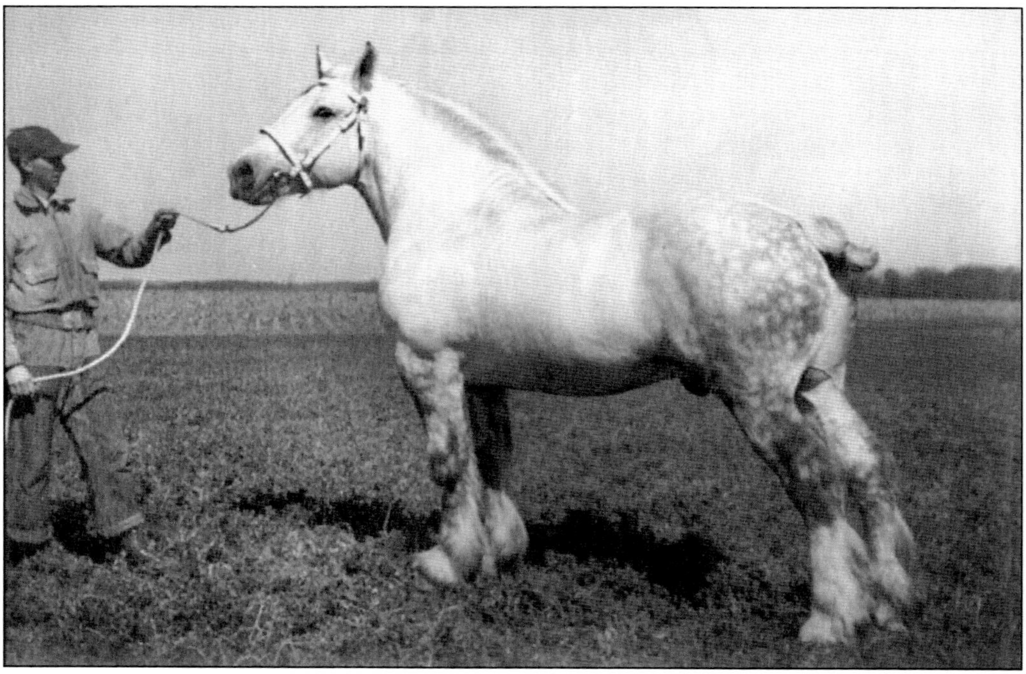

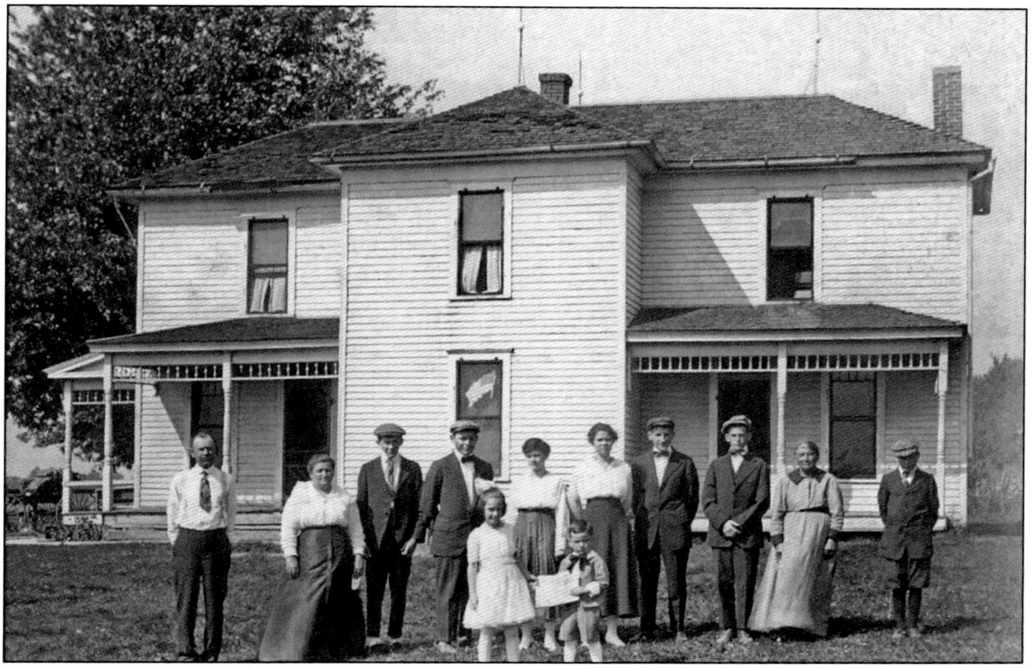

FURR FAMILY HOME. The Gordon Furr family poses in front of their home in 1910. This farm was located near Robinson Creek. George Furr is the man standing fourth from the right. He was one of the men in the courthouse photograph who was killed in action. His family commissioned a sculpture of him in uniform that marks his grave in Glenwood Cemetery. (Courtesy of Donna Lupton.)

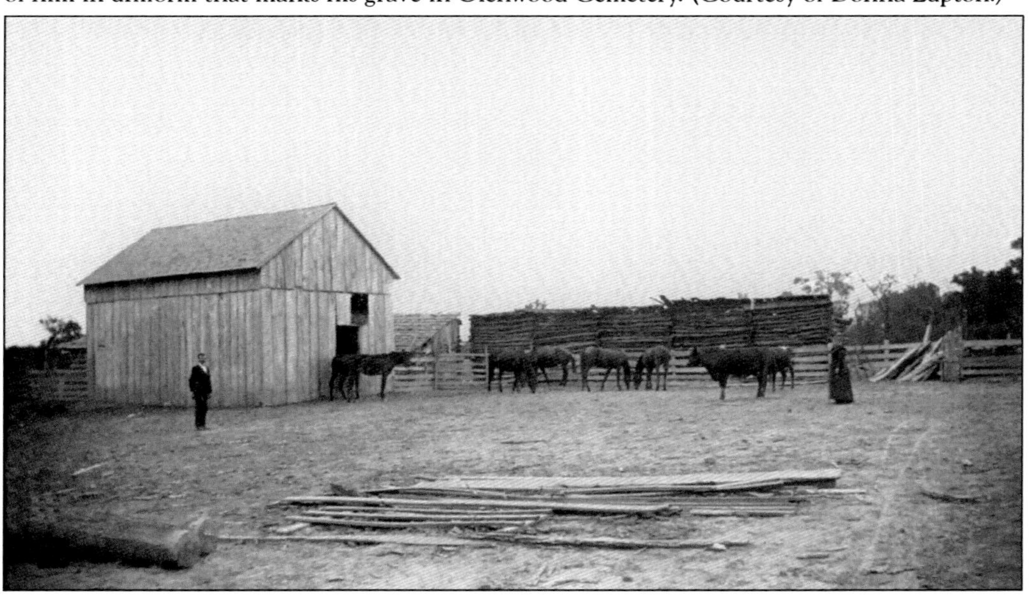

LIVESTOCK IN THE BARNYARD. This photograph was taken around 1900 at the Furr farm. Today this is the farm of Tom Horseman in Rose Township. Pictured is William Gordon Furr (left), along with his wife, Christine Luck Furr (right). There are lots of building materials stacked in the background. The materials in the foreground may indicate that the occasion for the photograph was in honor of a new barn. (Courtesy of Clark Furr family.)

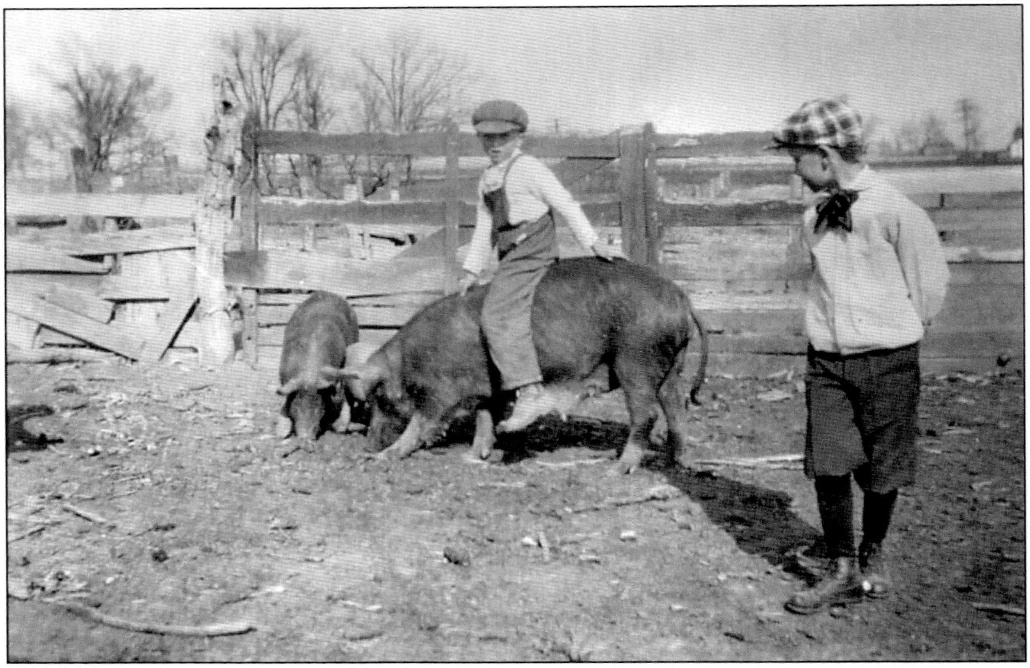

Boy Riding a Pig. Taken around 1915, this photograph shows Clarence Dagen on a pig. The other little boy is probably a visitor. His spotless attire would not last long in the pigpen. Unlike today, most farms had several types of livestock. (Courtesy of Clark Furr family.)

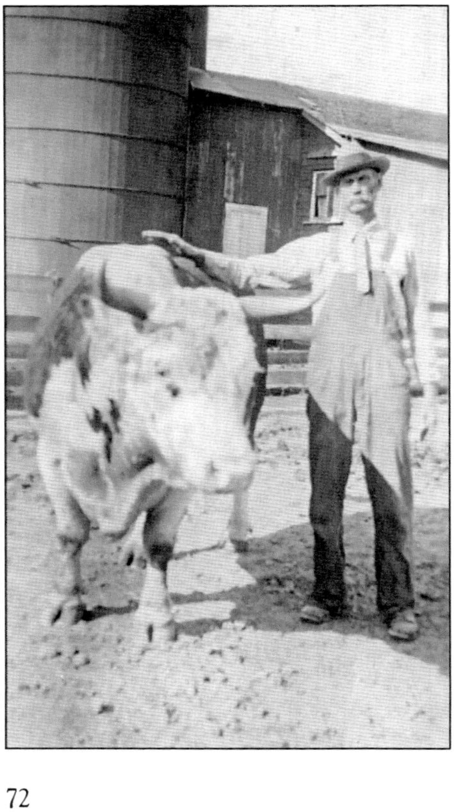

Farmer with Bull. Arthur Wilson poses with one of his favorite Hereford bulls. The bull seems rather tame and did a good job of posing for the photograph. Cattle breeders in Shelby County moved away from the horned breeds. (Courtesy of the Loren Wilson family.)

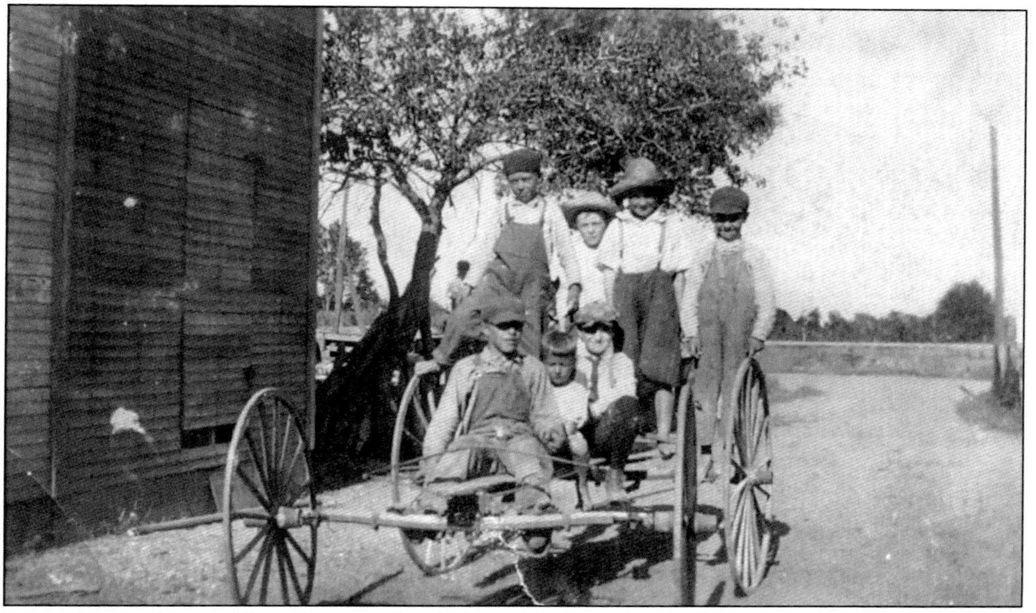

Seven Little Boys. This photograph is believed to have been taken in the 1920s at one of the Largent brother's farms in rural Shelbyville Township. Overalls were the fashion for boys, as all except the youngest has them on. Posing for the photograph probably kept them out of mischief for a few minutes. (Courtesy of Robert Largent family.)

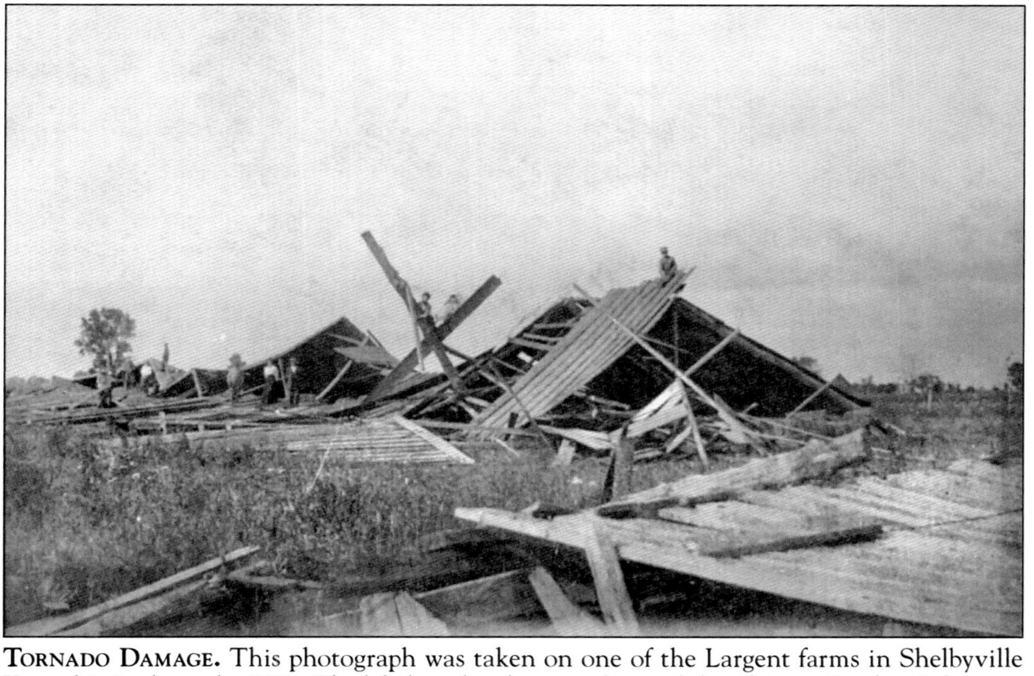

Tornado Damage. This photograph was taken on one of the Largent farms in Shelbyville Township in the early 1900s. The label on the photograph noted that this was "cyclone" damage. This was the term used for a tornado in the late 1800s and early 1900s. Today that term is used for other types of storms. The people are not identified but a large group can be seen within the damaged field. (Courtesy of Robert Largent family.)

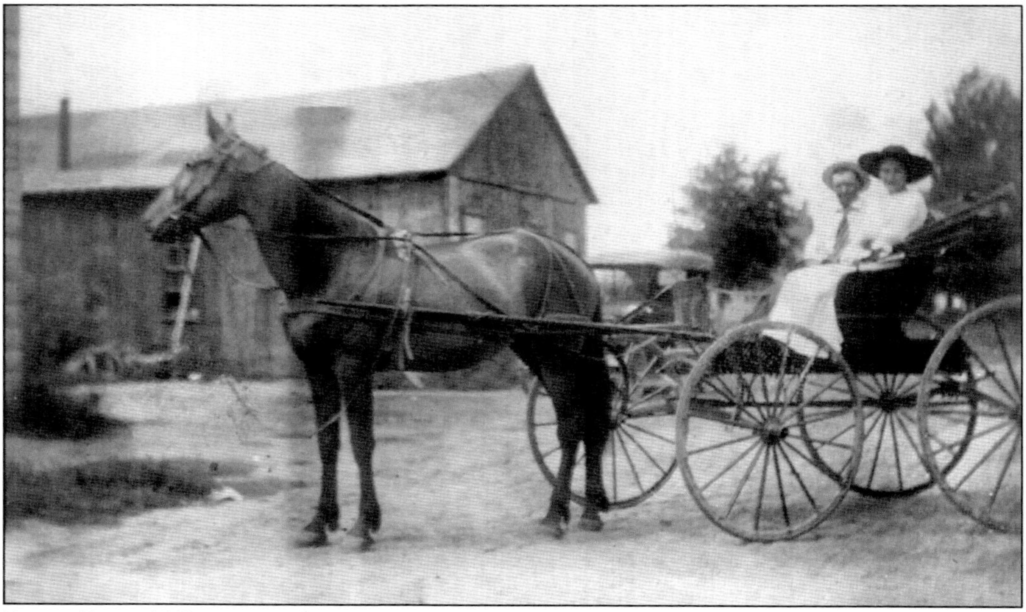

BUGGY RIDE. Alf Largent and Mary Largent are off for a buggy ride even though a car can be seen in the background. This photograph was probably taken in the 1920s. Alf Largent had returned from World War I (he is also one of the men in the courthouse photograph). This image demonstrates the transition in transportation from horses to vehicles. (Courtesy of Robert Largent family.)

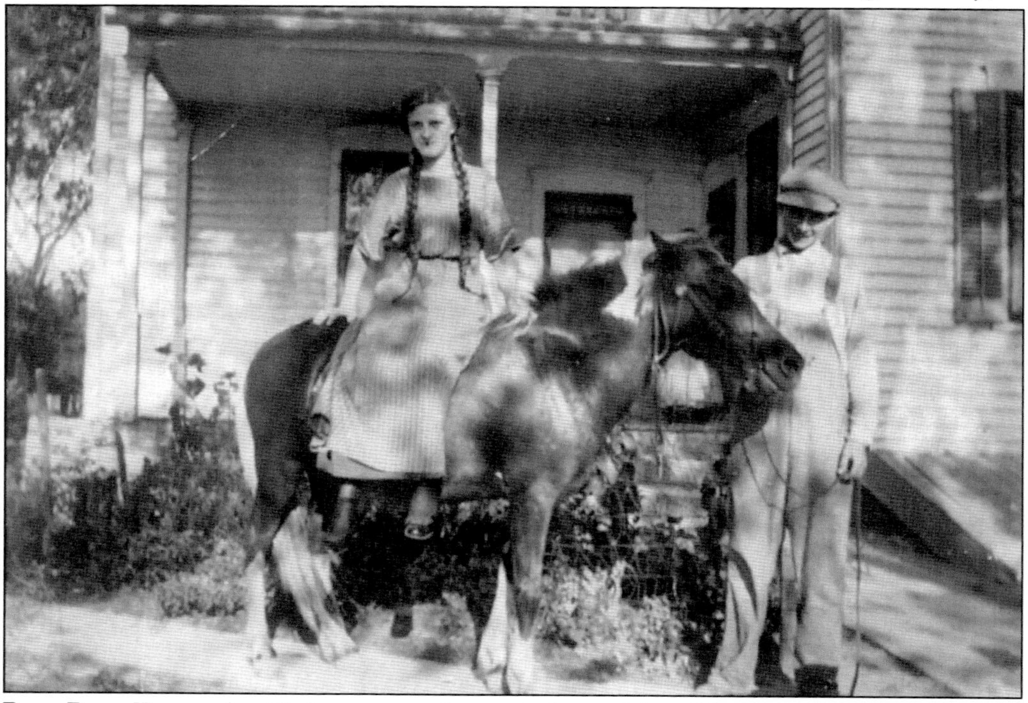

PONY RIDE. Two unidentified young people pose in front of the Alf Largent house, located in the northwest quarter of the southeast quarter of Section 22 in Shelbyville Township. The photograph was probably taken in the 1930s. (Courtesy of Robert Largent family.)

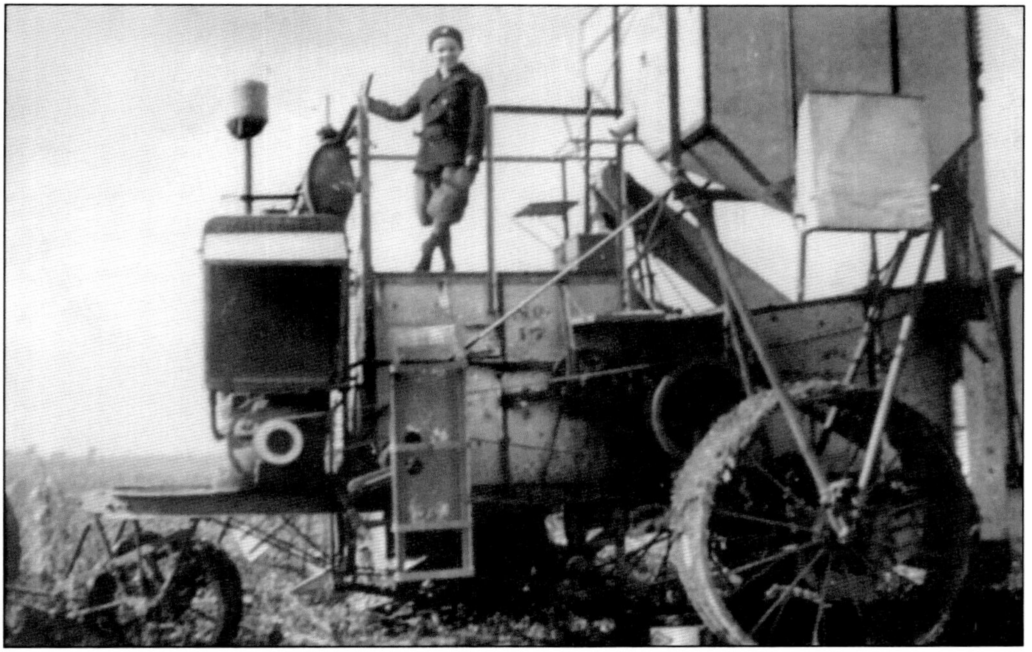

EARLY COMBINE. The term combine comes from "combined harvester–thresher." This photograph shows one of these "modern" harvesting machines, although this one is not self-propelled. It has larger metal wheels and a hopper for the grain. The threshing part of the machine is on the other side. Clarence Dagen climbed on the combine for the photograph. (Courtesy of Clark Furr family.)

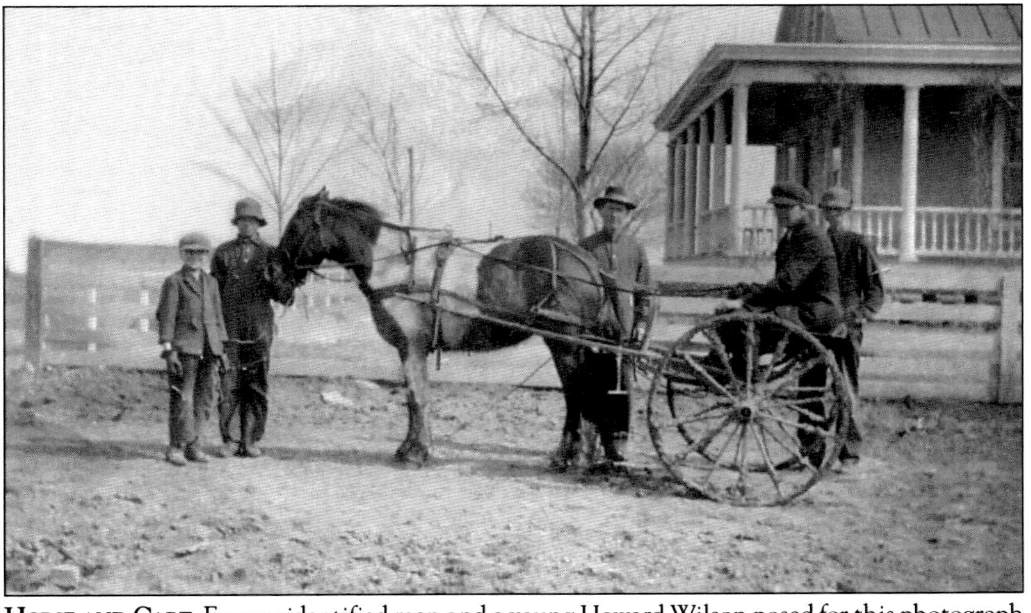

HORSE AND CART. Four unidentified men and a young Howard Wilson posed for this photograph in the barn lot of the A. J. Wilson farm. It was taken in about 1910 and shows the large buggy wheels needed for the muddy roads. If you look closely, quite a bit of mud can be seen on the wheels. (Courtesy of Clark Furr family.)

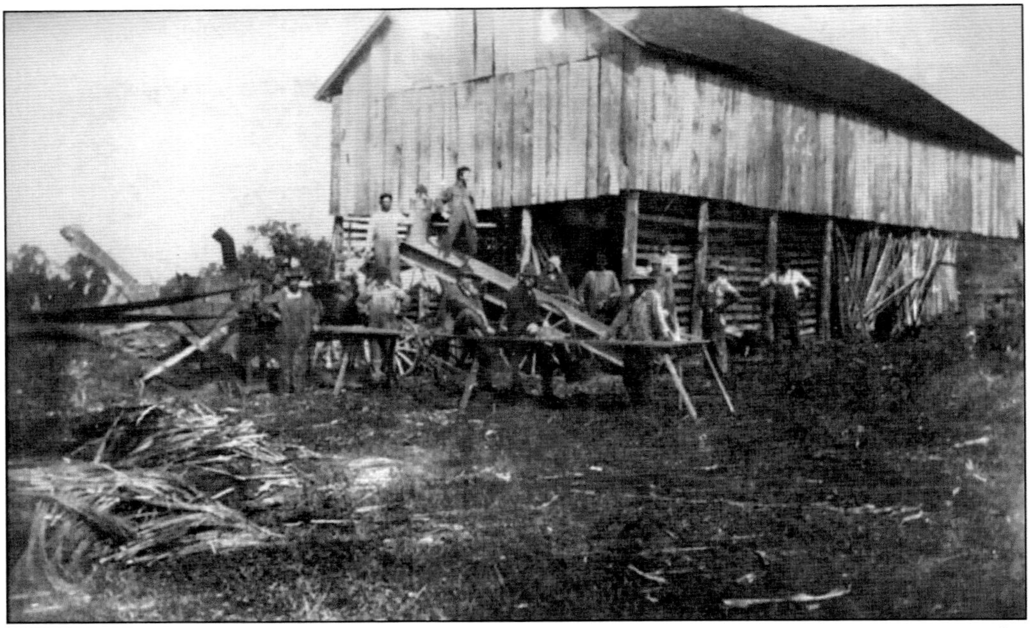

Working Hard. These men are using some implement that requires a steam engine to run the belt that powers the machine. They have a sorting table and there are materials in the foreground and background. (Courtesy of Robert Largent family.)

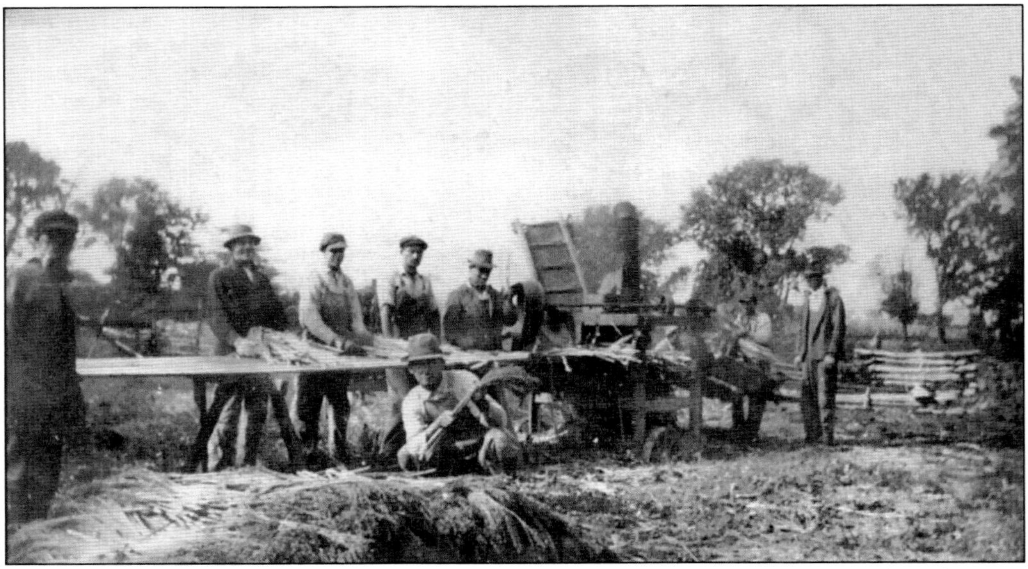

Making Brooms. On one of the Largent brother's farms, this group of men is making brooms. This photograph was taken prior to the 1930s, since it was out in the field, and it was not a permanent operation. A broom factory operated in Shelbyville in 1901 and sold brooms for 10 "Plunks." (Courtesy of Robert Largent family.)

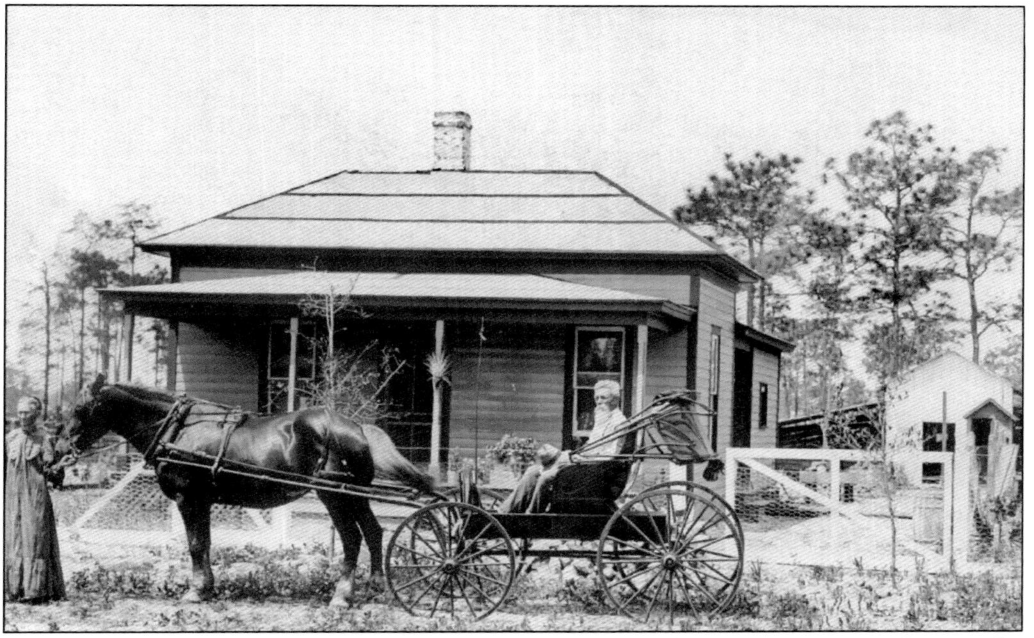

Barager House. This photograph was taken May 10, 1916, in front of the J. Barager house. The man and woman are Mr. and Mrs. J. Barager. Their house was not far from the A. C. Wilson farm in Section 36 of Ridge Township. (Courtesy of Clark Furr family.)

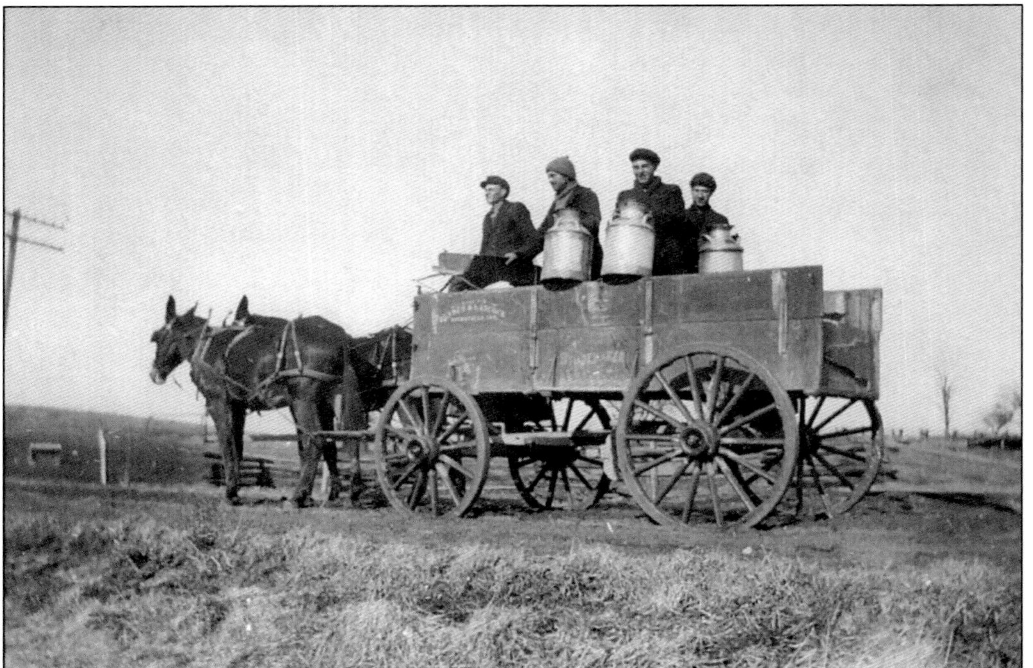

Milk Haulers. These young men photographed in the 1920s are hauling milk that they collected from Ridge Township. Its destination in Shelbyville is not known. (Courtesy of the Clark Furr family.)

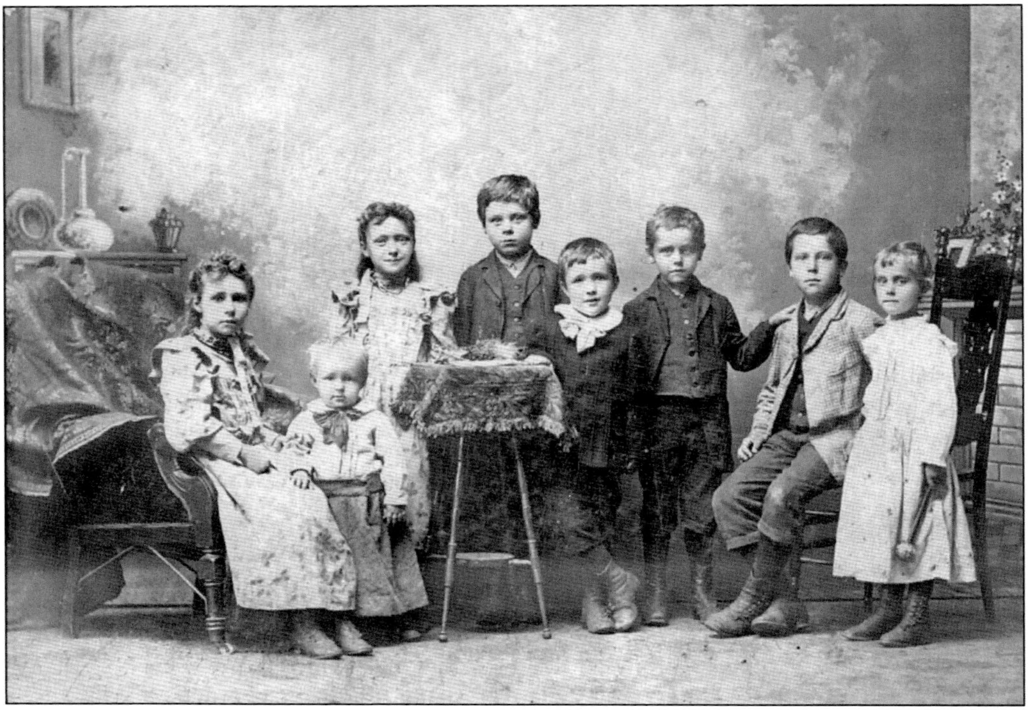

LARGENT CHILDREN. It is not known how many Largent families are represented in this photograph. The photograph is amazing because of the large number of children that held still. (Courtesy of Robert Largent family.)

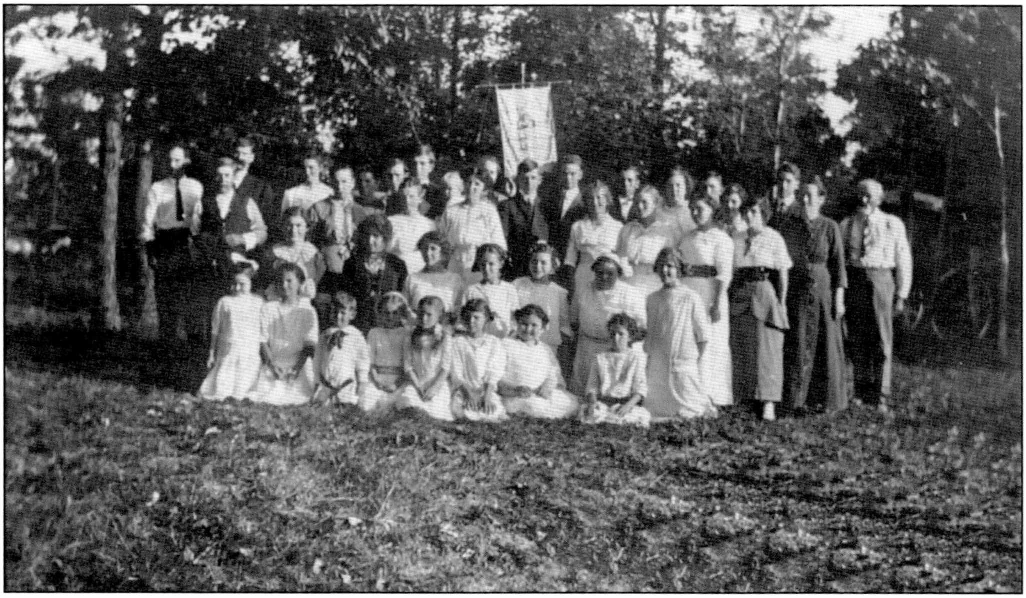

SUNDAY SCHOOL PICNIC. The Oak Grove Cemetery is all that is left of the Oak Grove Church. This picnic was held at the Oak Grove Church. The cemetery is located in southeast quarter of the northeast quarter of Section 22 in Shelbyville Township. The photograph was probably taken in the 1930s.

Three

Middlesworth, Westervelt, and Henton

The Middlesworth Post Office was first established on January 25, 1870. It was discontinued on May 13, 1875, re-established on January 21, 1876, discontinued on August 7, 1876, re-established on November 13, 1881, and then finally discontinued in 1931. Abraham Middlesworth purchased large tracts of land in many Shelby County Townships. The name of the town is thought to come from Abraham Middlesworth or one of his sons. The Terre Haute, Alton Railroad passed through Middlesworth. The shipping of livestock was the main business in the 1800s. Grain shipping became more prominent in the 1920s. After the Depression, the grain business made a comeback. In 1891, Jasper Douthit began the Lithia Springs Chautauqua. Each summer through the 1920s, classes, speakers, and many types of entertainment attracted large crowds. During this time, Middlesworth was a busy railroad stop. Other types of education and entertainment replaced the Chautauquas, and one of the few Chautauquas to be started in a rural area disappeared.

The village of Westervelt was surveyed for William Middlesworth in 1903. In 1904, the Chicago and Eastern Illinois Railroad was completed. The railroad brought growth. The names Middlesworth and Christman were suggested for the new town, but these were already taken. Dr. C. J. Westervelt was asked to name the town, and he called it Westervelt. Merchants moved in, and soon there was a restaurant, grocery, meat market, barbershop, lumberyard, elevator, general store, and doctor. The First Evangelical Church was dedicated on January 1, 1905. This church was completely destroyed along with 12 houses as a result of the Mattoon tornado in 1917. Five people were killed, and some of the debris from Westervelt was found as far away as Paris, Illinois.

Mr. Fulton was the first to establish a store in the village of Prairie Bird. A post office was established March 2, 1850, and discontinued on January 7, 1862. The name was eventually changed to Henton in honor of Isaiah Henton. On September 3, 1884, Isaiah Henton established a post office, and the village then went by the name of Henton, not Prairie Bird.

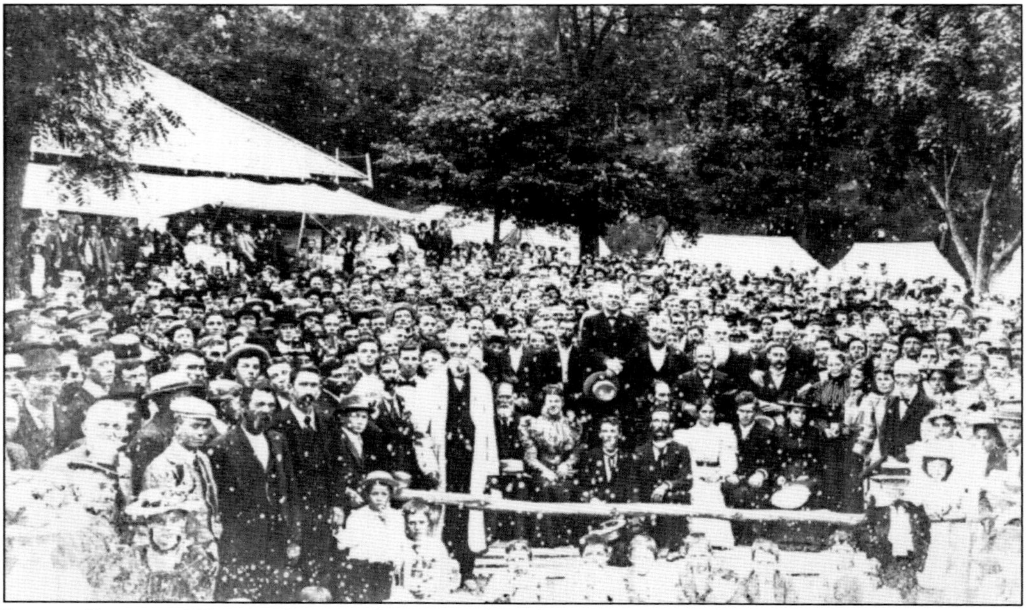

Lithia Springs. This is a large gathering at the Chautauqua in Lithia Springs. The photograph was taken about 1900 because of the presence of Anthony Thornton. The tall man in the long white coat is Judge Anthony Thornton, a prominent Shelbyville citizen and debate opponent of Abraham Lincoln. Most of the Chautauqua buildings at Lithia Springs were only temporary; the tents in the background are good examples.

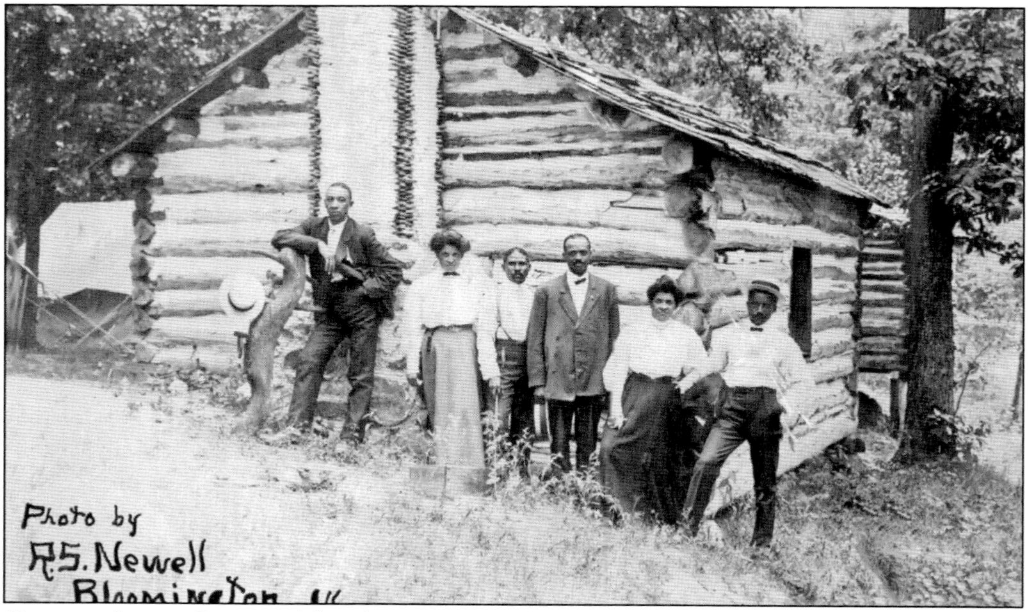

Carolina Jubilee Singers. A lot of singing groups from all over the country provided entertainment at the Chautauquas. The Jubilee Singers pose in front of one of the cabins owned by the Douthits. The photograph was taken around 1900. The man on the left is leaning on part of an old ox yoke. African American singing groups were popular with the Chautauquas, and their visits went without incident here.

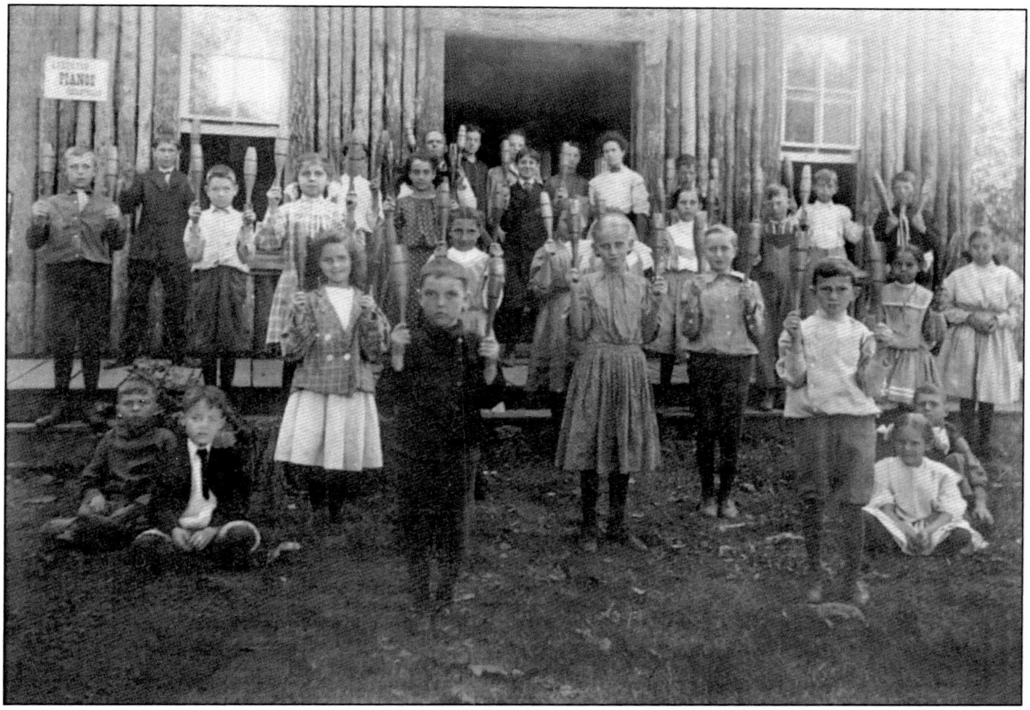

Physical Culture at Lithia. Taken in August of 1908, this photograph shows one of the classes for the small children. The children played games and activities while the adults went to classes. The pins in the children's hands look like small bowling pins but were actually made for exercise. Lithia Springs got its name from the lithium in the water in this area.

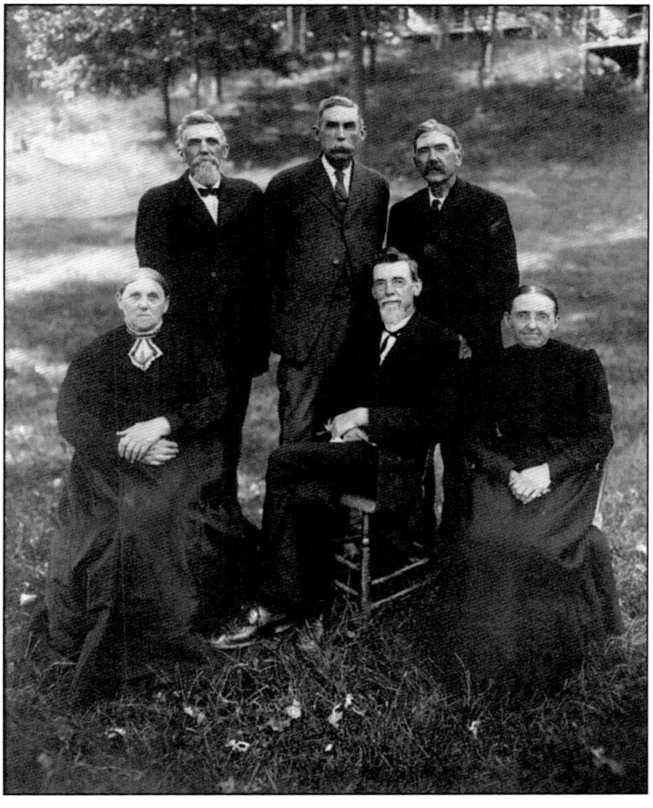

Douthit Family. This photograph was taken at Lithia Springs in 1905. Shown here are, from left to right, (first row) Nancy Thomas, Rev. Jasper Douthit, and Margaret Elliot; (second row) Samuel, William Franklin, and Levi Douthit. Reverend Douthit was a Unitarian minister in Shelbyville and the author of *Our Best Words*, published for over 30 years.

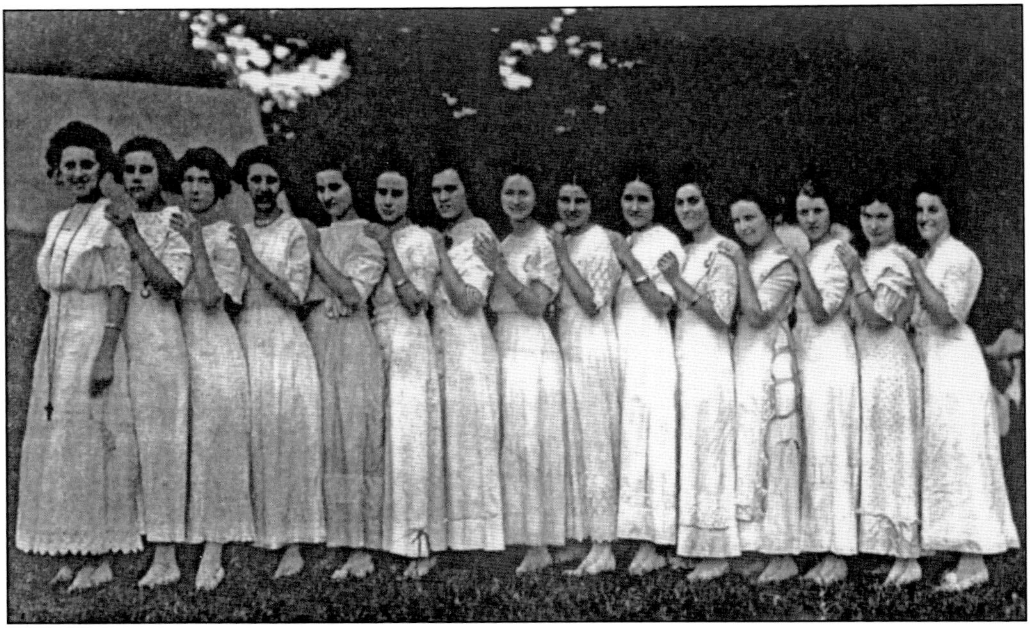

Girls in White. This group of girls posed for a photograph in 1910 during the Chautauqua at Lithia Springs. At the Chautauqua there was entertainment for everyone, and most people from around the area attended with their families. Most women and children stayed for the entire Chautauqua season even if the men did not.

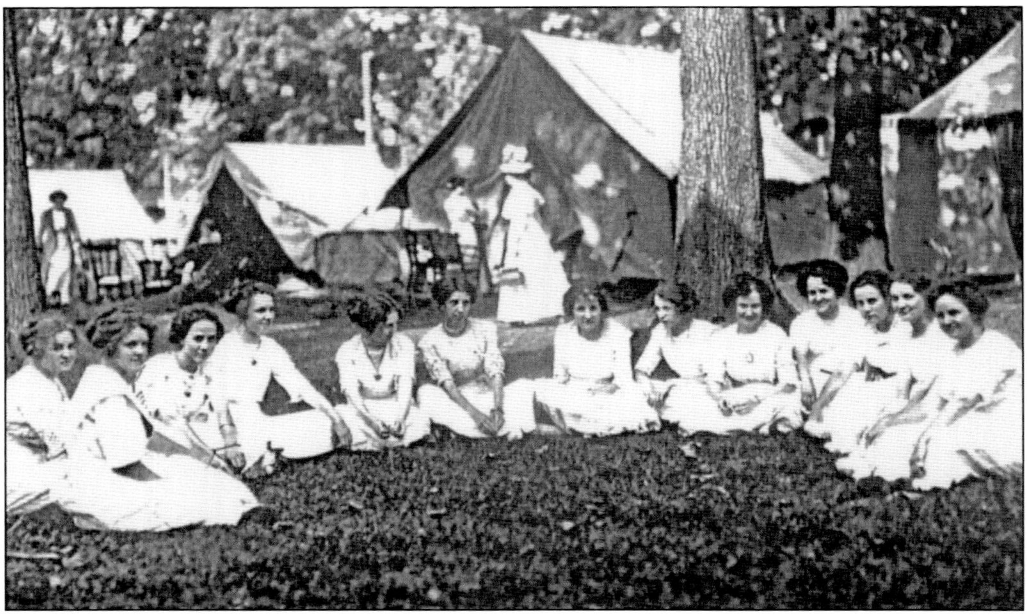

Tents at Lithia Springs. Most people who attended the Chautauqua stayed in tents on the grounds, as there were only a few cabins. It was the height of social interaction, and these girls seem excited to be at the Chautauqua.

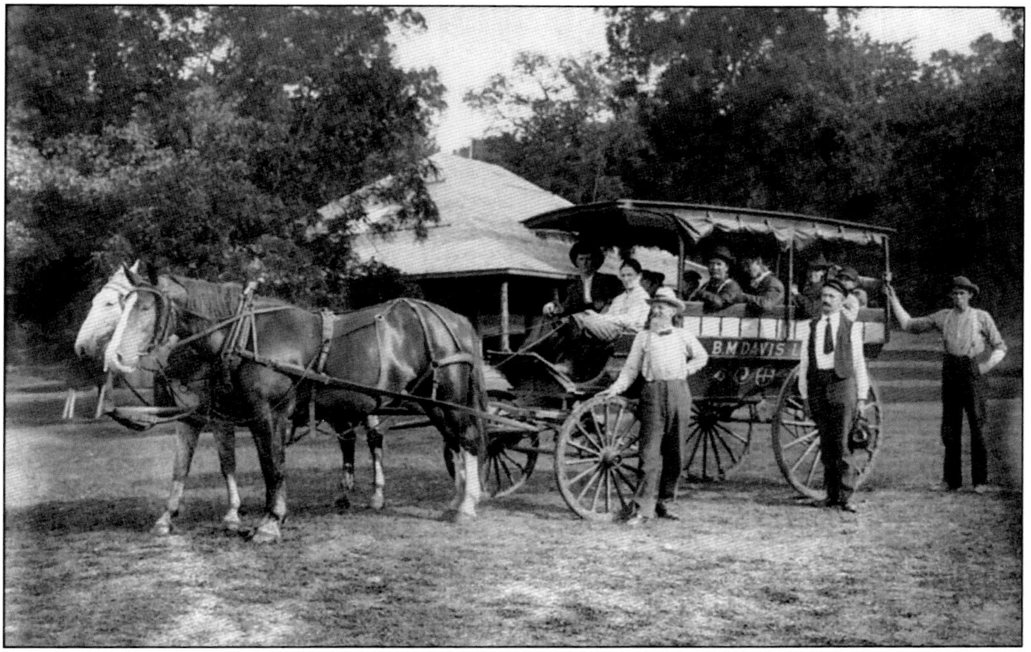

EARLY STATION WAGON. This dray was used to pick up passengers at the railroad depot in Middlesworth and take them to the Lithia Springs Chautauqua. In this 1901 photograph, the dray driver is John Cihak. The man at the front is William Thomas, and the man at the rear is Elmer Douthit.

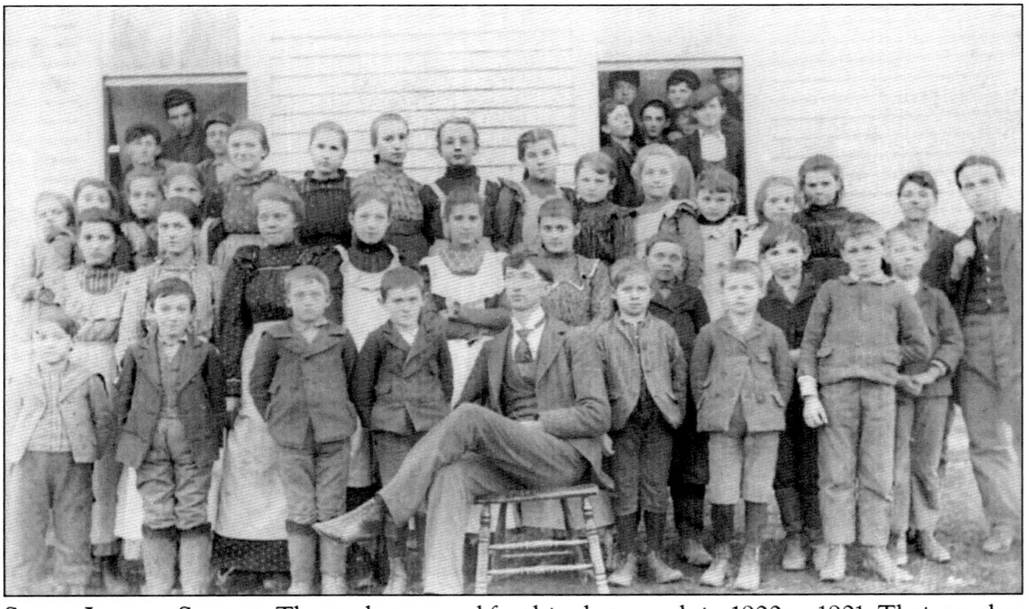

SOUTH LIBERTY SCHOOL. The students posed for this photograph in 1900 or 1901. Their teacher is in the front sitting on the chair but is unidentified. The number of students was quite large relative to the size of their school building. The children seem to be pushing to get in the window so they can be seen in the photograph.

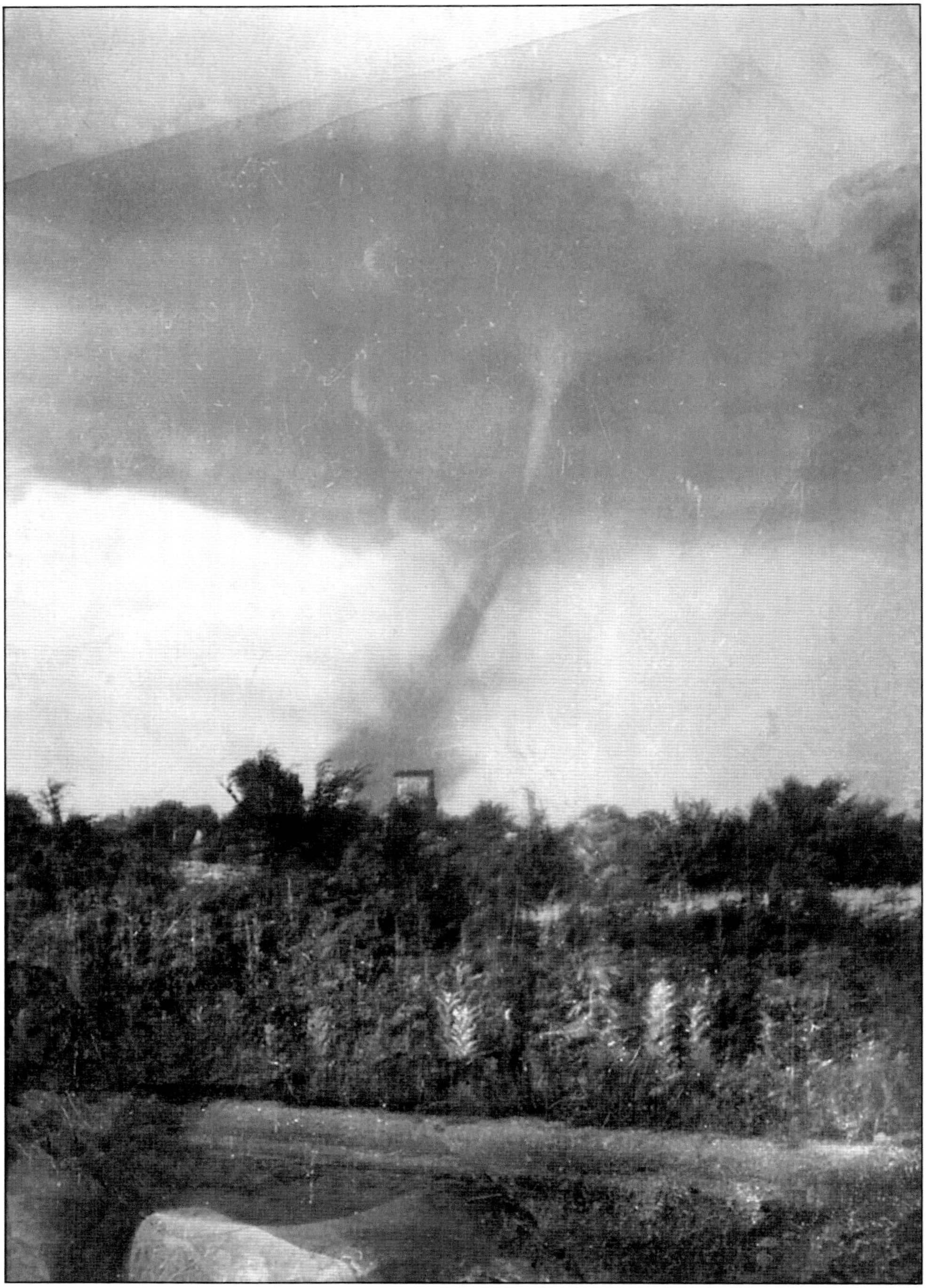

1917 Mattoon Tornado at Westervelt. This photograph was taken on May 26, 1917, at 3:00 p.m. The approaching tornado destroyed 12 houses, a church, and killed five people. In less than one hour, the tornado hit Mattoon and became known as the 1917 Mattoon Tornado because of the devastation that resulted. Early photographs of tornadoes are extremely rare, so this is all the more impressive.

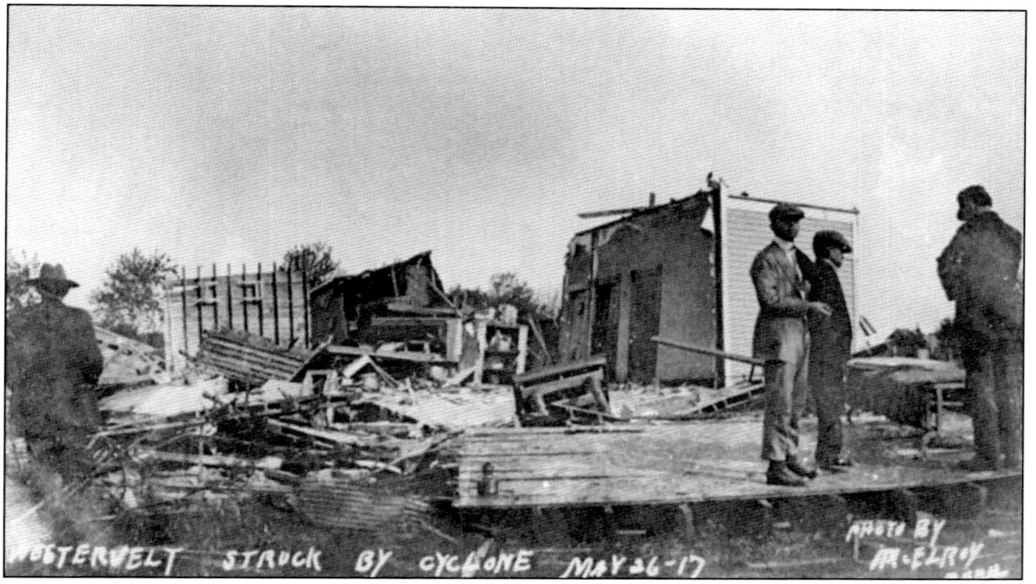

Tornado Damage at Westervelt. The 1917 Mattoon Tornado caused $50,000 worth of damage. The Evangelical church was completely destroyed. This photograph shows some of the destruction.

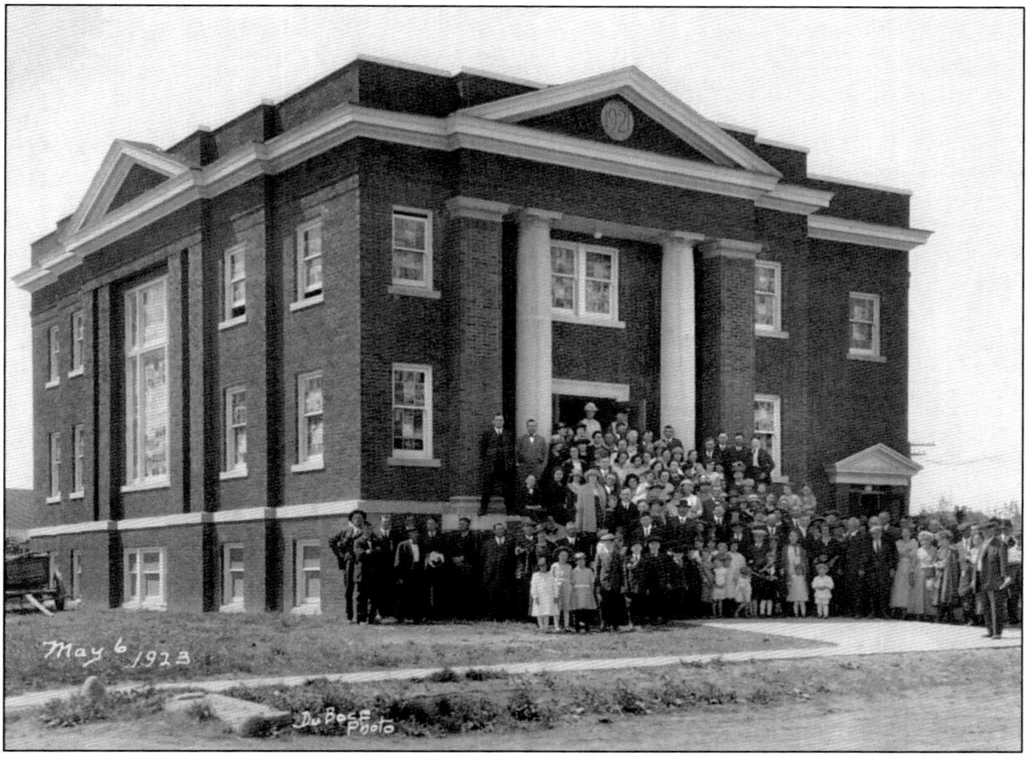

Westervelt Christian Church. This photograph was taken when the church was dedicated on May 6, 1923. The congregation proudly poses in front of the impressive church. Charles Harris of Urbana was the architect. The church is known for its fine acoustics.

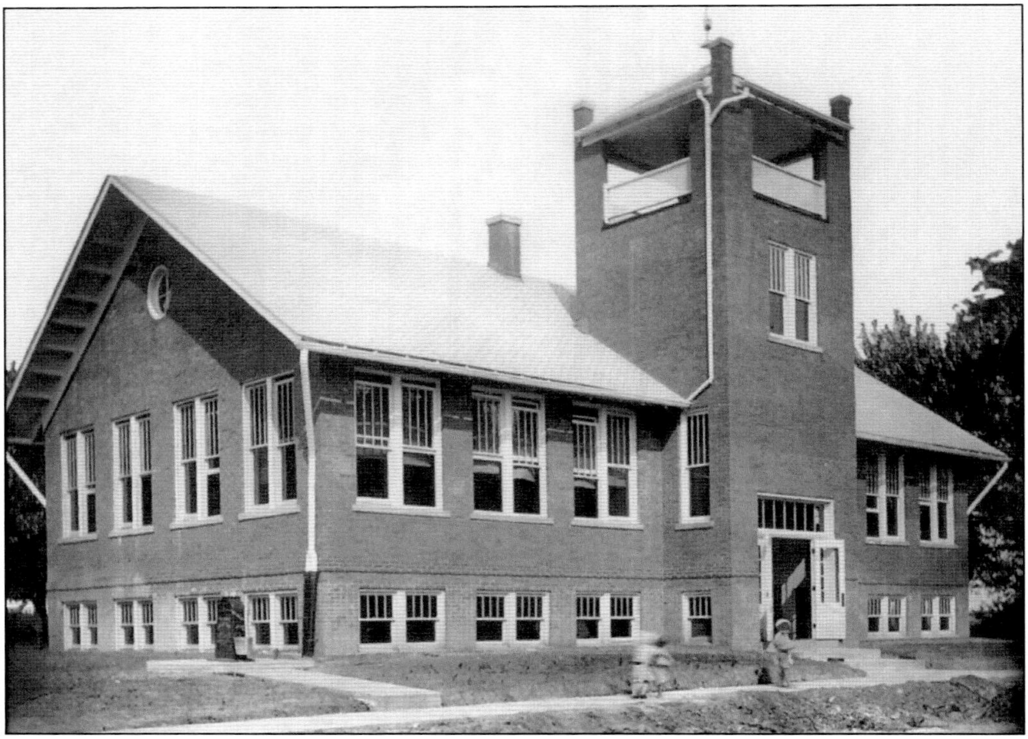

Westervelt Grade and High School. The four-room school was built in 1918, and this photograph was taken soon after, as the fire escapes and window screens were not yet installed. The upper floors were occupied by the lower grades and high school study hall while the other grades were downstairs.

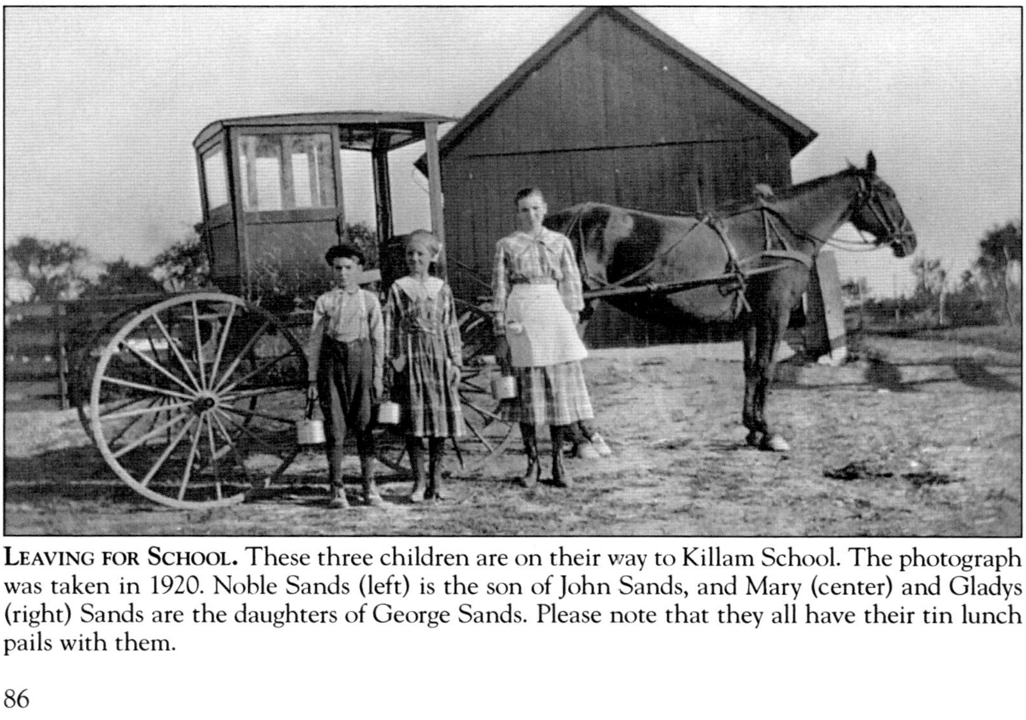

Leaving for School. These three children are on their way to Killam School. The photograph was taken in 1920. Noble Sands (left) is the son of John Sands, and Mary (center) and Gladys (right) Sands are the daughters of George Sands. Please note that they all have their tin lunch pails with them.

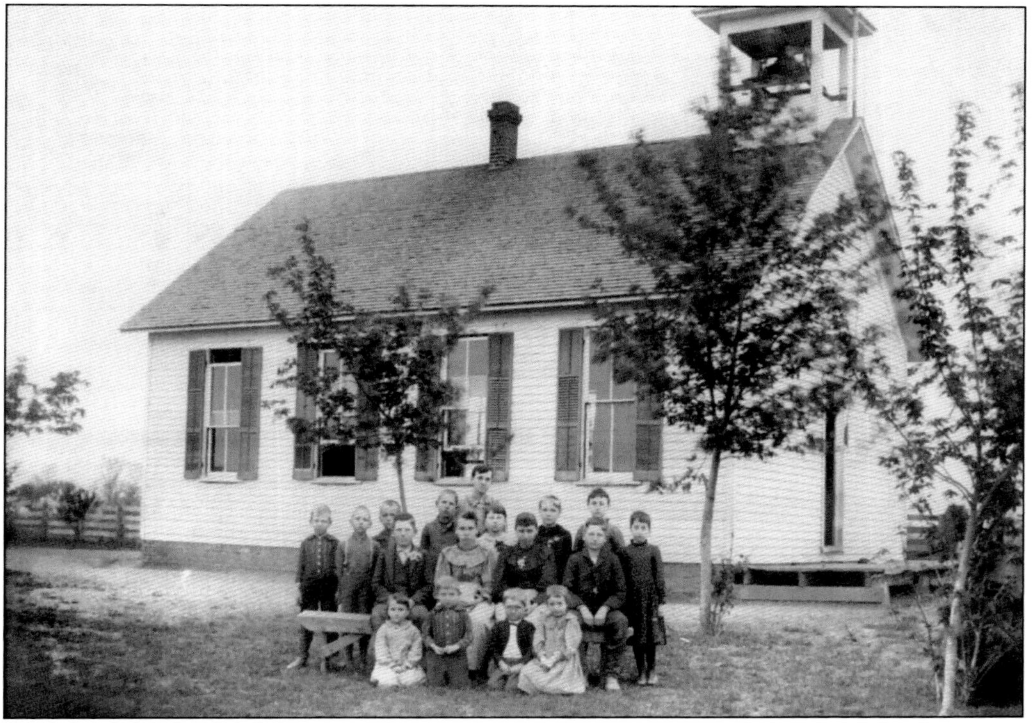

Buckeye School. The school was located on the west edge of Westervelt and on the north edge of the elevator property. The school was replaced with a brick building. Most of the children were from the Yost family, while others were from the Weakly, Miller, and Gladfelter families. The photograph was taken in the 1890s.

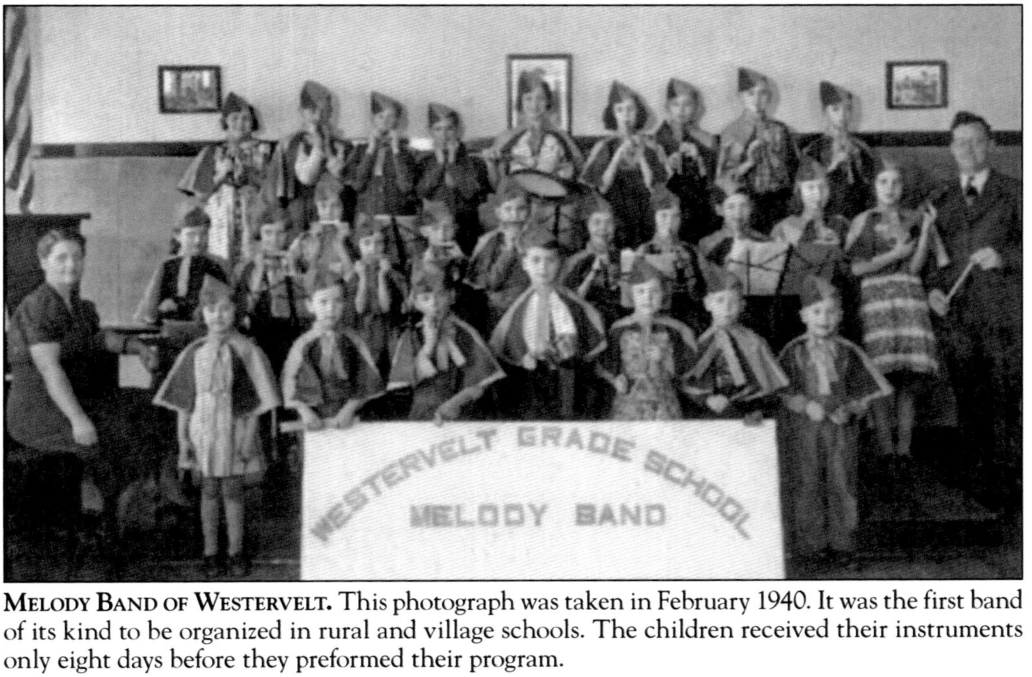

Melody Band of Westervelt. This photograph was taken in February 1940. It was the first band of its kind to be organized in rural and village schools. The children received their instruments only eight days before they preformed their program.

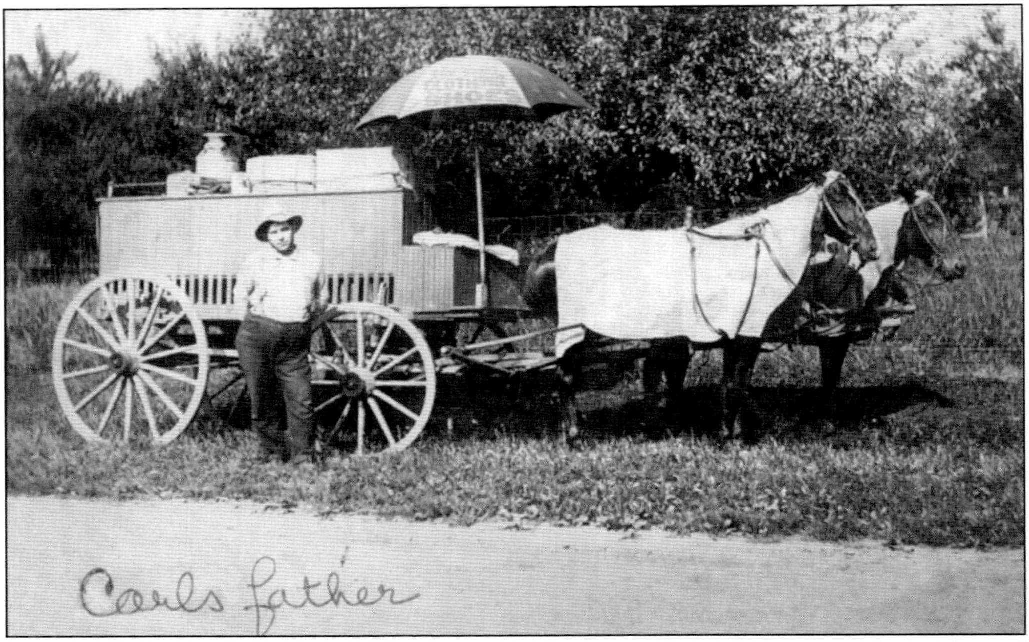

HUCKSTER WAGON. This photograph, taken in 1909, shows Anderson Rittgers standing in front of his huckster wagon. He is the father of Carl Rittgers. His route ran from Henton to Yantisville.

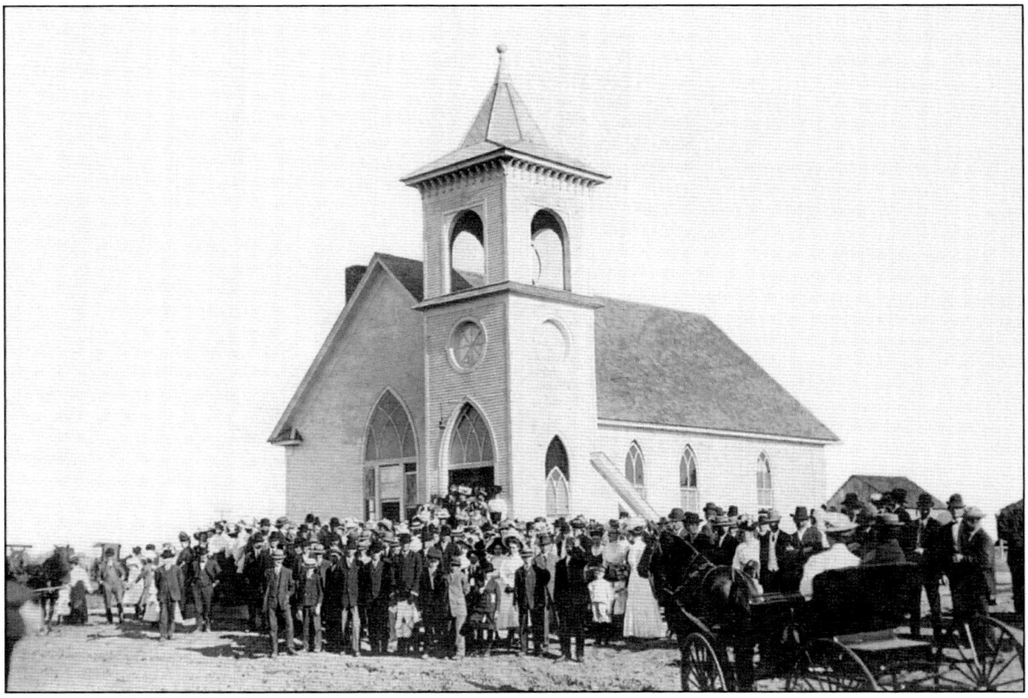

HENTON METHODIST CHURCH. This photograph was taken in 1909. The occasion is believed to be the church's dedication. It is unclear why the man and woman in the buggy on the right are there but are not a part of the group to be photographed.

Four

Stewardson, Strasburg, Sigel, and Herborn

When the Old Chicago and Paducah Railroad came to the Stewardson area, people decided there was a need for a town. William Stewartson had land where thousands of his sheep grazed, and voters chose this location for the town. The town was platted on January 10, 1874, but a controversy arose between the Germans and the English residents. The English preferred Stewartson named after the founder, while the Germans preferred Metz after Metz, Germany. The town was incorporated on September 30, 1874, as the Village of Stewartson but on June 25, 1883, the post office was changed to Stewardson. Mail could be sent to either Stewardson or Metz through the 1880s.

Charles Ostermeier constructed a store building where the Marathon Station is currently located. When the railroad began to pass through in 1874, he laid out 40 acres for a town around his store. Charles Ostermeier named it after his native Strasburg on the Rhine in Germany. He named the streets after those in St. Louis. The first crop grown in this area was wheat. The marshes around Strasburg were drained by tiling. The railroad provided transportation to the markets. Before incorporation, Strasburg split into a North Burg and a South Burg, but this was trouble for the village. An election was held and North Burg was incorporated as Strasburg in 1882, excluding South Burg.

In July 1863, Theodore Hoffman of Chicago purchased land for a town. Sigel was named after General Sigel, a famous Civil War general who was in the second Battle of Bull Run. In 1862 Sigel applied for a post office, but there was already a Sigel. Sigel became known as Hooker. Then when the northern Illinois Sigel lost its post office, Hooker changed back to Sigel.

The Wabash railroad agreed to put a switch at the present location of Herborn. In exchange H. W. Rinker would grant the Wabash Railroad a right of way through his land. He named Herborn after his hometown in Germany. The town had several business but in 1945 its decline began.

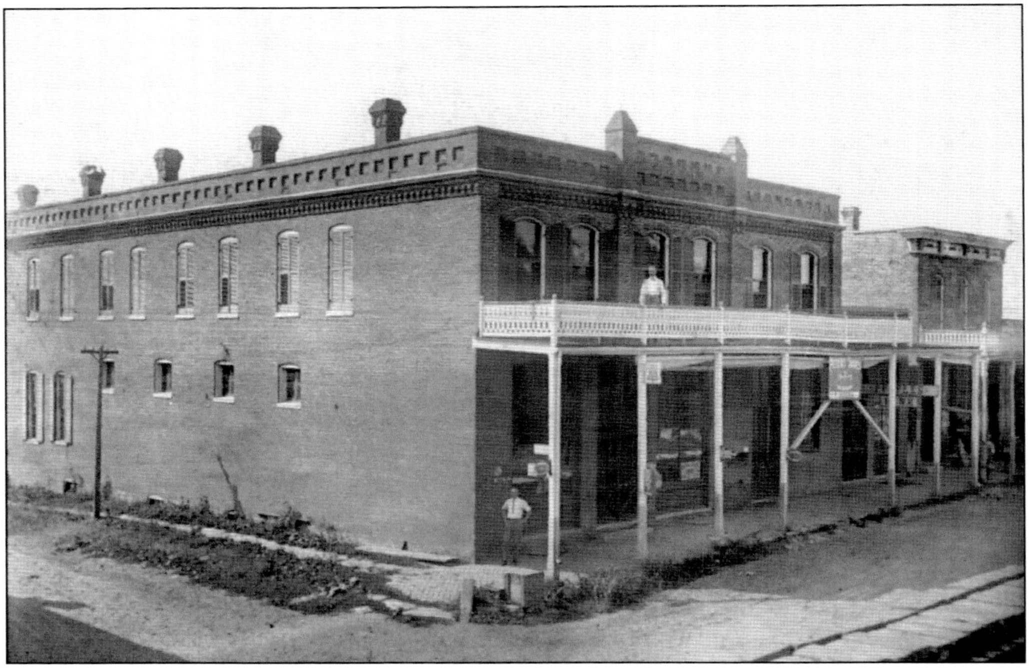

DIDDEA STORE. Peter Diddea opened a store in Stewardson in 1898. Diddea sold out in 1900 and went to Shelbyville. The store was located on South Pine Street. In Shelbyville, he opened a livery stable and feed store with M. O. Finks of Shelbyville.

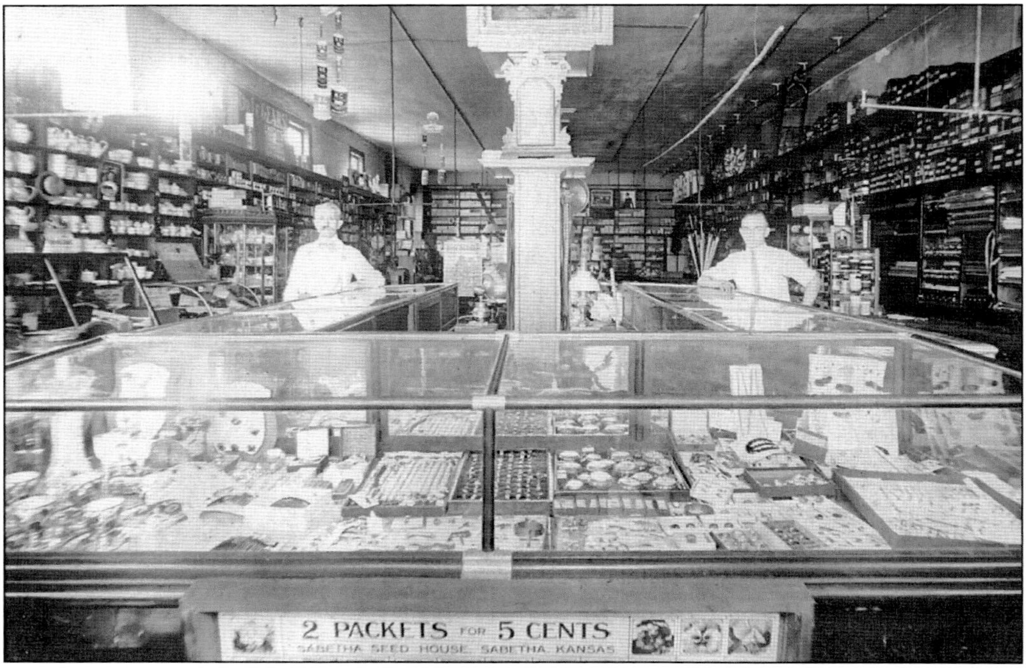

INSIDE DIDDEA STORE. Mr. York sold the store to Diddea in 1881. It continued as Mautz and Diddea until Diddea moved to Shelbyville. It was a general merchandise store, but it also kept hardware, tinware, and pumps.

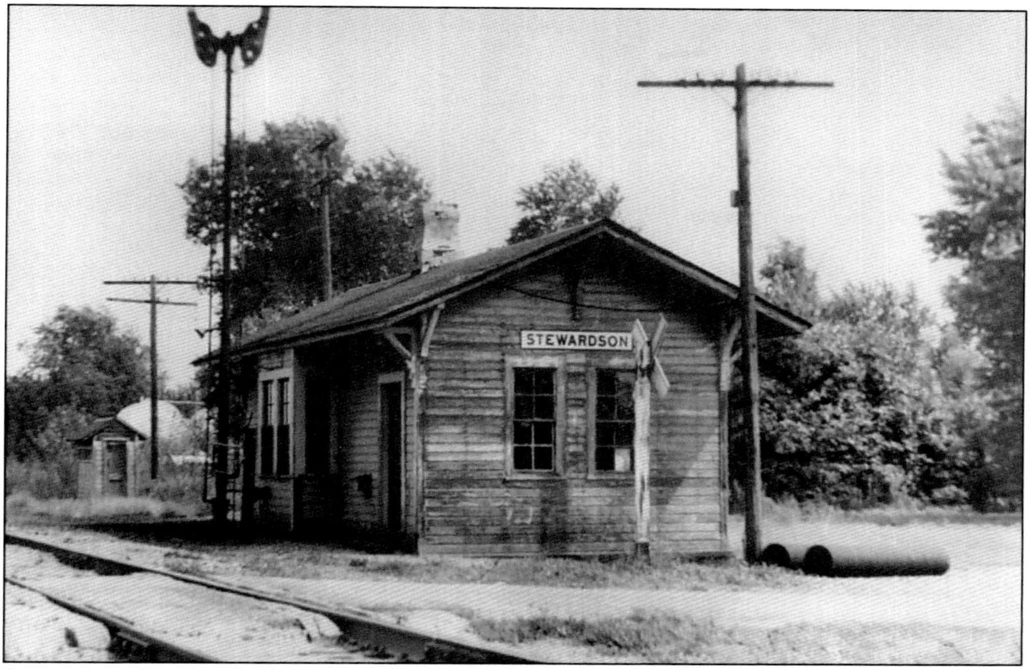

STEWARDSON DEPOT. The depot is pictured by the railroad tracks. In 1970, John Falk, a former Herborn resident, moved the abandoned Nickel Plate Depot to the corner of Main and Cedar Streets.

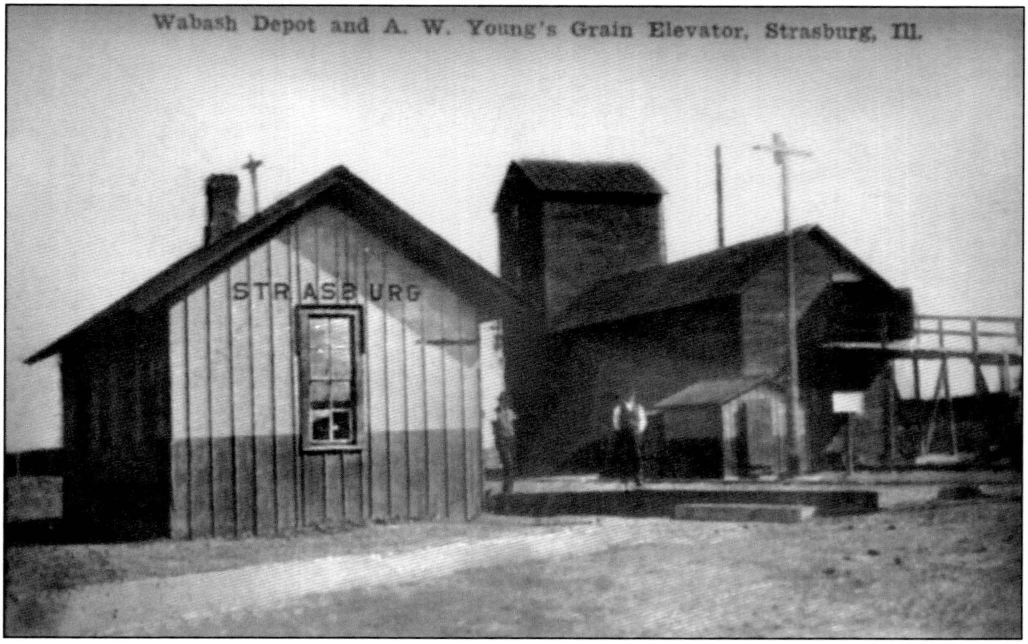

STRASBURG DEPOT. The freight was hauled north to south in the morning and reversed in the afternoon. Passenger trains went in the opposite directions. After 1880, the passenger service resulted in this depot being built near the present ballpark restrooms. A. W. Young's grain elevator is in the background. Passenger service was discontinued in 1930, and two years later the railroad ceased to exist and the depot was torn down.

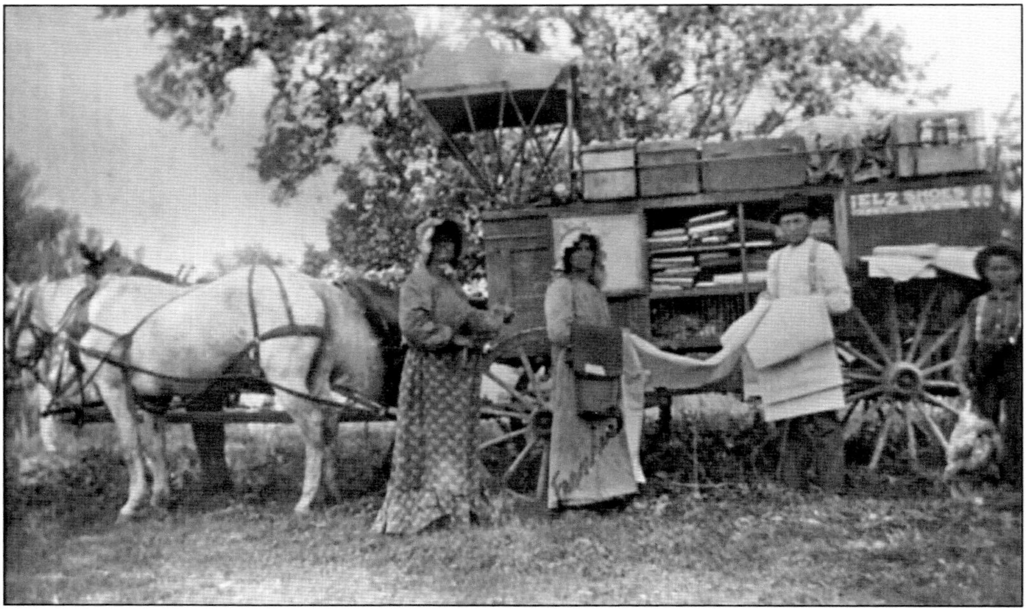

Huckster Wagon. The Huffers—Cassie, Francis, and Herrick—are buying goods from Elmer York's Huckster wagon. They met York at Hazen's corner at Route 16. The photograph was taken in 1898. With poor transportation options at this time, the "store" traveling to you must have been very efficient. John Falk, the man who moved the Stewardson Depot, helped his father with a Huckster wagon in the area.

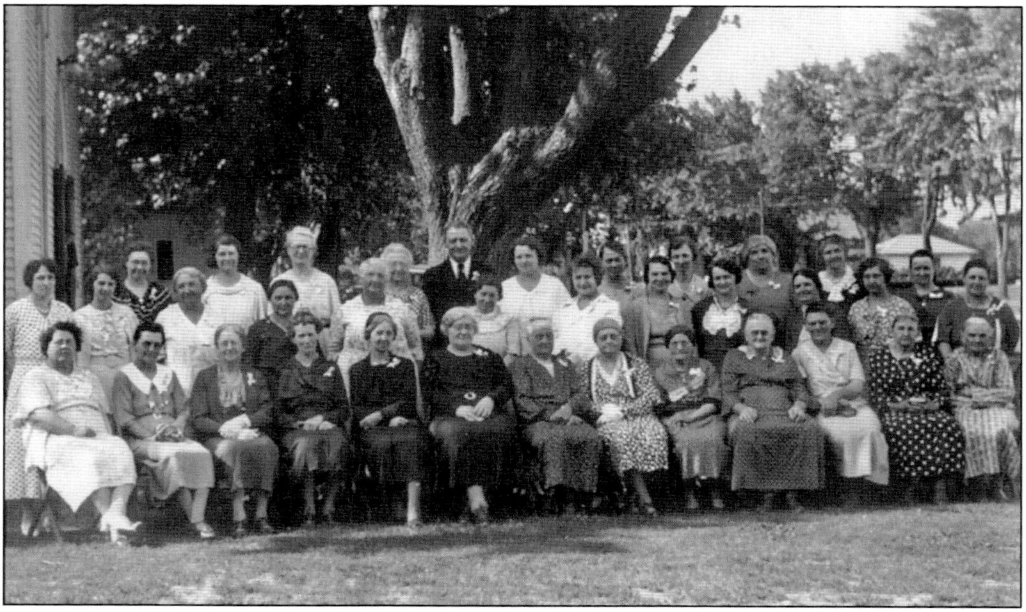

Ladies Aide. Photographed in 1935, this is the Ladies Aide of Strasburg. Ladies organizations were very popular in the first half of the 1900s. This photograph was probably taken in front of one of the churches with the pastor standing in the middle of all the ladies. Collars and dots were fashionable during this time period, and these ladies are showing quite a variety. (Courtesy of Gene Kull family.)

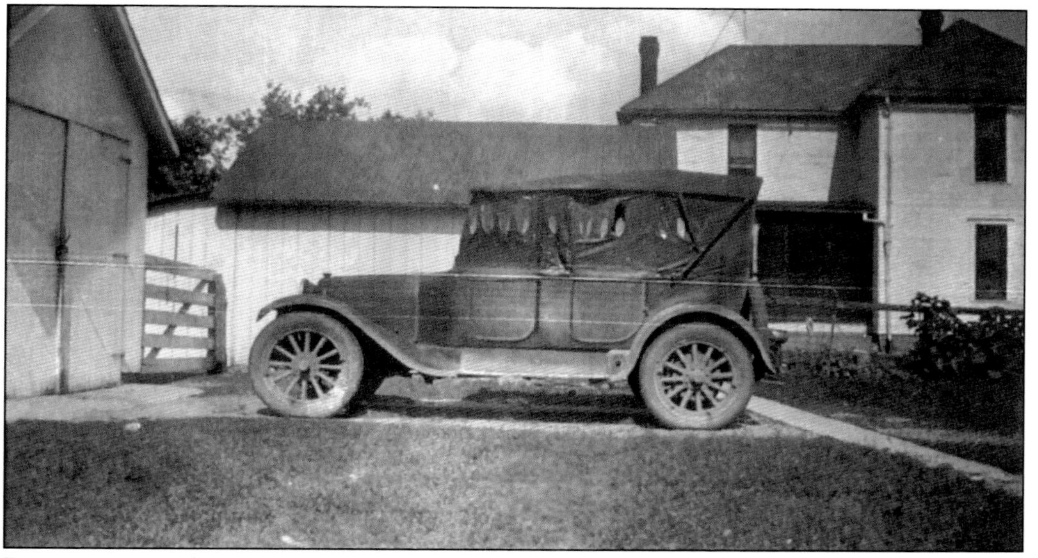

Reel's Dodge. This is Louis Reel's Dodge, parked outside his house. The side curtains were a special option; many photographs of cars similar to it around 1917 did not have the side curtains. (Courtesy of Gene Kull family.)

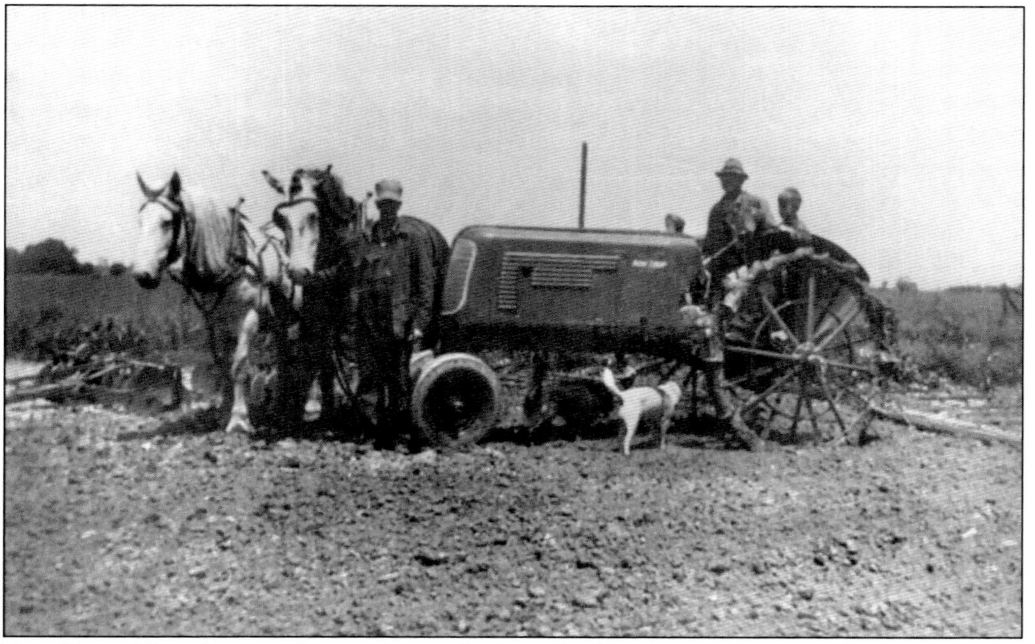

Reel Farm. This photograph was taken at the Louis Reel Farm in 1940. Pictured with the tractor are Roscoe Hash and David Schmitt. Reel is holding the reins of his horses, Flora and Ribbon. The handwriting also looks like Bob is the name of the dog. (Courtesy of Gene Kull family.)

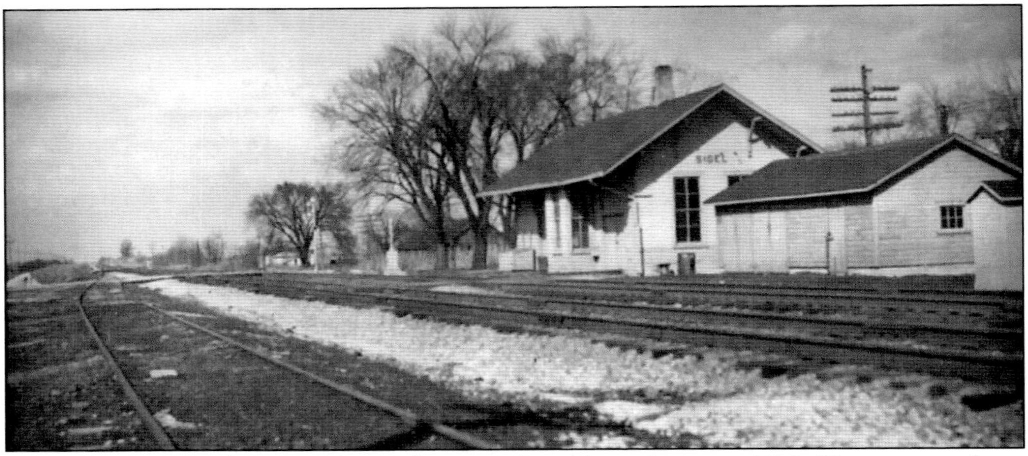

Sigel Depot. The depot was located next to East Front Street in 1895. There were sidings stretching in both directions on the Illinois Central Railroad. By 1914 the depot was gone. When the passenger trains were running, the depot was the place to be on Sunday afternoon. The trip to Effingham cost 35¢. Train No. 34 was the express and carried mail, milk, and cream.

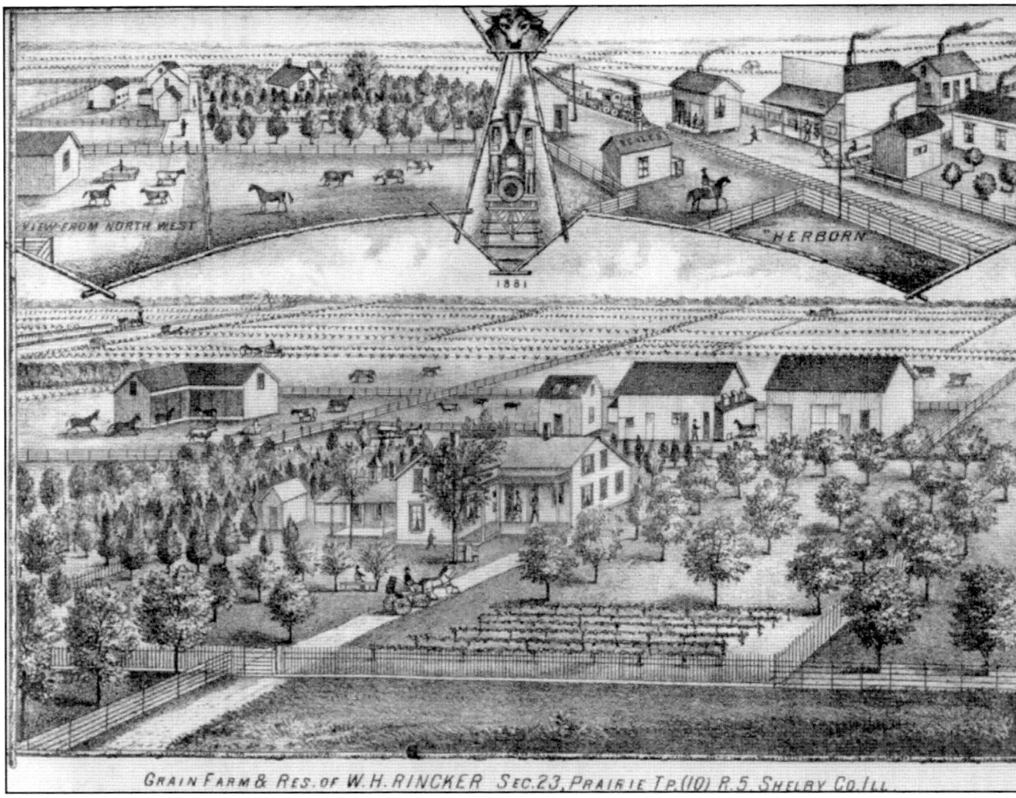

Herborn at its Peak. This sketch from 1881 shows a thriving village on the railroad. There is a general store and a variety of businesses and houses. Most are simple wood structures, and the prominence of the railroad can be seen in the drawing. Note the sheep head at the top of the page. No sheep are pictured in the fields, but Herborn is close to the thousands of sheep that grazed on Stewartson land.

Five

Moweaqua

The history of Moweaqua is a lesson in the importance of spelling. Mattie Wells, an early settler, named the village. She chose a Native American word, Moawequa, for the village name. One of the meanings is "muddy water" and was probably chosen because of the location of the village, near the muddy Flat Branch Creek. Two other meanings are possible: "She that weeps" or "Wolves always weeping." The original spelling lasted until the name of the town had to be registered for placement on an official map in 1890. The clerk mistakenly spelled Moawequa as Moweaqua. Once the name was recorded it could not be changed, so the village and township had to change their names. Because of this error in spelling, the village of Moweaqua is the only one in the world.

Michael Snyder laid out the village of Moweaqua in the fall of 1852. Soon after, Chester Wells built the first sawmill to supply railroad ties to the Illinois Central Railroad Company. Store buildings, a brickyard, and a flouring mill then came to the village. Michael Snyder secured that the railroad would pass by the village by giving the railroad every other block of 40 acres. The numerous acres of land that were not used by the railroad were eventually sold for $2.50 an acre.

Immediately after the Civil War, the railroad traffic passing by Moweaqua increased due to the large stock shipments. Agriculture also prospered, as the Centennial Program noted the soil in that area was so fertile that residents only had to "tickle it with a hoe and it will laugh with a harvest." Coal was also an important economic activity. Early mining dated back to 1891, and coal mining continued in this community until 1935. The 1932 Christmas Eve mine disaster was essentially the end of mining. The methane explosion killed 54 miners and took a year to clean up. The mine operated for two more years before closing.

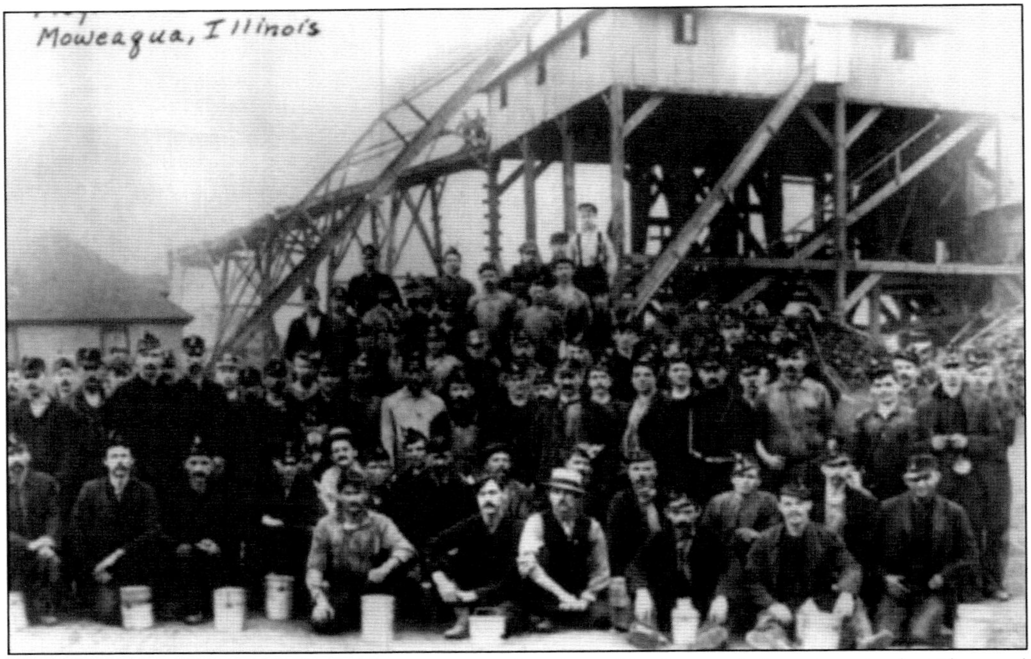

Progressive Miners. Coal miners are pictured gathered in front of the mine tipple. The coal was conveyed up into the structure, and then it was poured down the chute into the railroad cars. The mine was run by the Moweaqua Coal Corporation. This must have been the beginning or the end of the shift, as all the miners have their lunch boxes.

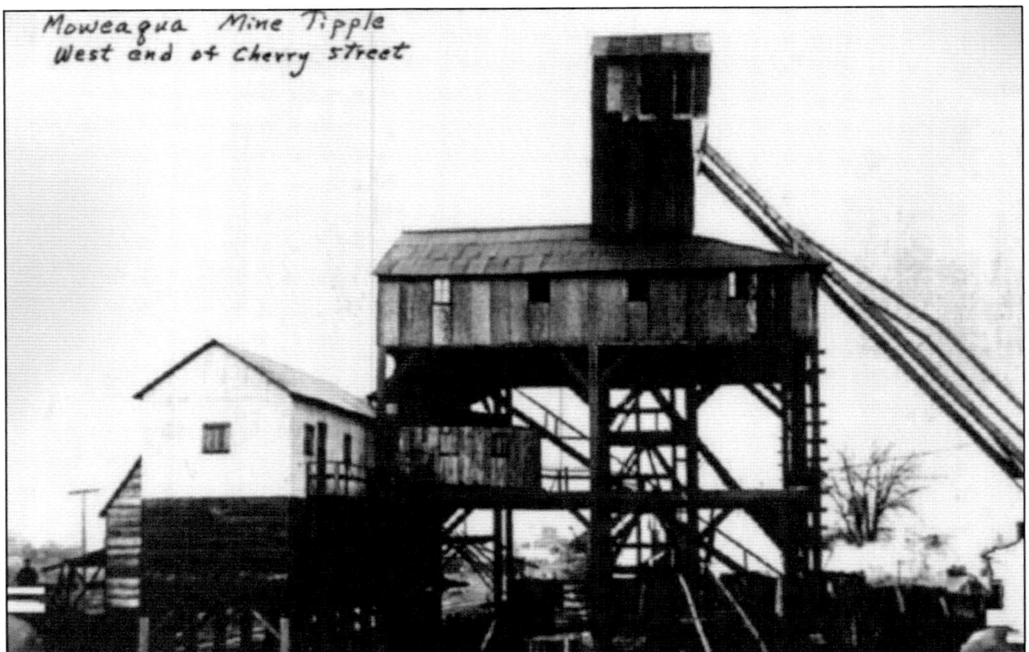

Cherry Street Tipple. This view of the mine tipple setup is better at conveying the coal to railroad car loading system. The mine tipple was located at the west end of Cherry Street.

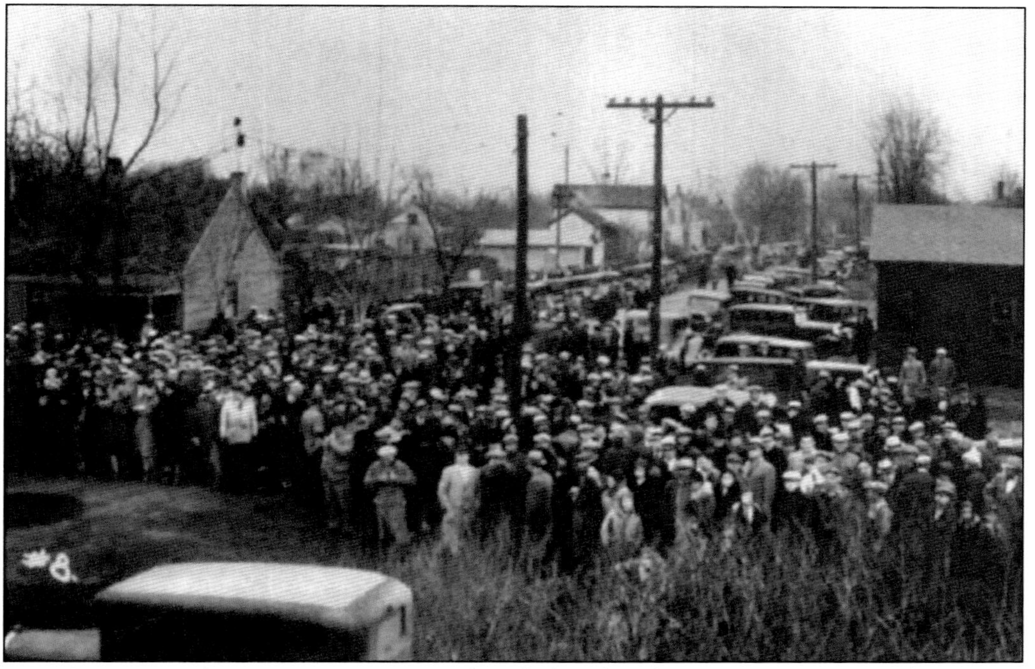

MINE DISASTER. The entire community gathered after the Christmas Eve mine accident. Many speculated that a carbide lamp was responsible for the methane gas explosion. The accident claimed the lives of 54 miners.

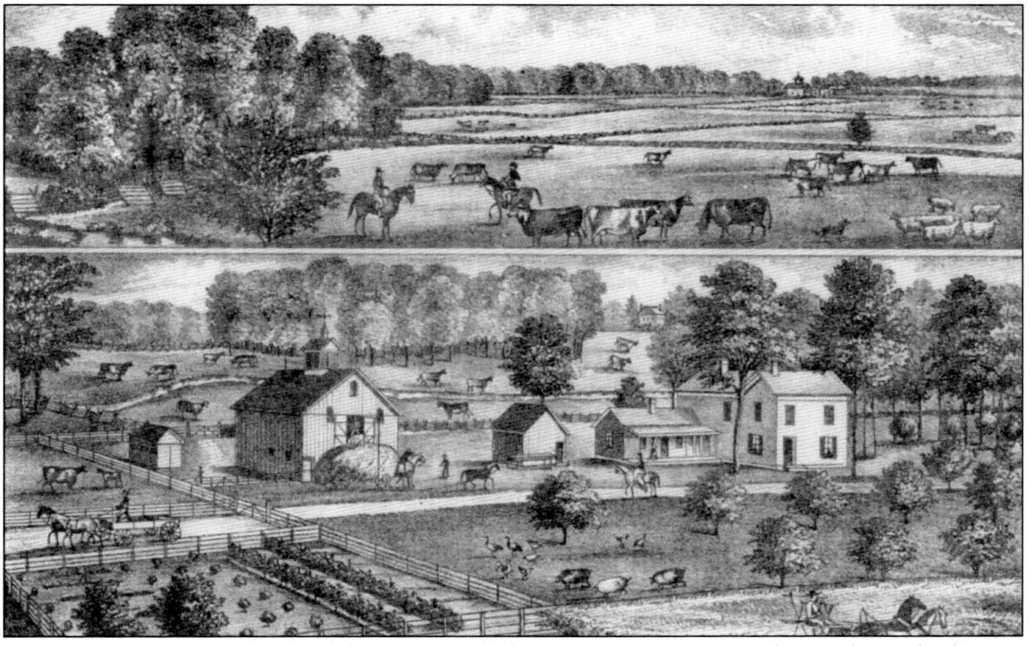

DOYLE FARM. This is a sketch of the E. M. Doyle farm in Moawequa Township. It shows the farm as it was in the 1870s. The spelling demonstrates that it was before the township name change. Doyle gave up the stage business to start farming, and he eventually built it up to this farm. Doyle had 17 children and was in the Missouri Regiment that was a part of Shermans' March to the Sea.

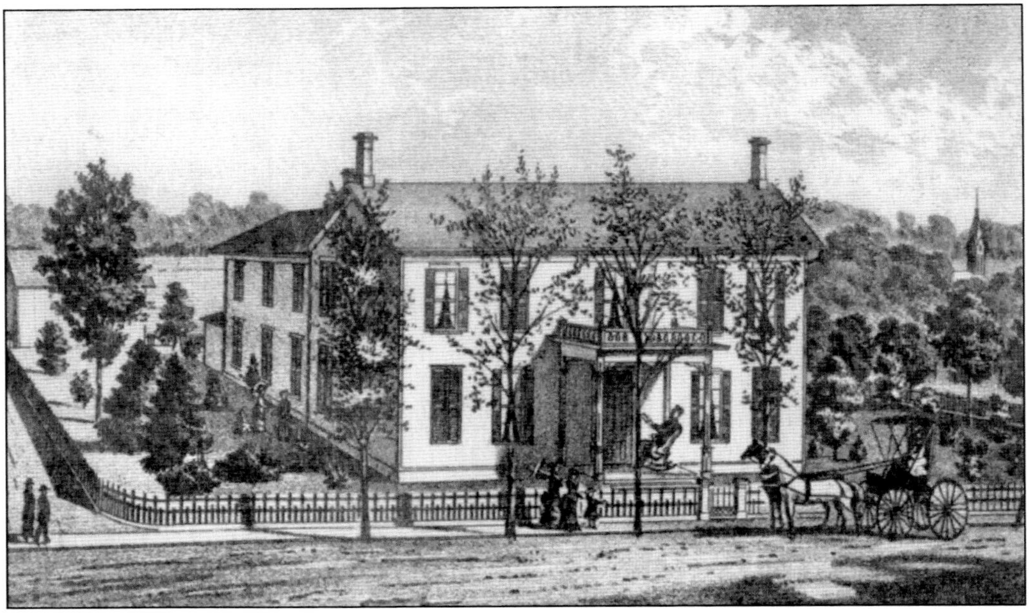

A. C. CAMPBELL RESIDENCE IN MOAWEQUA. Campbell's farm was successful, and in 1856 he moved to this residence in Moawequa. He fought in the Spanish–American War and then enlisted in the U.S. Army and was captain of Company E, 32nd Regiment Illinois Volunteers. During his three years of service he was at Shiloh, the Siege of Corinth, Vicksburg, and Shermans' March to the Sea. In 1880, he won a seat in the 33rd senatorial district.

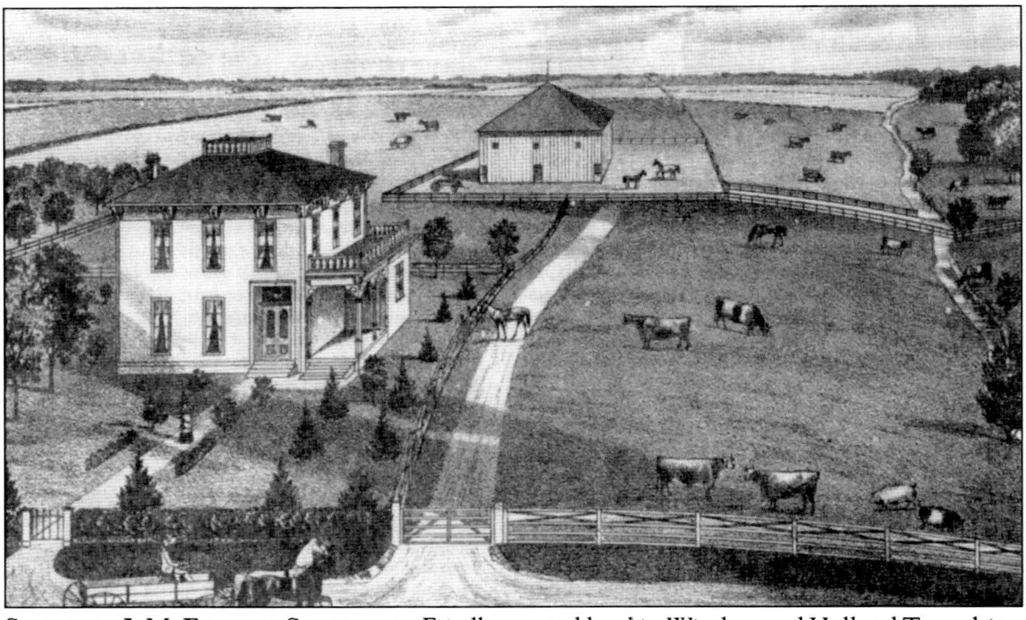

SKETCH OF J. M. FRIEDLEY STOCKFARM. Friedley rented land in Windsor and Holland Townships. His farming enterprises then improved, and he bought land near Moawequa. Because of his wife's poor health, he moved to Moawequa in the spring of 1867. In 1874, Friedley and two partners opened the Bank of Moawequa. He was involved in the development of the area and was a "straightforward and honorable businessman."

Six

Cowden, Herrick, and Lakewood

Marcus Cowden was a mechanic in Dry Point Township. In the spring, his shop was a busy place. Farmers traveled there to have their plows, harrows, and cultivators repaired, and it was also a place to visit and discuss current affairs. Marcus Cowden heard that there were plans to build a railroad from Shawneetown to Beardstown. He checked his map and was certain the railroad would go through his farm. He wanted to build a station and then a city on his farm. The more he discussed his plans, the more ridicule he received. One day he heard the railroad surveyors were 20 miles to the south. He rode to meet them and stayed with them as they approached his farm. He had the last laugh because the railroad went through his farm just as he had predicted. The town was platted in 1872, and it officially became a village on June 4, 1875. The town of Cowden grew, and Cowden was involved in this growth.

Near the present town of Herrick, there were lots of towns that were created but did not survive. In 1881 a town named New London began near Herrick, and it thrived for a few years. Margaret Basye, a daughter of General Thornton, owned land that J. T. Herrick managed for her. In July 1883, he had land surveyed for a town. He offered the railroad $1,000 to build a depot on this land, among other inducements. On August 14, 1883, the town of New London moved to Herrick, and in 1888, Herrick was incorporated. From the 1900s to the 1950s, Herrick was known as "dog town U.S." Hounds were raised here and shipped to every state and many foreign countries. Coonhounds, foxhounds, and beagles were the most popular breeds. However once the Railway Express office closed, shipping by air became too expensive and that brought an end to the dog business.

The Lakewood Post Office was established on July 26, 1872. The area was wet and contained wood, so Lakewood was a logical choice for the name.

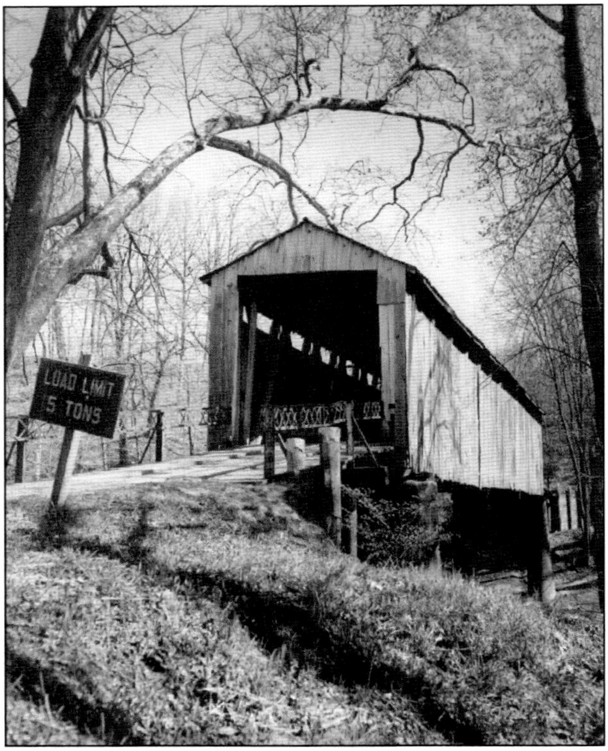

COVERED BRIDGE. The bridge was erected in 1868 downstream from the old Thompson Mill. The bridge was thought to be covered for protection from the weather, or another suggestion was that the horses thought it was a barn and were less likely to shy away from the bridge and the running water of the Kaskaskia beneath. This is one of the few covered bridges left in the state of Illinois.

THOMPSON MILL. The first mill, built in 1843, was located north of the covered bridge. During these days the flies were so bad on the prairie that people had to travel to the mill at night. The first mill was destroyed, and the second Thompson Mill was built in 1862. In 1900, Minton Lankford bought the mill and added a general store. Thompson Mill was torn down in 1914.

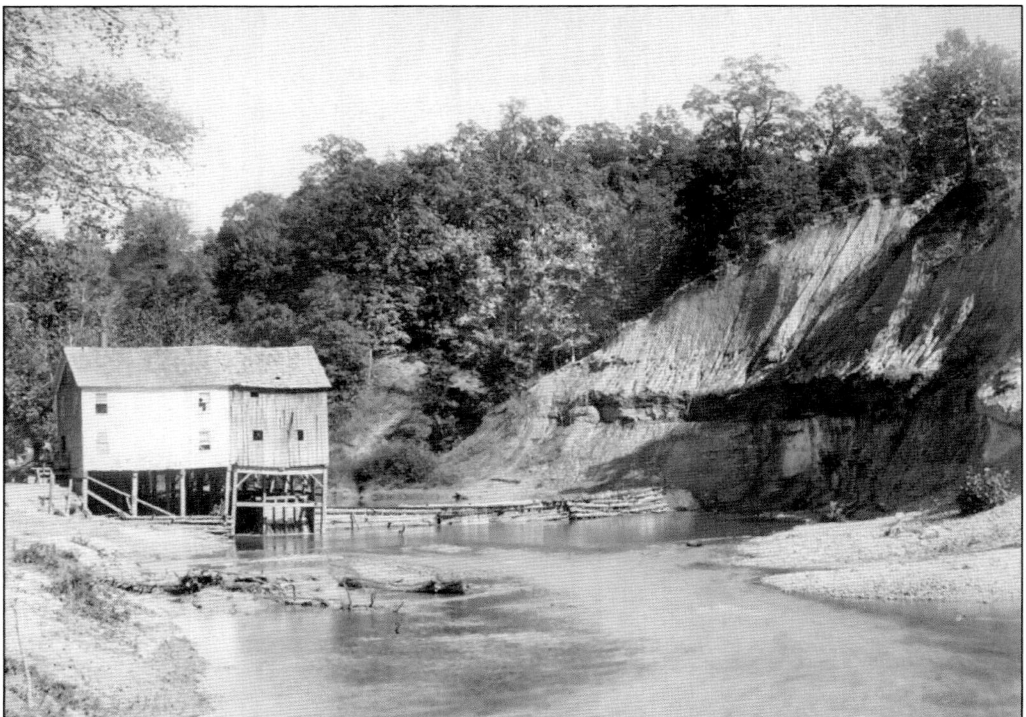

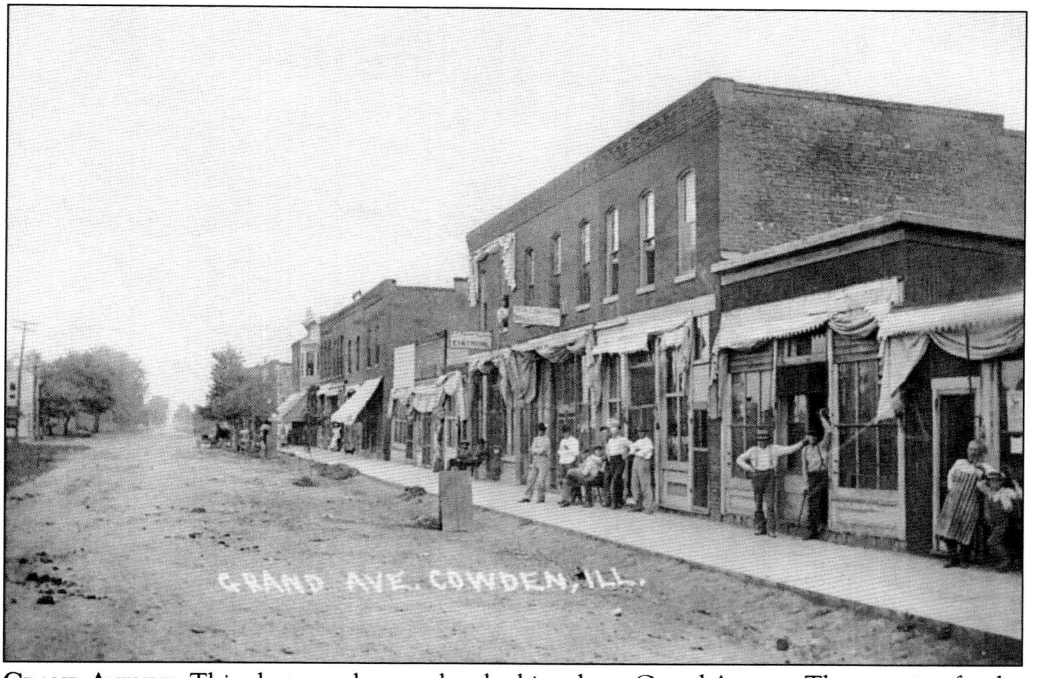

GRAND AVENUE. This photograph was taken looking down Grand Avenue. The occasion for the photograph is unknown but several individuals—including a storekeeper, young boy, and a man hanging out a window—have gathered for the occasion.

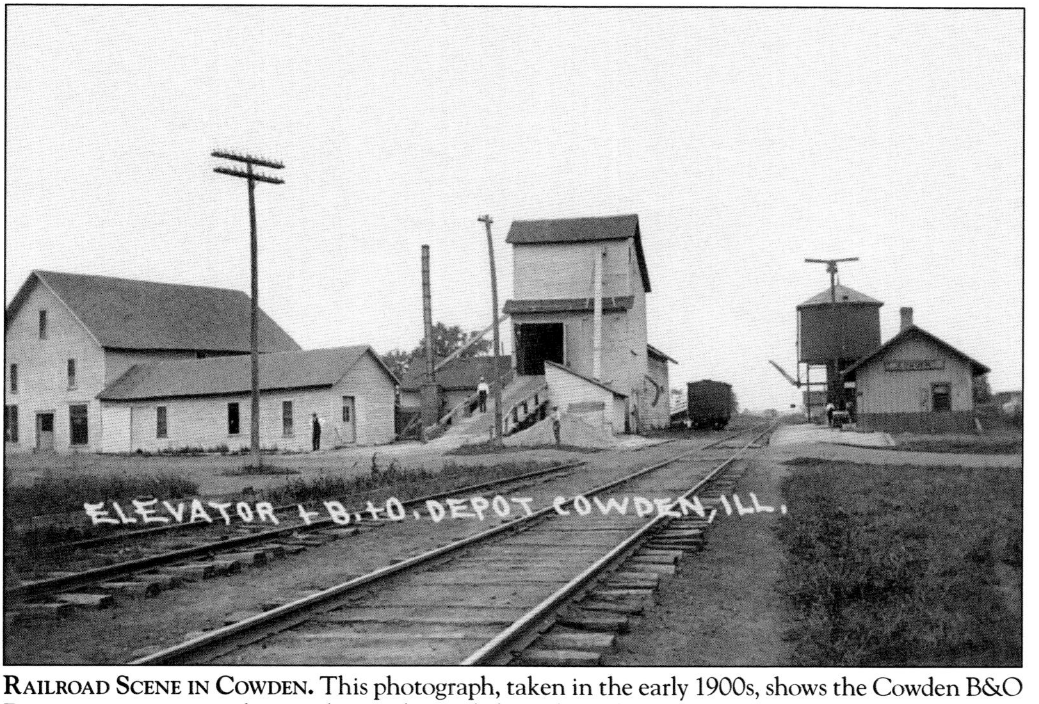

RAILROAD SCENE IN COWDEN. This photograph, taken in the early 1900s, shows the Cowden B&O Depot, water tower, and grain elevator located along the railroad. The railroads' arrival encouraged growth of the town. Today Cowden has a large grain elevator operated by Tate and Lyle.

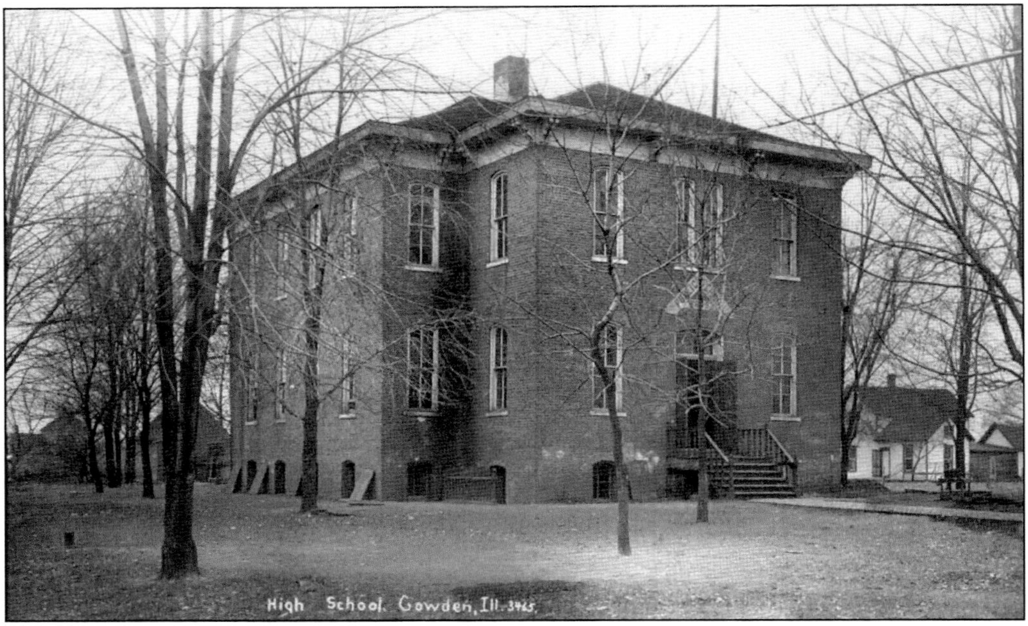

Cowden High School. This brick high school was built in the 1920s. The number of large brick structures demonstrated that Cowden was prosperous. The residential location, almost on first glance, makes it look like a large residence.

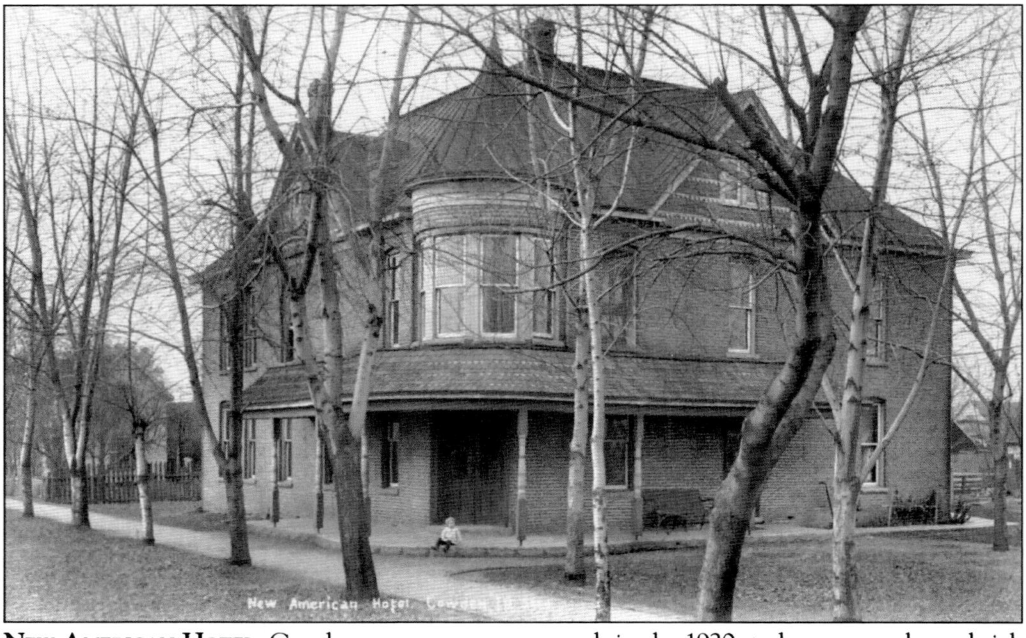

New American Hotel. Cowden was prosperous enough in the 1920s to have a very large, brick structure for a hotel. The little girl in the photograph looks small compared to the large hotel.

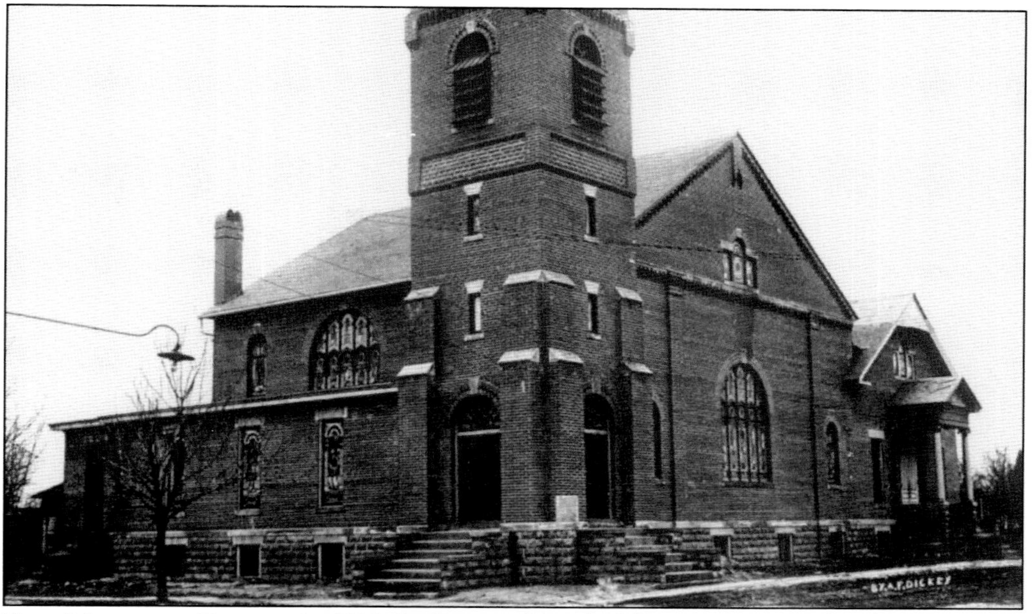

First Methodist Church. In 1866, the Reverend Isaiah Villars was appointed as the first regular preacher. The previous church built in 1866 was moved west and remodeled for Sunday school use when the pictured church was built. This church was dedicated on April 24, 1910. At the end of the evening services, $11,185 had been pledged to cover the entire cost of the building. This photograph was probably taken in the early 1920s.

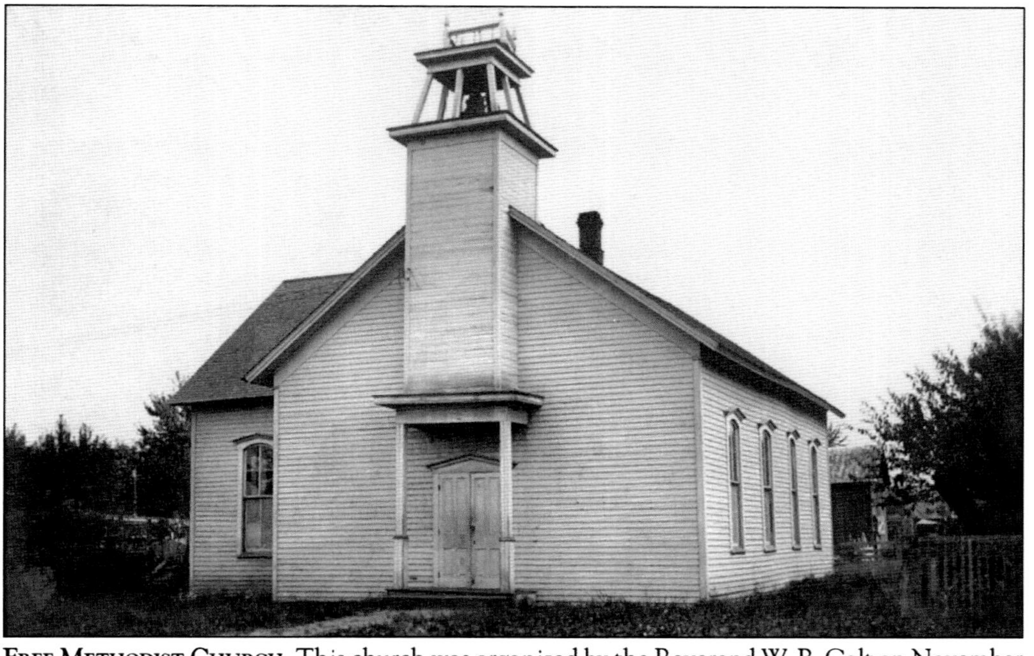

Free Methodist Church. This church was organized by the Reverend W. B. Colt on November 20, 1881. The first church was erected in 1882 and was located across the street from the church in the photograph. The pictured church was erected in 1915. This photograph was taken not long after this. The frame church was destroyed by fire on January 27, 1963.

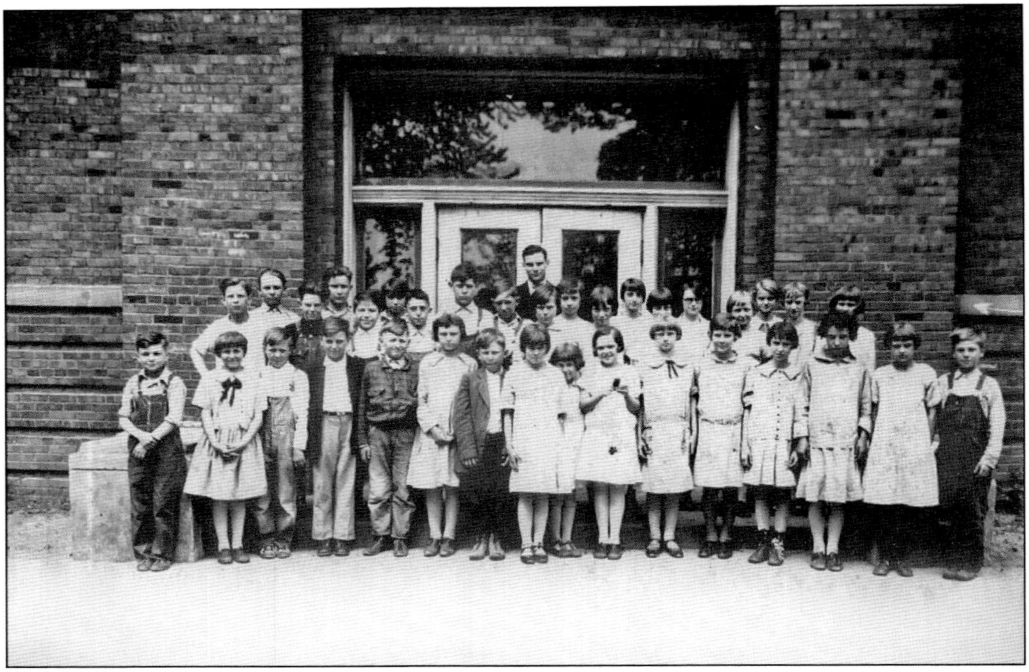

COWDEN GRADE SCHOOL. Students are gathered for a photograph in 1926. They are posing in front of the grade school that was in use until a new one was built a few years later. Bib overalls were common for the boys, and the fashion for girls included bows and wide collars on their dresses.

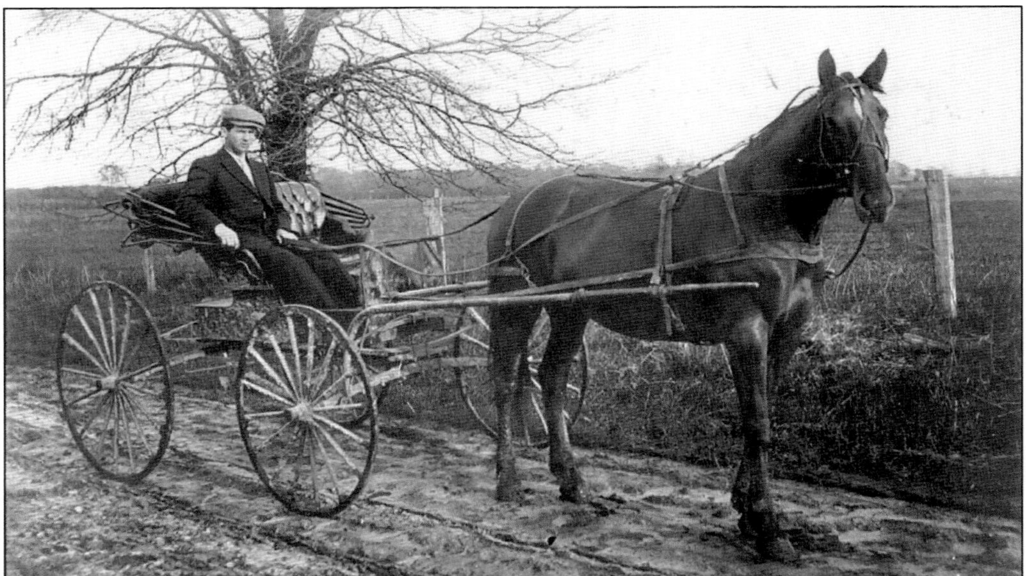

CECIL CORLEY, 1913. Corley is striking a fashionable pose. The lighter buggies, like the one in this photograph, replaced the heavy, cumbersome wagons of the past. Cecil is one of the sons of Frank and Ella Corley. After attending grade school in Herrick, he and his brother Ennis left the farm and studied medicine. He began his practice in Michigan in 1921. He was named Michigan's Outstanding Physician in 1969. (Courtesy of Buchanan family of Herrick.)

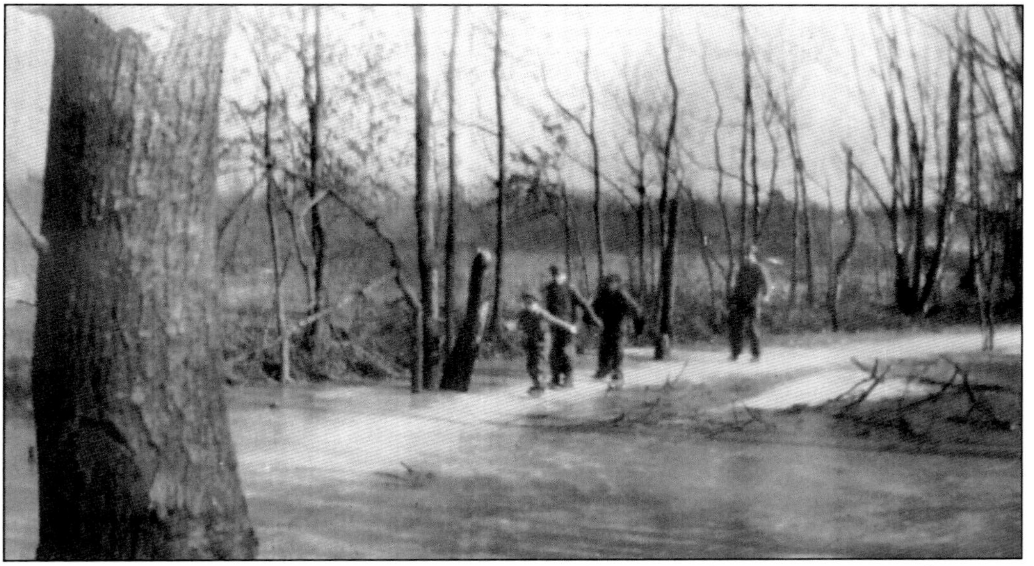

Frozen Creek Fun. Several young boys, pictured in the winter of 1922, are creating their own fun. It was cold enough and the creeks had enough ice for skating. This is just one of several photographs of the boys skating, so it must have been a rare event to warrant several photographs. (Courtesy of Buchanan family of Herrick.)

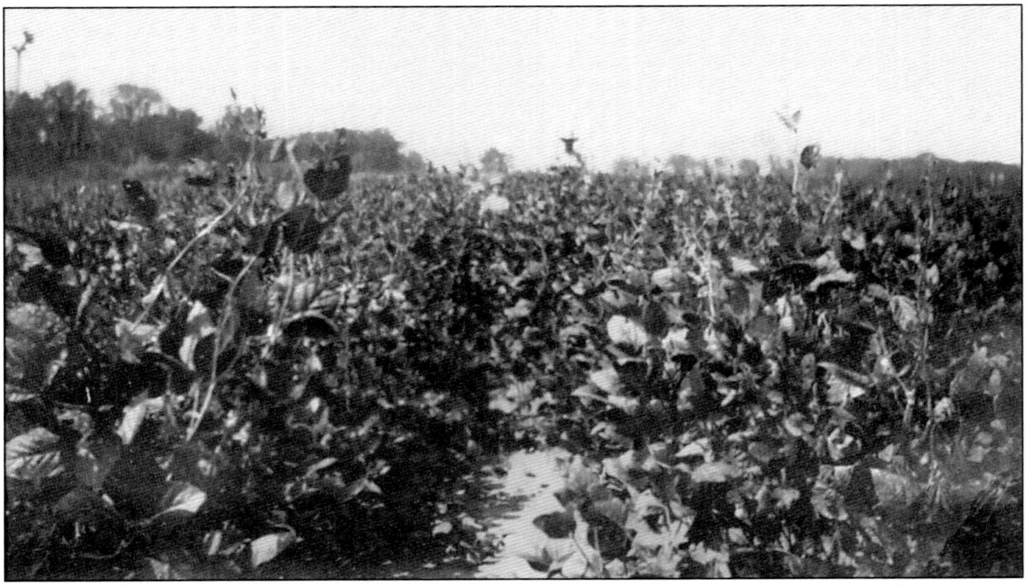

Early Soybeans. Soybeans were not as common a crop as they are today in Shelby County. This photograph, taken in the 1920s, shows how much different the soybean plants looked then compared to those today. Farmers in the early days of soybeans had to harvest them by hand, similar to how one would harvest beans from his or her own garden. They would even get young people to help in the harvest. (Courtesy of Buchanan family of Herrick.)

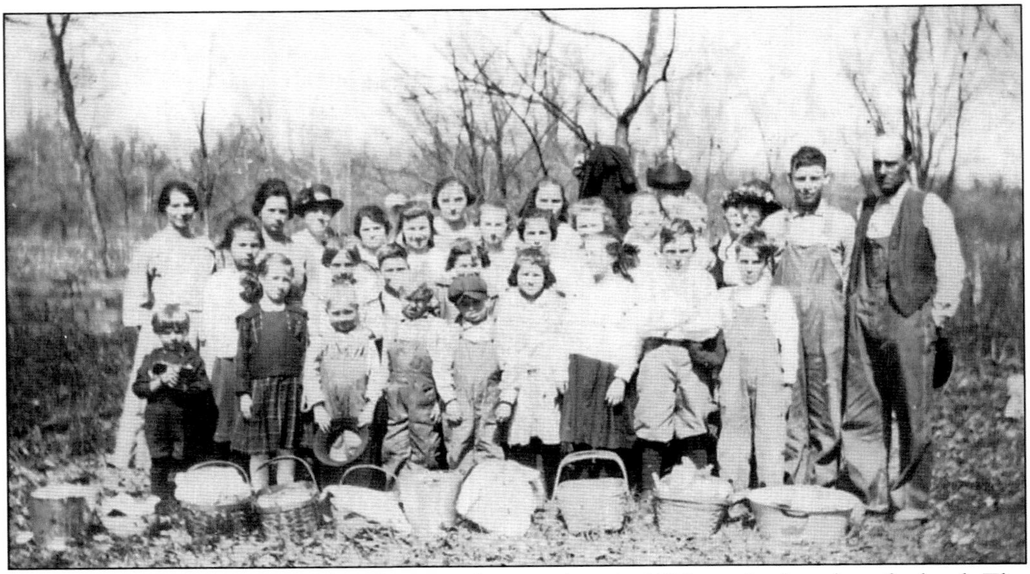

Pleasant Union School. This photograph was taken in 1926 on the last day of school. The Pleasant Union students are shown with their parents. It was common to have a basket dinner with the parents on the last day of school. Looking at the size of the baskets and tubs, it must have been quite a lunch. (Courtesy of Buchanan family of Herrick.)

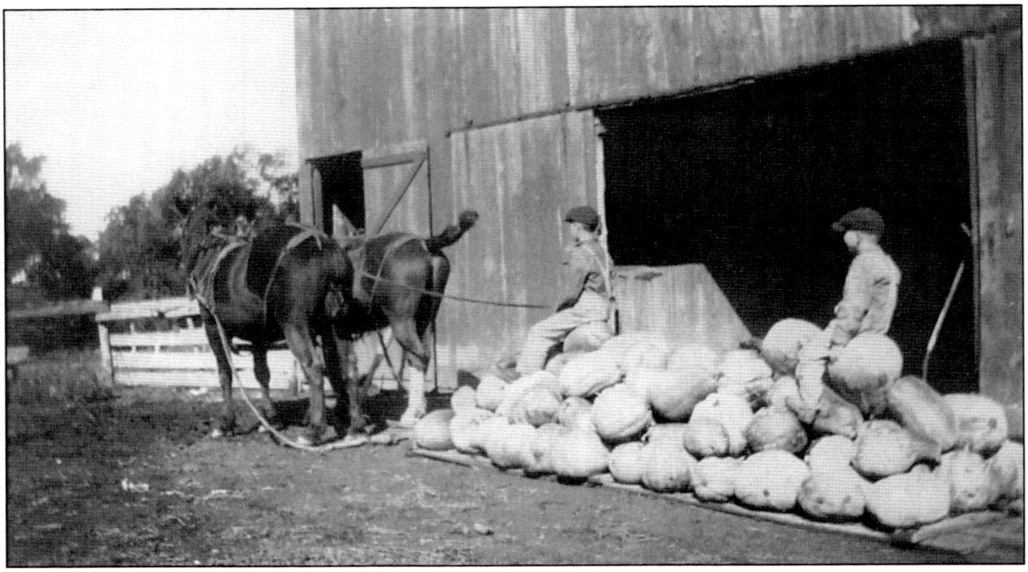

Pumpkin Kings. Reid "Buck" and Ross "Bud" Buchanan, two sons of Claude and Lola Buchanan, are shown with a load of pumpkins in 1921. Pumpkins grow well in Illinois, and it is a little known fact that today Illinois is the nation's leading producer of pumpkins. (Courtesy of Buchanan family of Herrick.)

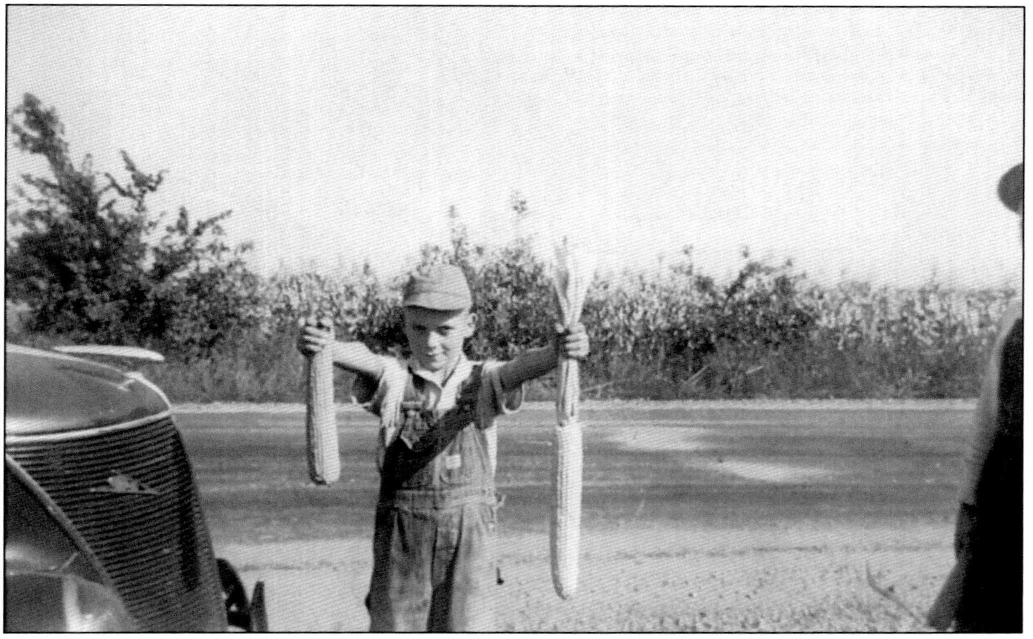

BIG EARS OF CORN. The 1940 corn harvest was memorable for the Buchanans. Maurice, son of Claude and Lola Buchanan, is pictured displaying huge ears of corn. This is from the cornfield north of Meyers Cemetery on the Whittington farm that the Buchanans rented. (Courtesy of Buchanan family of Herrick.)

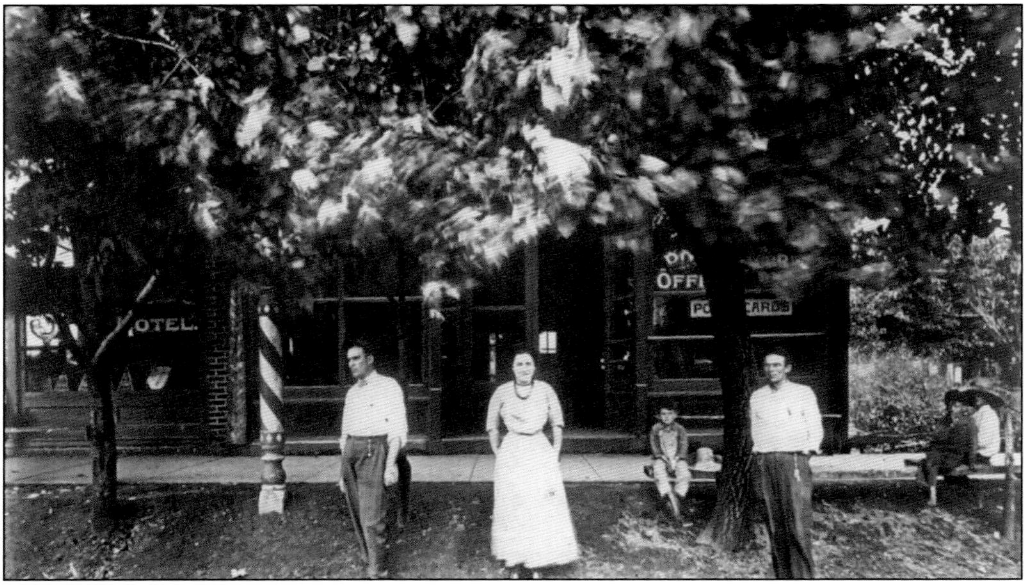

HERRICK POST OFFICE, 1942. This is the second location of the post office. Pictured here are, from left to right, Bill Oare, Winnie Frailey, seated Oren Oare, Charles Oare, and an unidentified person with hat. The Oares migrated to Illinois from the South after the Civil War. Charles, the eldest, was born in 1881. He was a teacher and worked at the post office. Oren, born in 1906, is Charles's son. His other son, Charlie, born in 1916, would eventually become postmaster. (Courtesy Buchanan family of Herrick.)

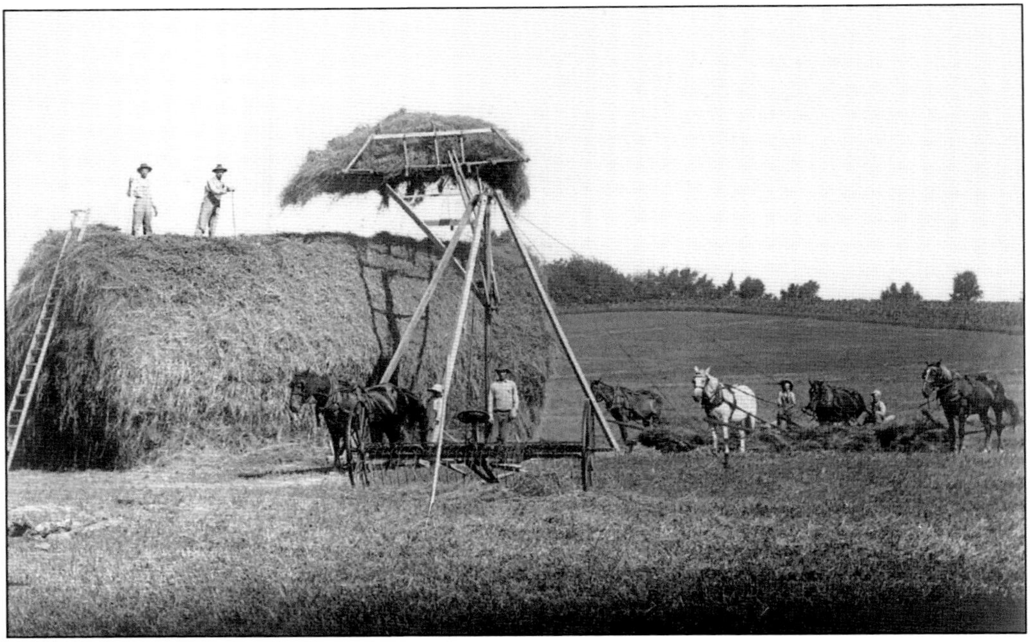

Stacking Hay at the Lankford Farm north of Herrick, 1916. The horses on the right side pull, which raises the hay derrick. Men usually stack the hay by hand with pitchforks until it gets too high and then they have to use the derrick. Stacking the hay is an "art." It has to be stacked so that it will settle straight and shed water. (Courtesy of Buchanan family of Herrick.)

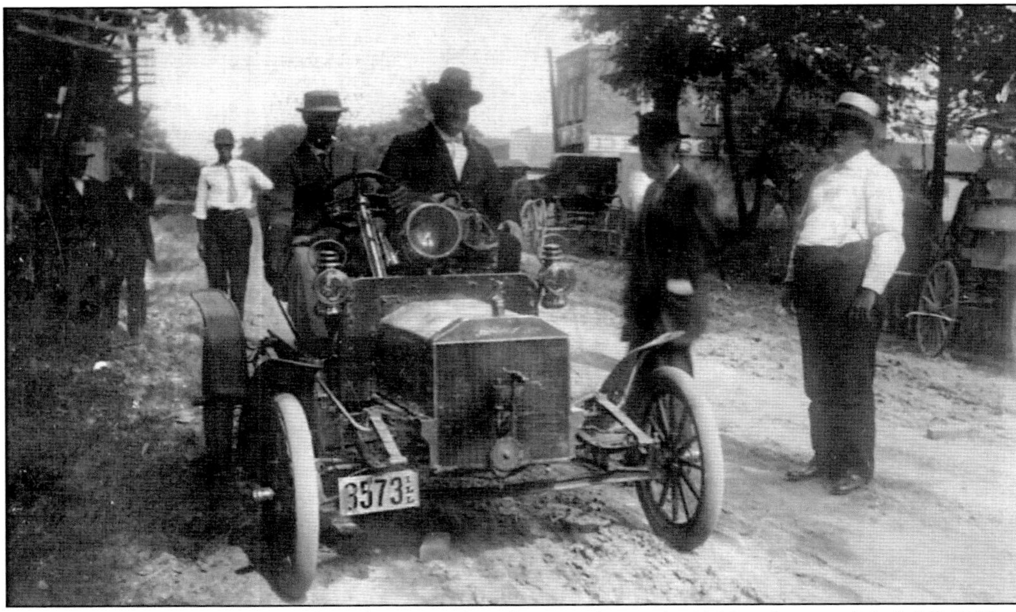

Main Street Lakewood. This photograph, taken in the early 1900s, shows a Model "N" Ford owned by M. A. Harmon. The men are very interested in the car. Please note the steering wheel on the right—it was not moved to the left until 1908. The headlamps and hood on this car were "options" at the time. A new Model "N" cost $500 and although only a two-seater, they were very popular and sold well.

Seven

Windsor, Findlay, and Quigley

In 1853 the Terre Haute, Alton, and St. Louis Railroad began construction. The tracks were joined in Shelbyville in early 1856. P. C. Higgins of Bunker Hill and Simeon Ryder of Alton purchased land and laid out several towns. Windsor's survey was filed on May 16, 1865. Prior to this, Windsor was called Cochran's Grove and Illiopolis. In 1856, Jonathan Bruce of Sand Creek was constructing a hotel to be named Wilson Illiopolis. The railroad was installing a switch and on his first night of business on March 31, 1856, he had 10 railroad workers as customers. Even though the hotel was not completely finished, the workers probably did not mind since there was 14 inches of snow on the ground. While campaigning against Stephen Douglas in 1858 for the U.S. Senate, Abraham Lincoln spent the night in the Windsor House, formerly Illiopolis House. While Mrs. Bruce made breakfast for Lincoln, her daughter Belle sat on Lincoln's lap. They had a wonderful story to tell once he became president.

L. H. Keller opened a general store when the railroad began construction and bought wool from up to 25 miles away. He also sold New Orleans sugar right out of a barrel in the street, as it was being unloaded. People were that desperate to buy. Other businesses soon followed, including: a saloon, drugstore, grocery, post office, and doctor's office.

In 1883 George Mauzey built the first general store in Findlay. Michael Bare, a store employee, would entertain people in the evenings with his storytelling. A frequent topic included what was happening "back yonder" in Findlay, Ohio where he was from. People began calling the store Findlay. When George Mauzey applied for a post office, he named it Findlay. On December 18, 1884, the Findlay Post Office opened. Growth was slow, but the arrival of the railroad in 1891 brought more growth, since Findlay was now connected to Chicago. The village incorporated on April 29, 1892.

Quigley was a small community that had a post office from 1890 to 1904. It was named for a family in the area.

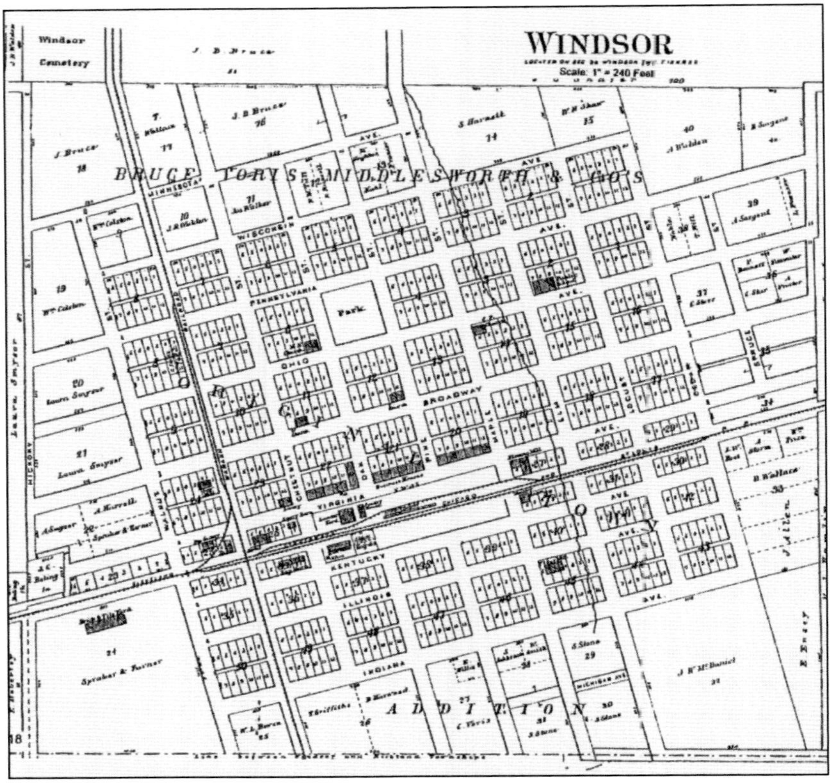

PLAT, 1895. This plat demonstrates how the City of Windsor was laid out relative to the railroad, not in relationship to the compass directions. Several locations are still current, such as the Methodist church and the original part of the Windsor Cemetery. The business district is in the same location, but the stockyards along the railroad are gone.

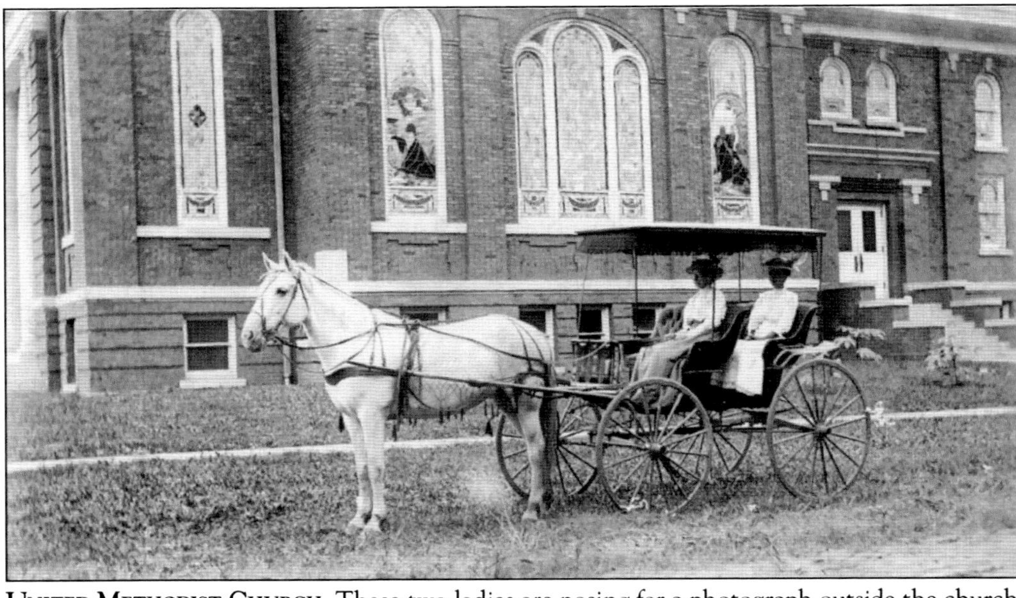

UNITED METHODIST CHURCH. These two ladies are posing for a photograph outside the church. The church was dedicated on March 9, 1913 and this photograph was probably taken soon after. The stained glass windows are brilliantly colored, and even in this black and white image they are impressive. Please note that the horse has a fly net on, which can be clearly seen because of his white color.

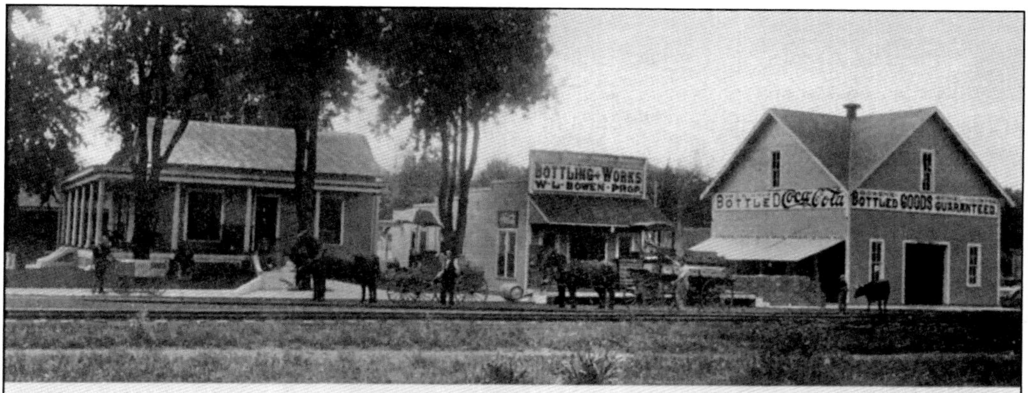

THE WINDSOR BOTTLING WORKS.

WINDSOR BOTTLING. Members of the Bowen family owned the bottling works. It started in 1894, but this photograph was taken in 1903. Edwin Cassell was a partner but was killed in 1894 when an exploding bottle severed his jugular vein. Bowen held a franchise for exclusive bottling of Coca-Cola, which covered several counties. In 1925, the franchise was sold to the Mattoon Coca-Cola Bottling works.

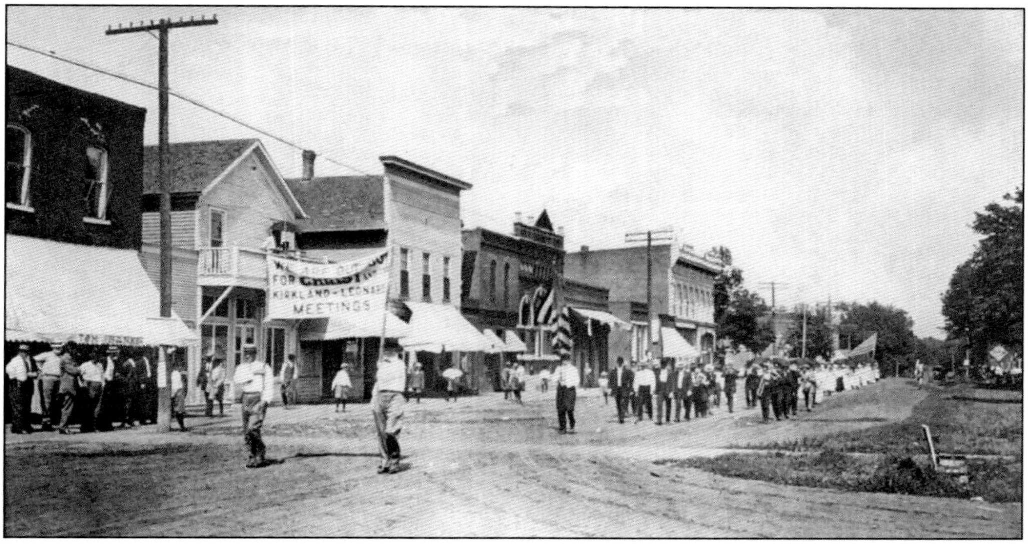

REVIVAL PARADE. A large union tent revival was held for four weeks in 1911. The parade occurred on August 6, 1911. Over 1,500 people participated in the parade, and the procession was four blocks long. It was led by Evangelist Sam Kirkland and his wife riding on white horses. Kirkland was the organizer of the tent revival.

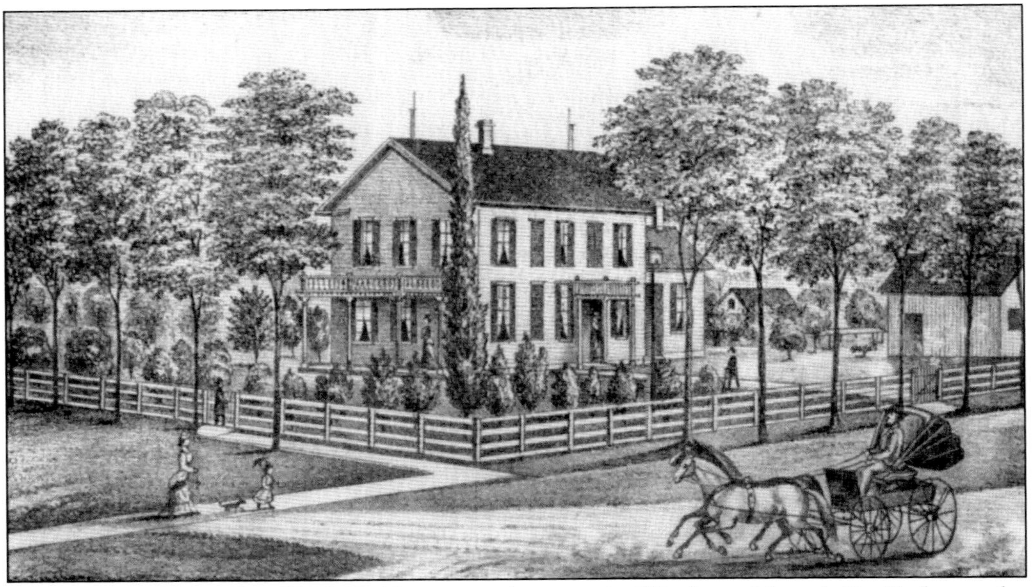

Dubler Residence. Dr. W. H. Dubler was a physician in Windsor, although Dr. York was the first physician to settle in Windsor and the first to build a house in the 1850s. Dr. Dubler came to Windsor in the 1870s and built this large residence in the city.

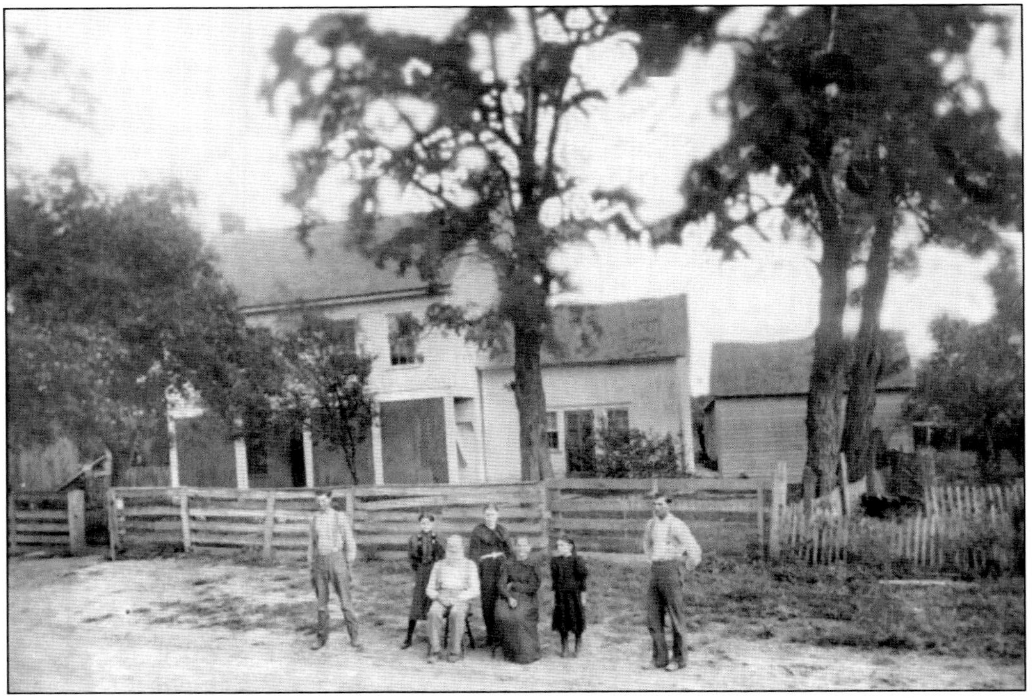

Black Horse Tavern. Mr. and Mrs. Valentine Tressler purchased the log tavern in the 1840s. It was mainly a drovers inn, but other guests on their way to Shelbyville or Charleston were common customers. Famous guests were Martin Van Buren, Judge David Davis (later chief justice of the Supreme Court), Samuel Moulton, Judge Anthony Thornton, and Abraham Lincoln. Abraham Lincoln enjoyed the Tressler's sauerkraut.

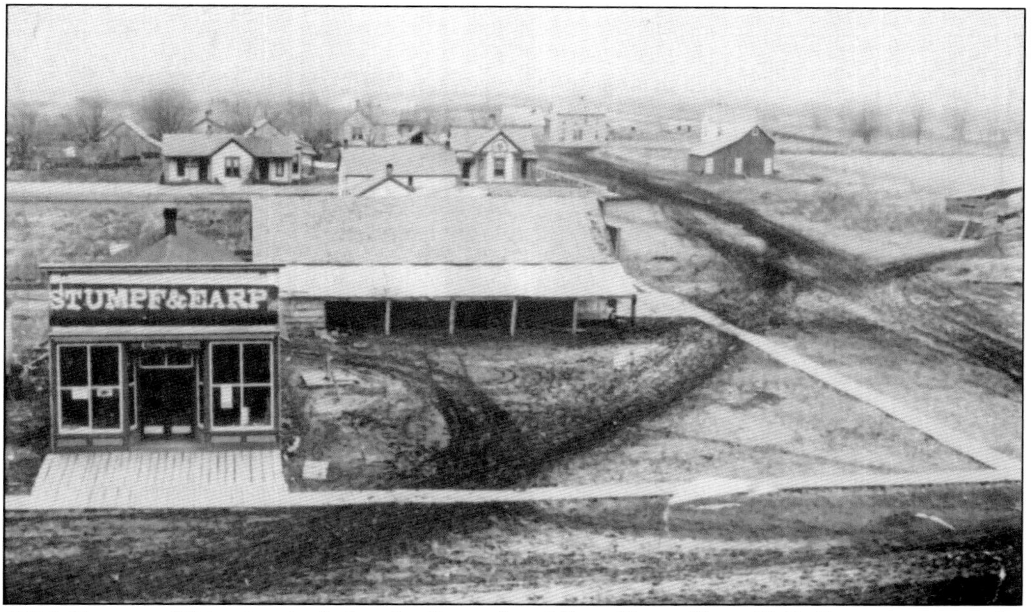

1900 FINDLAY. This view includes the Stumpf and Earp Dram Shop. E. E. Earp was granted a right to run a dram shop for a year and then on April 30, 1898, he purchased a saloon license for $483.95. O. E. Stumpf joined the enterprise sometime between 1898 and 1900. Dram shop is a legal term for a tavern. The name came from the fact that these shops sold spirits by the "dram." (Courtesy of Lois Cruitt.)

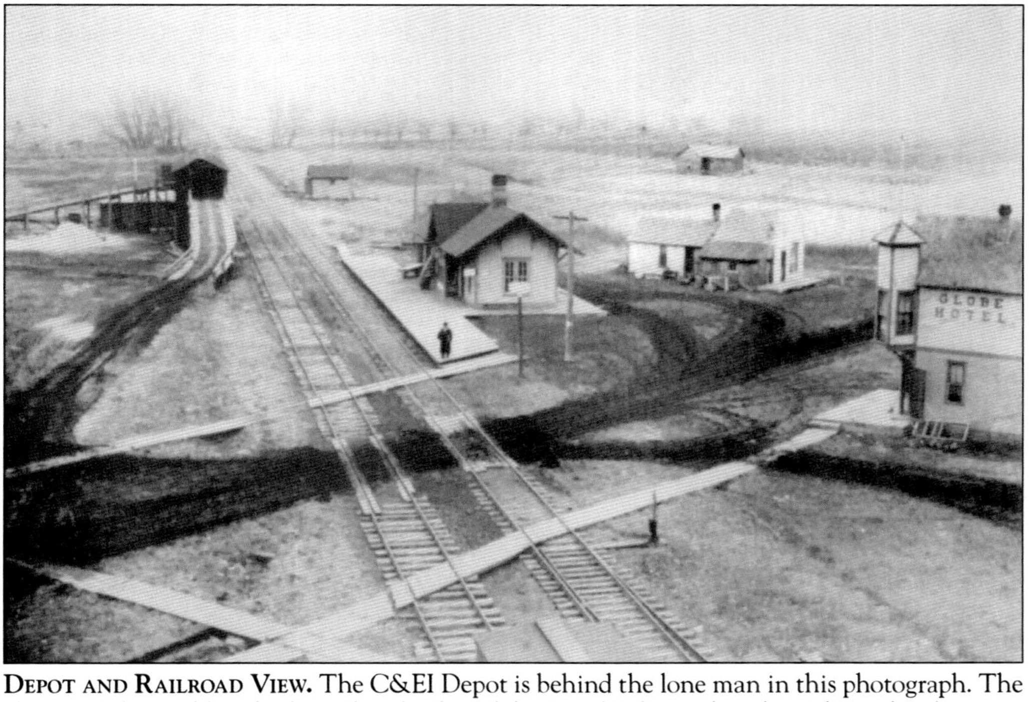

DEPOT AND RAILROAD VIEW. The C&EI Depot is behind the lone man in this photograph. The elevator is located beside the railroad. The Globe Hotel is located at the right and in between the hotel and depot is a restaurant. (Courtesy of Lois Cruitt.)

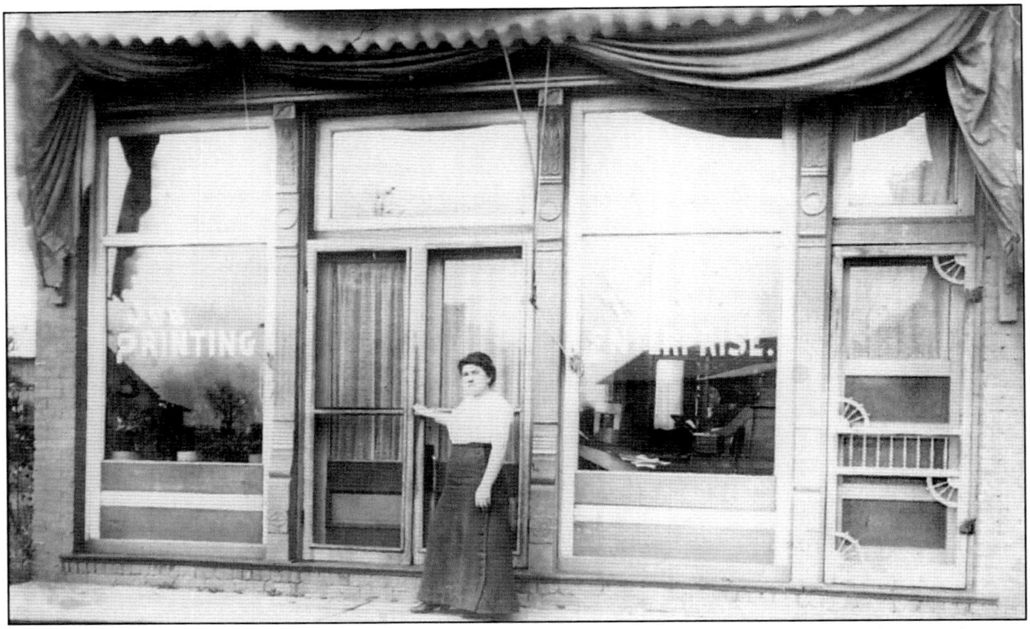

Mrs. Worley at *Enterprise* Office, 1904. William Johns sold the paper to the Worleys in 1903. Mr. Worley worked at the *Shelbyville Democrat* and Mrs. Worley taught school. Mr. Worley died on March 9, 1904, and Mrs. Worley became the editor, and her daughter and her ran the paper. Her daughter, Bonnie, continued the paper after her mother's death. In 1947 she sold it to Elmer McIlwain and continued as a reporter. (Courtesy of Lois Cruitt.)

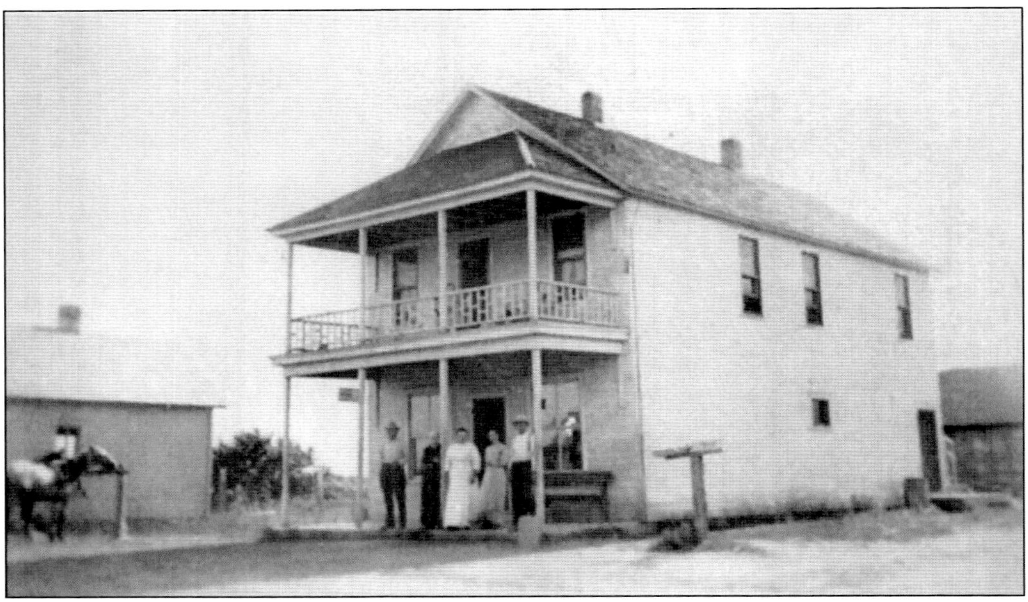

Quigley Store. This store was one of the few buildings in Quigley. Store owners and employees pose for a photograph. This photograph was probably taken in the late 1890s when Quigley was at its peak. The balcony is quite ornate, and the second floor was used for living quarters. There is someone sitting on the balcony.

Eight

Oconee and Tower Hill

Dr. Ballard laid out a town called Luro. Although it was located on the Illinois Central Railroad, the railroad company refused to put in a switch. Without the switch, the few businesses located here quickly died out. In April 1855, a year after Luro was laid out, the town of Oconee was surveyed. The businesses from Luro moved to the new town, and the town began to grow. Oconee is the name of the daughter of a Native American chief. It is Shawanese for "bone." The Oconee tribe became part of the Creek and Seminole Nations. In Creek, *o* means people or nation and *conee* means skunk.

In 1830 or 1831, Burrell Massey homesteaded on one of the mounds lifted by the glaciers, and it became known as Massey's Knobs. In 1848, Washbourne Wade laid out a village on part of his land and called it Manyawper but later changed the name to Westminster. This was a good location for trading, as it was on the Shelbyville to Hillsboro stagecoach road. After the Terre Haute, Alton, and St. Louis Railroad bypassed Westminster, it was abandoned. Tower Hill was surveyed in June 1857 by P. C. Huggins and Simeon Ryder. These are the same men who laid out Windsor and Gays. The town was built nearly in the center of the township and just south of one of the largest knobs in the township. The township was originally called Pilot Knob. A general store, houses, post office, hotel, and mill were soon added to the town. Beulah Gordon told an interesting story of an event during the Civil War. The Knights of the Golden Circle, composed of Southern sympathizers, decided to ride to Shelbyville. The group met Judge Anthony Thornton who immediately ordered them "to disperse and go home." In 1891 flying kites was prohibited in Tower Hill and the penalty could be from $1 to $10. The city council was serious about not flying kites.

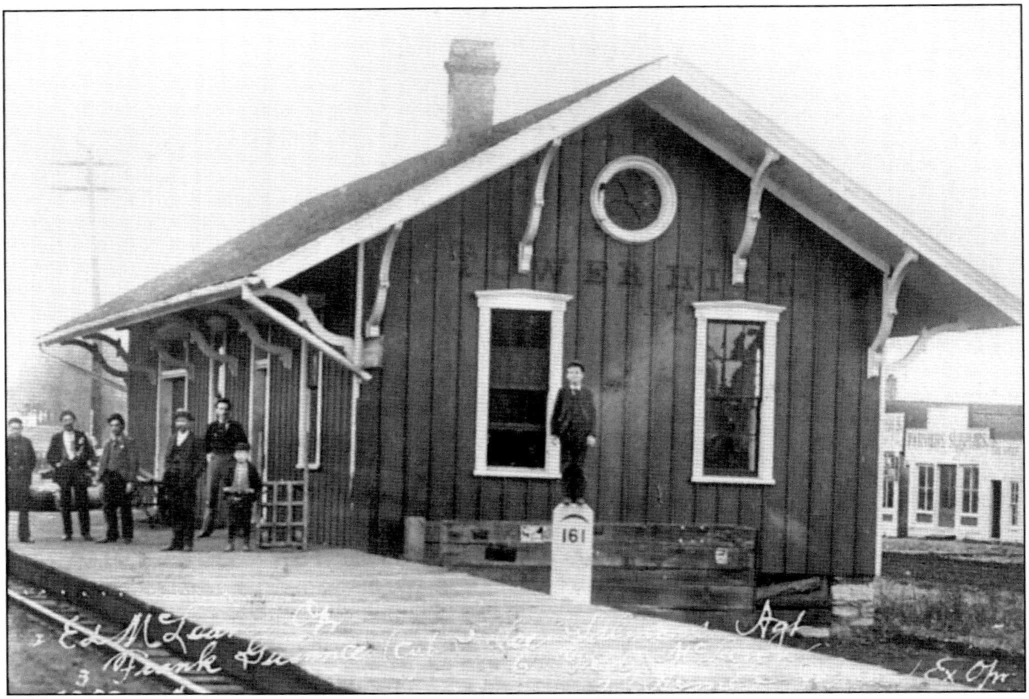

TOWER HILL DEPOT. This photograph was taken in 1893. Several names are handwritten on the photograph; the order of identification is unknown.

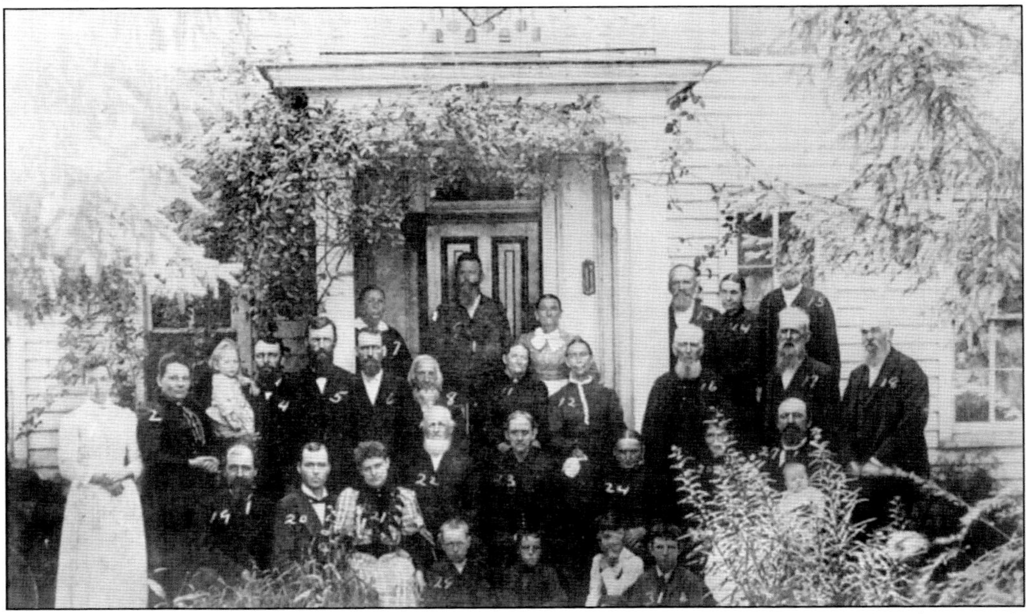

50TH ANNIVERSARY. The anniversary couple is Conrad and Mary Anderson Eiler. The photograph was taken at their anniversary party on August 26, 1891. The back of the photograph documents the names of all but a few of those shown. In addition, there are details of the relationship to the couple, marital status, family order, and even occupation. D. Brownback is even noted as a pioneer.

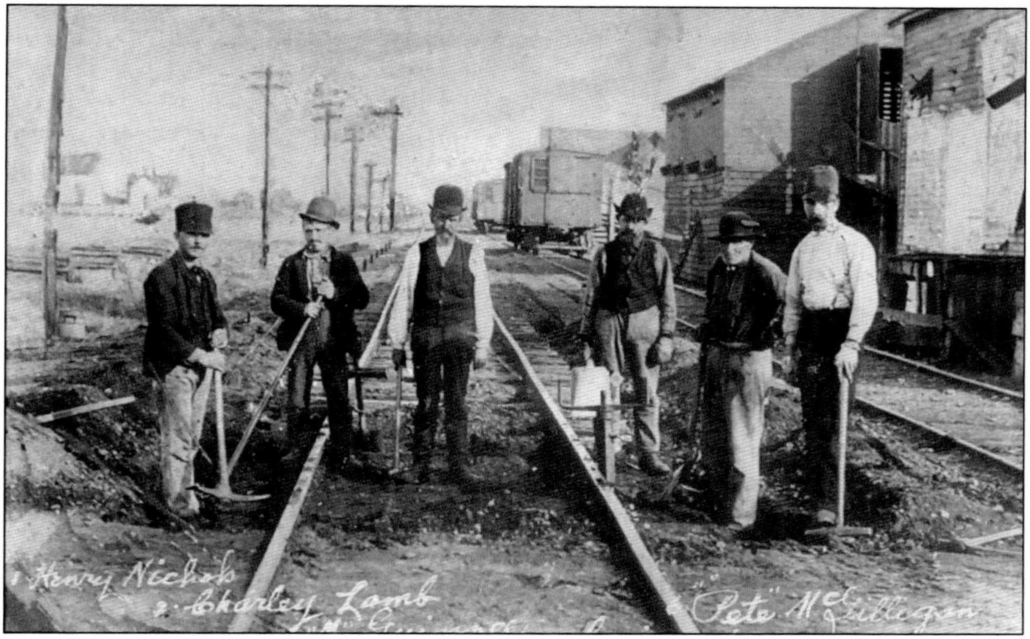

SECTION CREW. This photograph was taken in the summer of 1893 in Tower Hill at the same time as the depot photograph. This section crew is from the Cleveland, Cincinnati, Chicago, and St. Louis (Big Four) Railroad. The men are, from left to right, Henry Nichols, Charley Lamb, Michael Guinnee, Dan Guinnee, Jerry Lenihan, and Pete McGilligan.

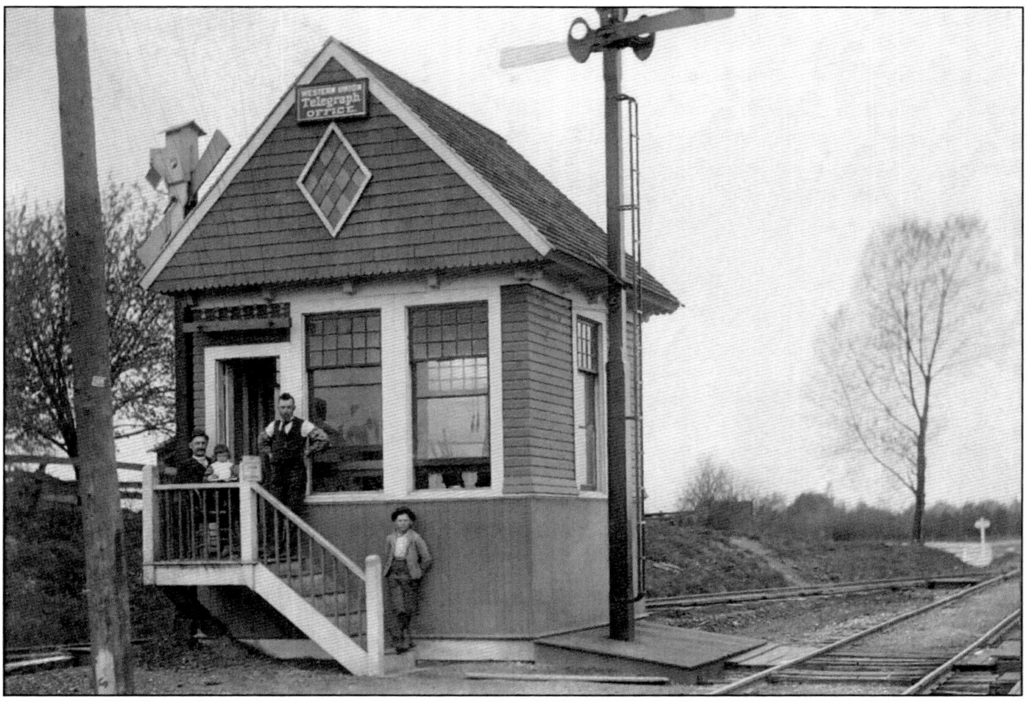

TELEGRAPH OFFICE. This photograph of the Western Union Telegraph office in Tower Hill was taken in 1896. There is a lot of gingerbread on this office.

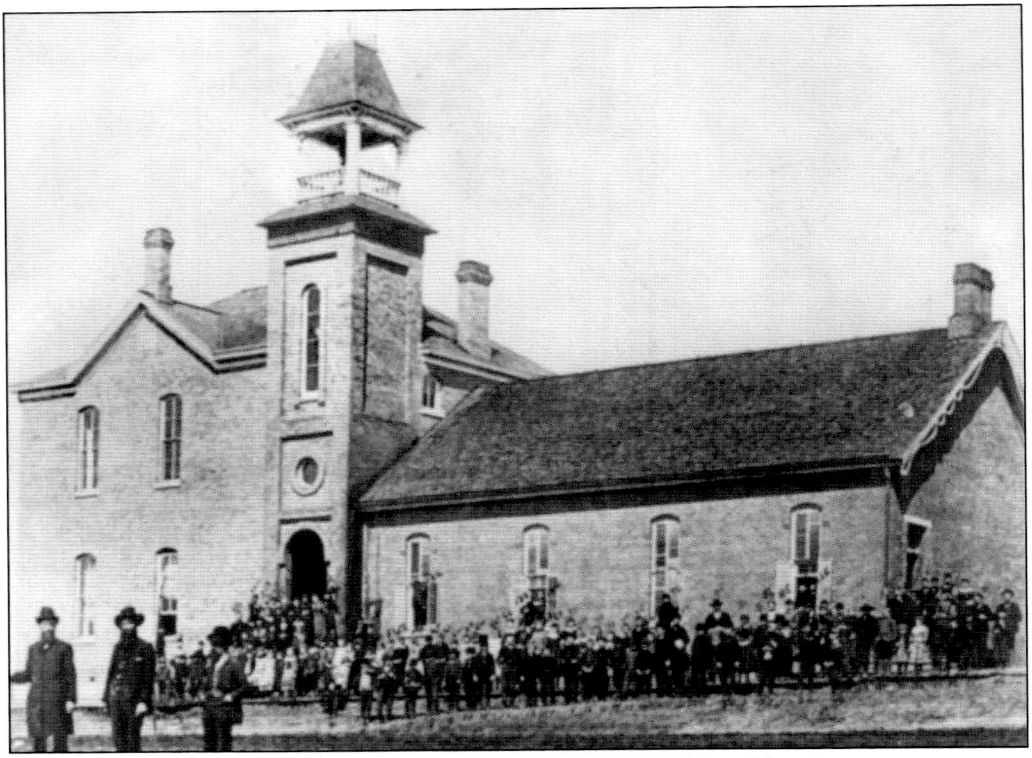

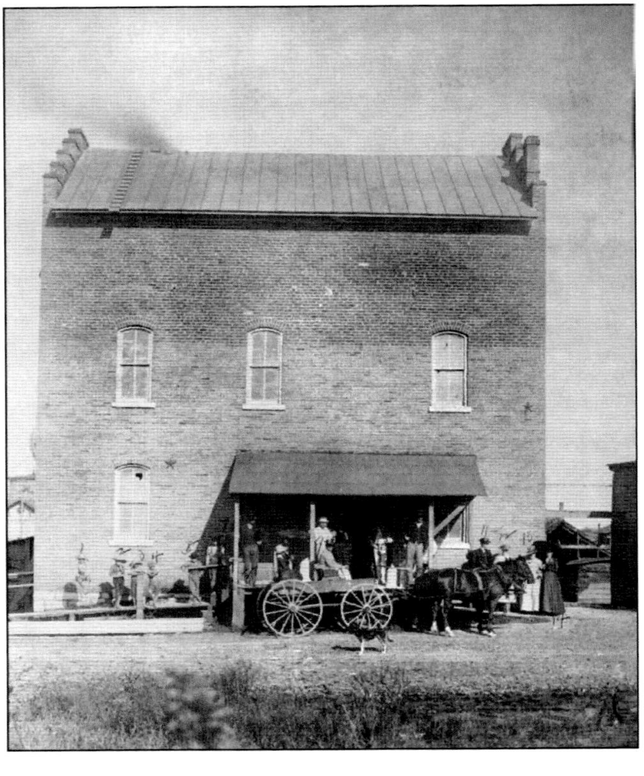

TOWER HILL SCHOOL BEFORE 1895. In 1872 Tower Hill had a one-room frame school. A second frame room and a brick room were added. Two more rooms were then added, one frame and one brick. A new seven-room brick school was added to the one room brick building built in the 1880s. The school is shown here. This building burned in 1895, and salvaged material from the school was used for building the new school.

OLD RED FRAME MILL. This photograph was taken before the mill burned in the winter of 1883. Pictured here are, from left to right, Warren Weeks, Fred Stumpf, Chase Weeks, Boyd Weeks, Horner Runkle, Charles Sibbitt, Pete Stumpf, Cully Guinnee, Jacob Runkle-the proprietor, Horner Eiler, Margaret McIlwain, Ida Conrad, and Loella Andes.

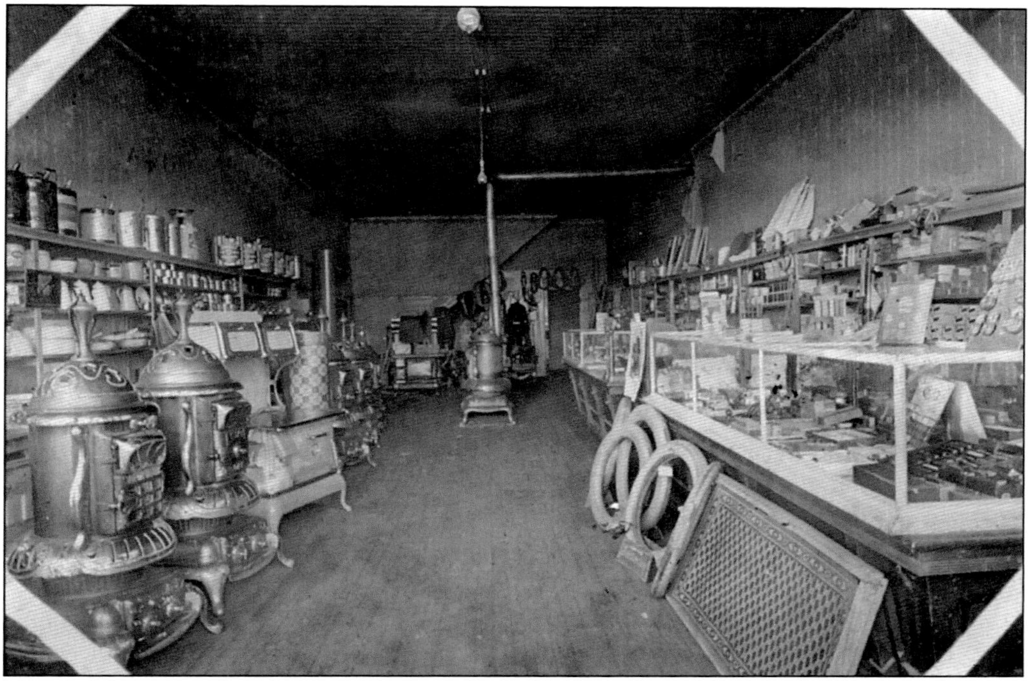

HARDWARE STORE. This is the interior of the O. C. Mage store taken in 1924. The variety of stoves is very interesting. Horse collars and clothing can be seen in the rear of the store.

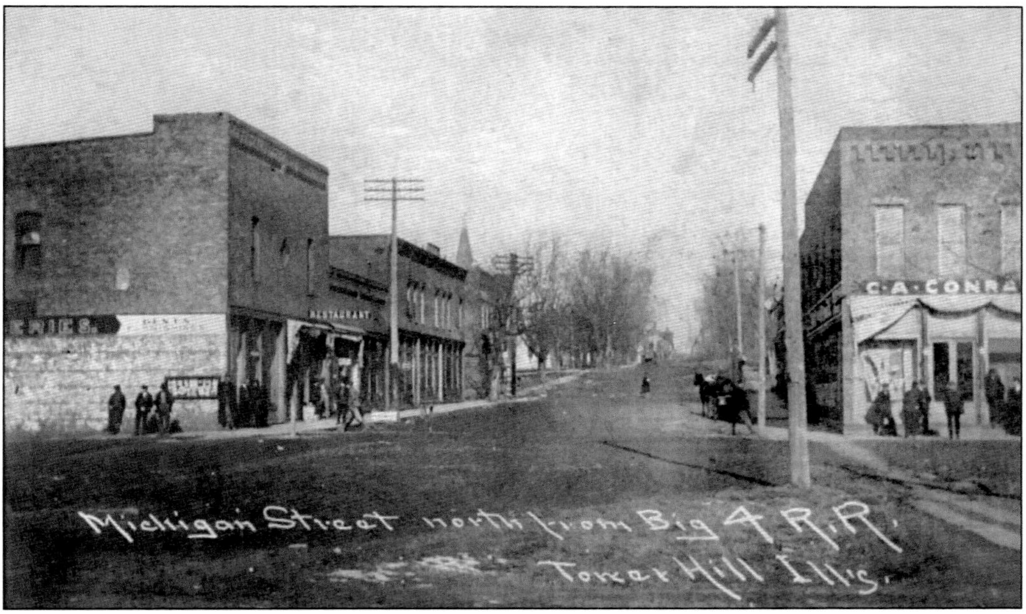

DOWNTOWN TOWER HILL. The view is Michigan Street north from the Big Four Railroad. There appears to be no occasion for the photograph, as no one seems to be posing.

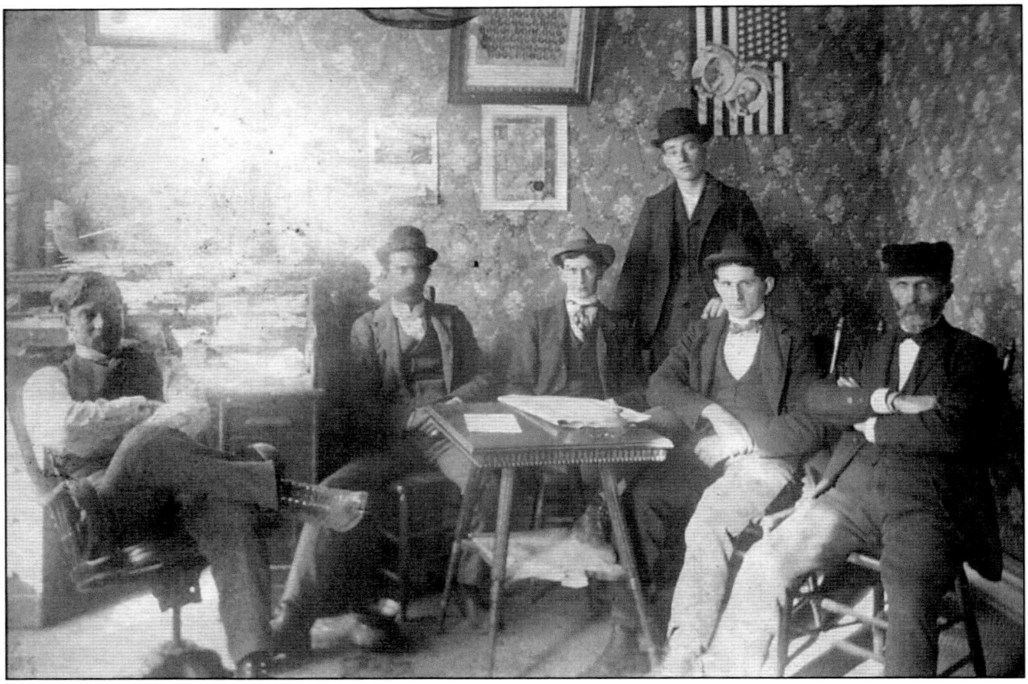

Campaign Committee, 1900. The committee was involved in the campaign of McKinley and Roosevelt. President McKinley was in a rematch with William Jennings Bryan. He chose Theodore Roosevelt as his running mate. Pictured here are, from left to right, Homer Carley, Roy Miller, Charley Holt, Clarence Inman, Charles Weeks, and postmaster Pugh Faught. Please note the campaign memorabilia on the back wall.

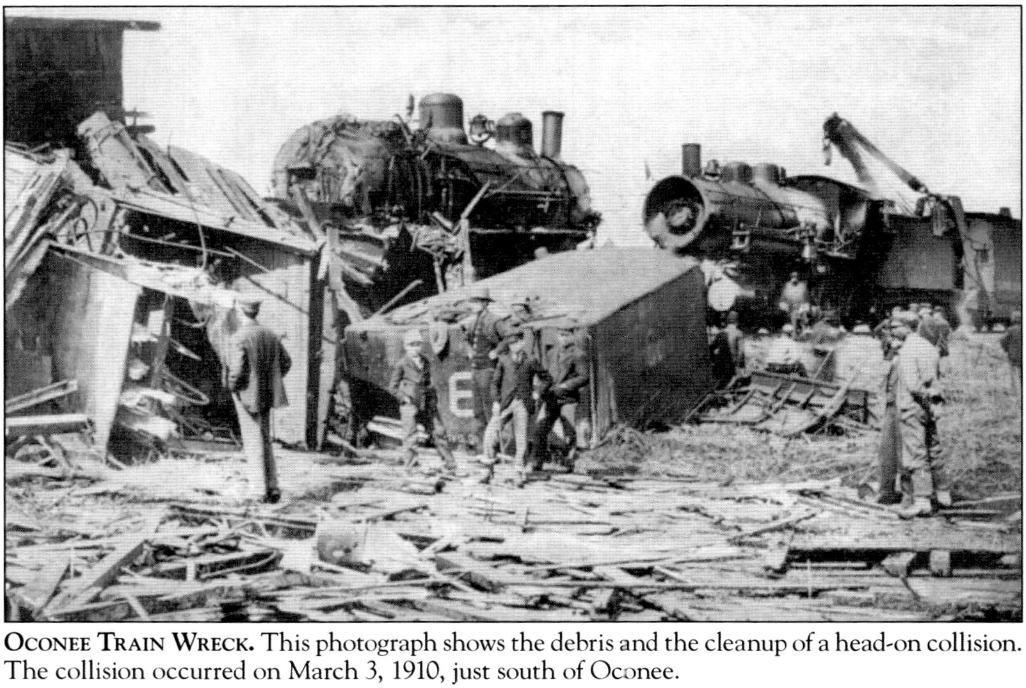

Oconee Train Wreck. This photograph shows the debris and the cleanup of a head-on collision. The collision occurred on March 3, 1910, just south of Oconee.

Nine

Clarksburg, Holland, and Mode

To the south of Shelbyville, several towns were formed. Two of those towns used to be in the Holland Township. Clarksburg split into another township. In 1880, Theodore Dove bought a tract of land from John W. Johnson. Dove commissioned George W. Dickinson to layout the town of Clarksburg on 22 acres. The village is named after Theodore Dove's wife, Alta Clark. The village of Clarksburg became official on May 7, 1897, at 1:45 p.m. The railroad was integral to the village's success. In the 1920s, it was a busy village. There were two restaurants, a garage, a general merchandise store, doctor, post office, church, and two lodges. Near the depot there were stock pens, scales, and a hay barn. Clarksburg declined due to the rural to urban migration of the 1920s and faster transportation to larger towns like Shelbyville.

In 1898 Mary Burke commissioned the layout of the village of Holland. Prior to this, Holland had been known as Barlow. The people who live on the north side of town are residents of Shelby County. Those who live on the south side of town are residents of Effingham County.

The history of Mode begins with the history of Old Mode. Old Mode was laid out by Jacob Smith in 1866 and was called Smithville. The post office was a half mile south and was called Mode. This gradually became the name of the village. The Illinois Central Railroad owned the land where Mode was located. The railroad then sold it to Jacob Gallagher in 1871. He gave the land to his son S. D. Gallagher in 1878. His son divided the land into village lots and New Mode was formed. Dr. Duncan built the first house, and one of the rooms became the first Sunday school and also the first school. Old Mode faded as New Mode grew because of its location near the railroad. Today, there are still several residences, and the W. R. Yakey Grain Company is also located there.

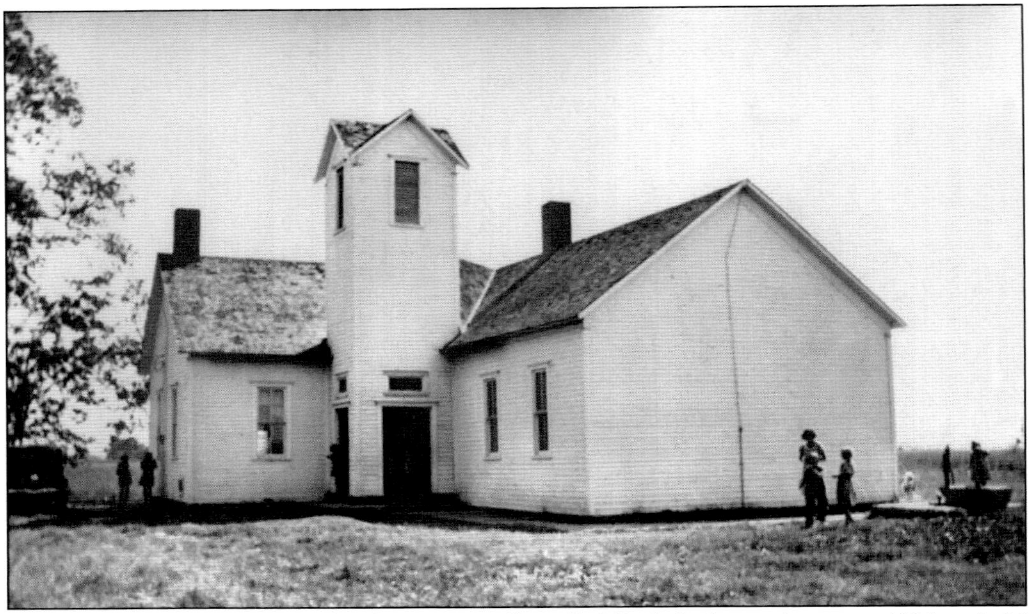

Clarksburg School. The school was originally called Bethel when it began in 1925 with 26 pupils. This photograph was taken in the 1920s or 1930s. Clarksburg consolidated in 1947, and in 1950 it became only an elementary school. The last year of the school was 1961 when it was consolidated into the Shelbyville School District. In 2001, it was put on the National Register of Historic Places.

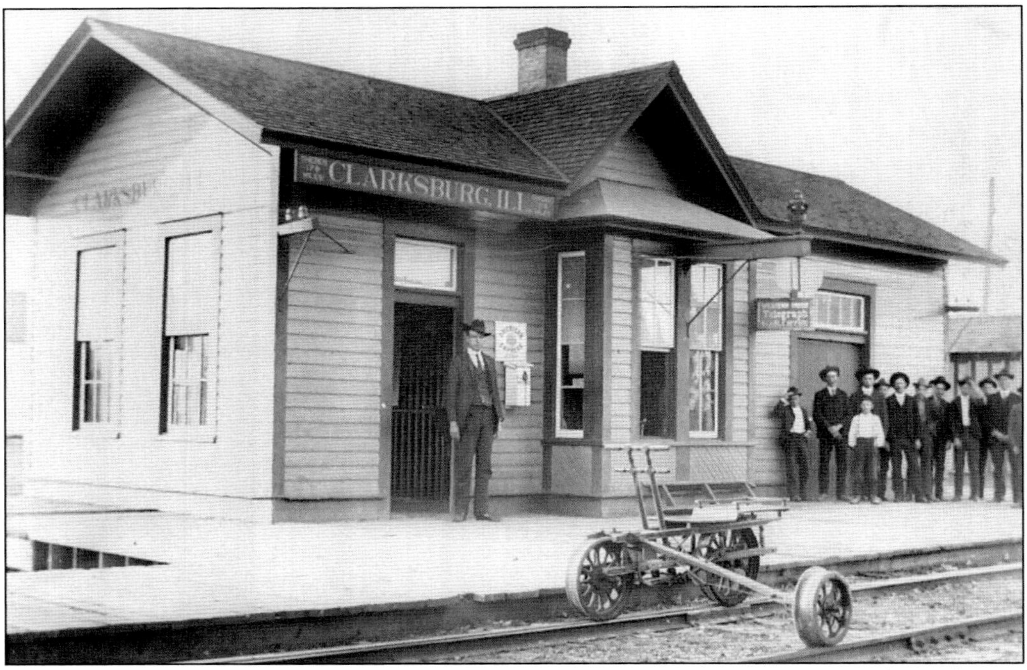

Clarksburg Depot. This photograph was probably taken when Clarksburg was a busy place in the 1930s. The CE&I Railroad ran along the east side of town. The depot was located just across from the siding beside the railroad and at the end of Main Street. (Courtesy of the author.)

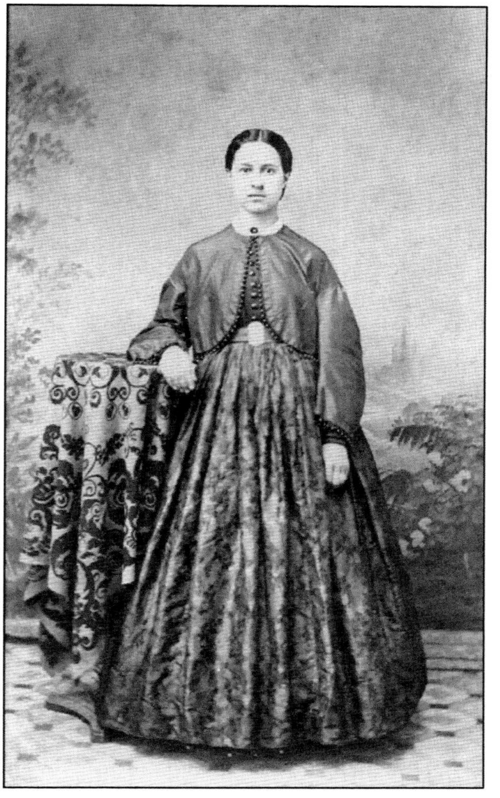

Frances Westenhaver Gallagher. This is the wife of Henry Gallagher and mother of Jacob E. Gallagher. The photograph was taken by G. Hannaman in Shelbyville in the 1860s. Please note the heavy and shiny dress material. (Courtesy of Jacob E. Gallagher family.)

Soybean Demonstration. Soybeans were still a relatively new crop when this photograph was taken in the 1940s. The soybean plants look different from today's plants. The demonstration field was on Jacob E. Gallagher's farm in southern Clarksburg Township. (Courtesy of Jacob E. Gallagher family.)

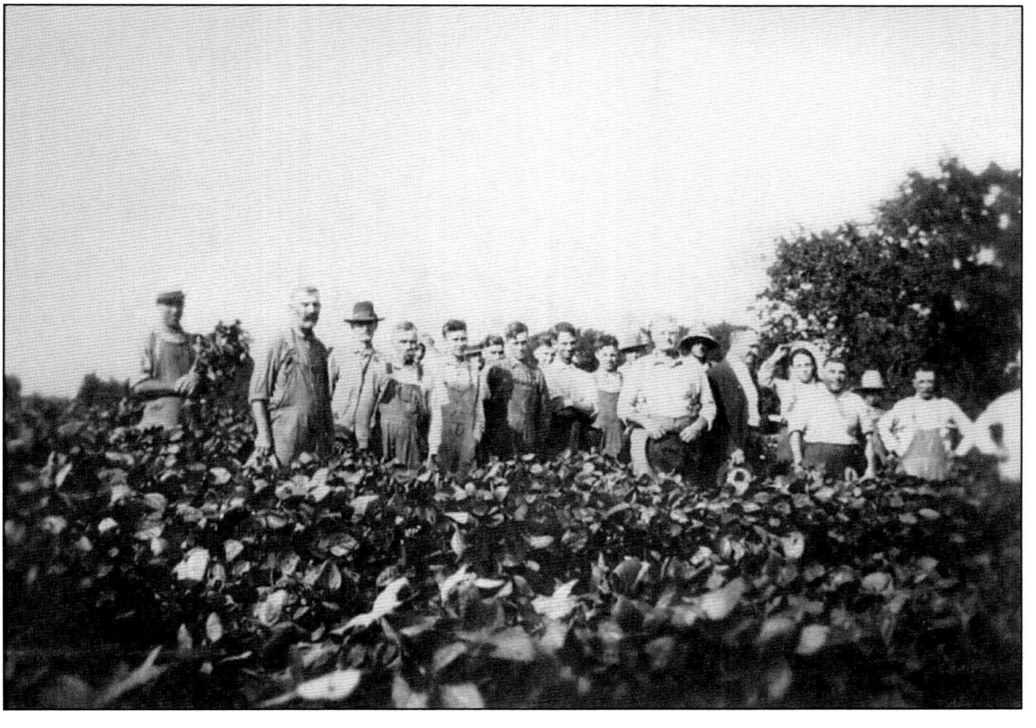

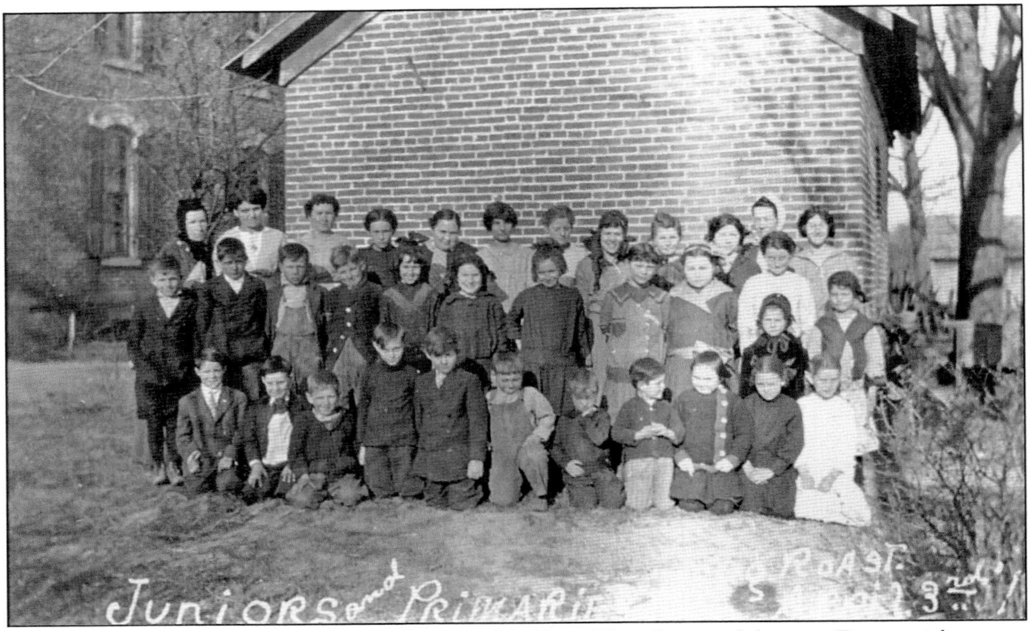

Egg Roast. The junior and primary classes at Mt. Zion Church are celebrating Easter with an egg roast. This photograph was taken on April 3, 1915, at the home Flora Allen in rural Clarksburg Township. (Courtesy of Jacob E. Gallagher family.)

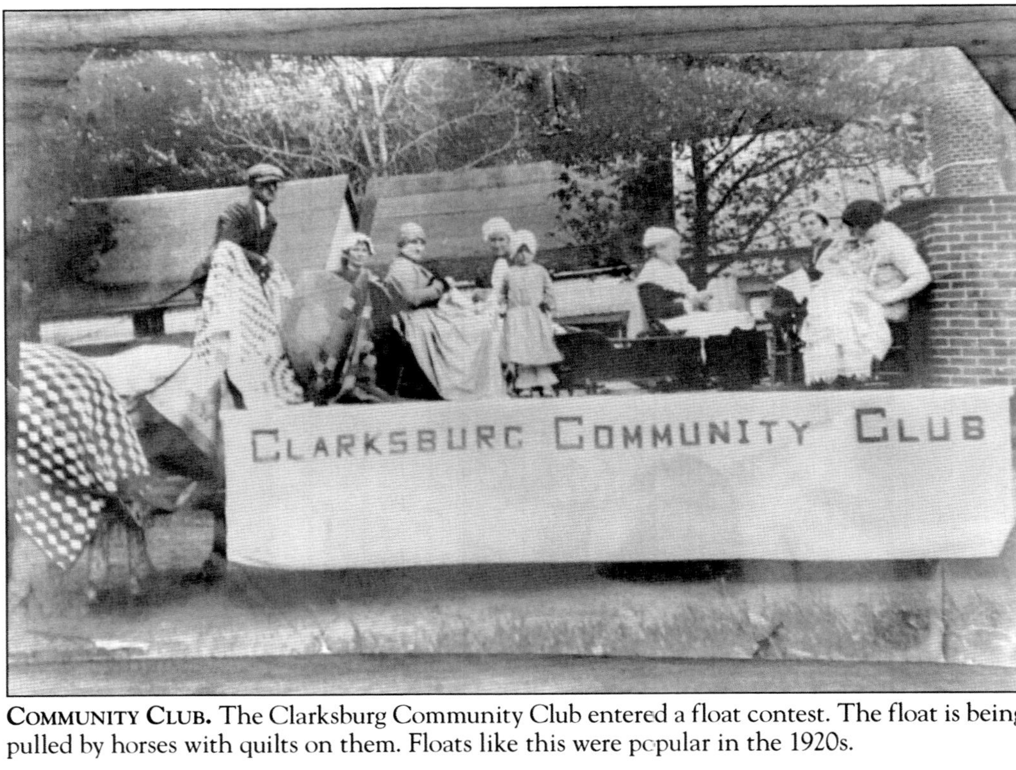

Community Club. The Clarksburg Community Club entered a float contest. The float is being pulled by horses with quilts on them. Floats like this were popular in the 1920s.

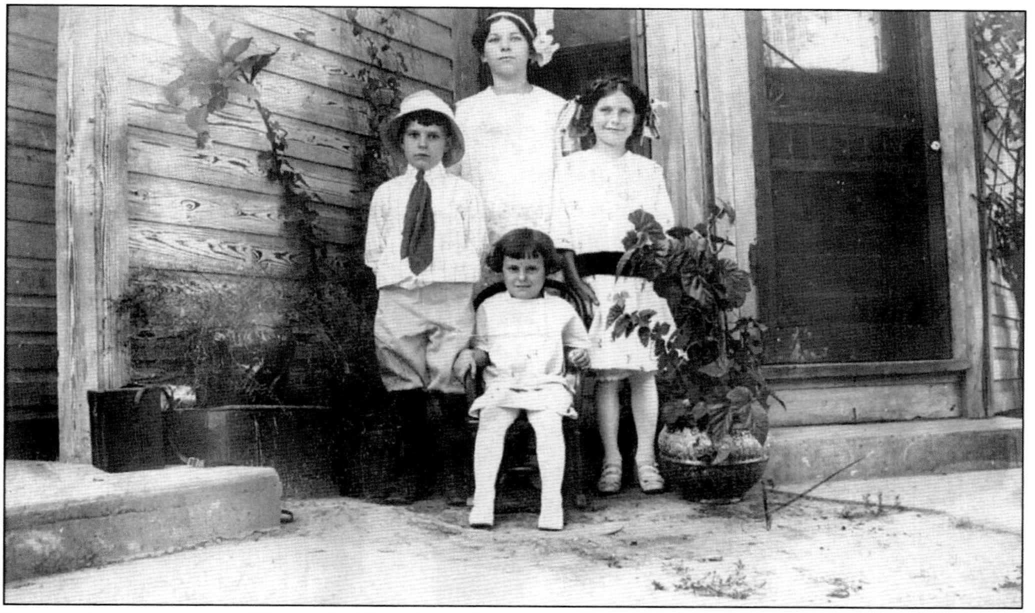

Little Adventurers. These children have dressed up for a photograph on the back steps of their home in rural Clarksburg Township. This photograph was taken c. 1910. The children are, from left to right, Tom, Florence, Frances, and Louise Gallagher (sitting). Their parents were Jacob E. and Fannie Gallagher. (Courtesy of Jacob E. Gallagher family.)

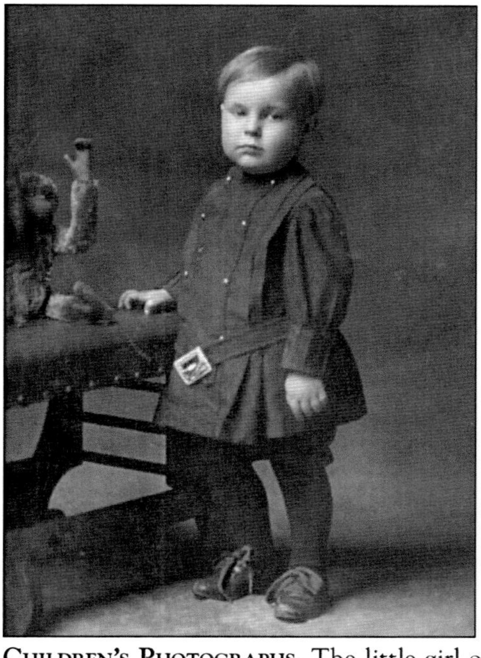

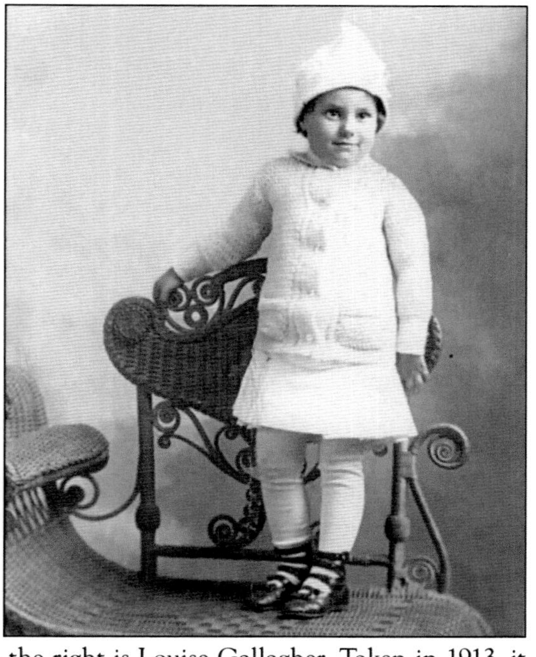

Children's Photographs. The little girl on the right is Louise Gallagher. Taken in 1913, it shows the types of props that were used in photographs. Taken in 1908, the photograph on the left is of her brother Tom Gallagher. During this time it was hard to distinguish boys from girls due to their clothing. The monkey on the left kept him still for the photograph, but he still did not keep his belt buckled. (Courtesy Jacob E. Gallagher family.)

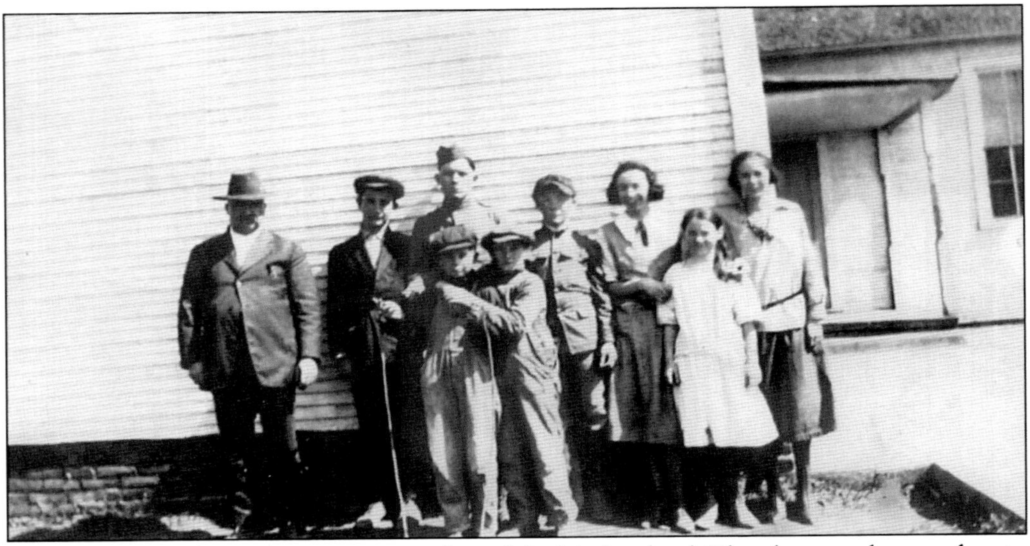

Mode School. This is the upper room class of the Mode school. The photograph was taken in 1920, and the school is located in Holland Township. The teacher on the far left is Mr. Riechel. (Courtesy of Author.)

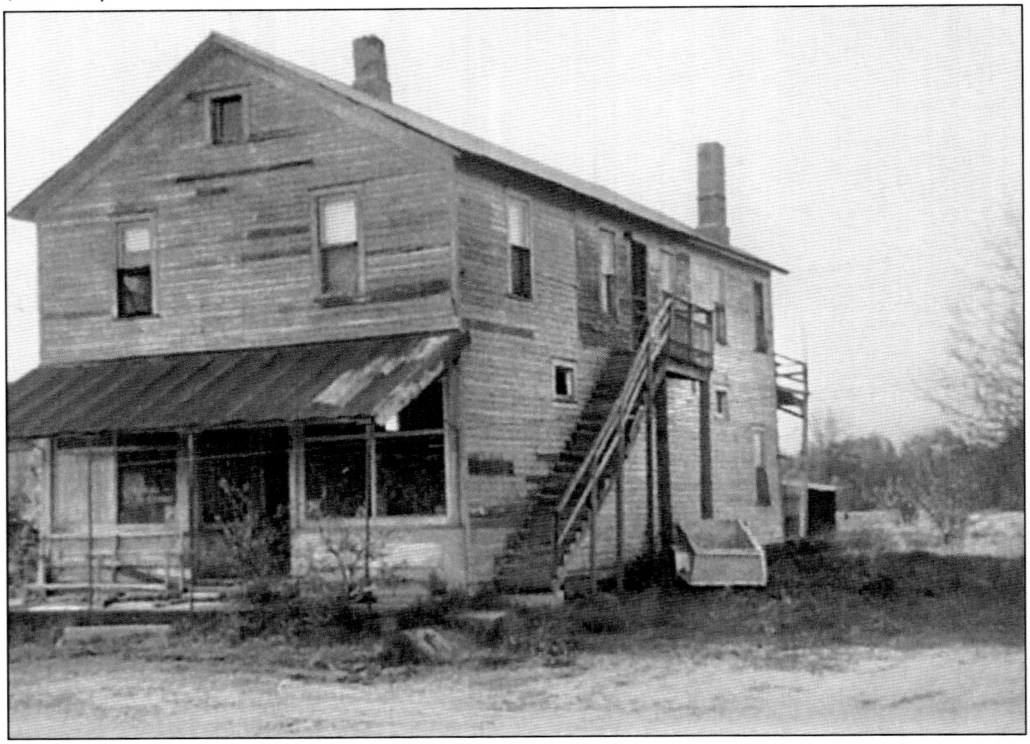

Holland Store. Tabor's General Store was located in the village of Holland. There was a post office in the store until 1922. This photograph is probably from the 1940s. Tyne Dial built a two-story general store— she used the upper story as her residence. It has seen several owners: Jess Jennings in 1918, then Jake and Frank Musser, Roy Slifer, and then the last owners, Earl and Sadie Lutz, who closed the store in 1965.

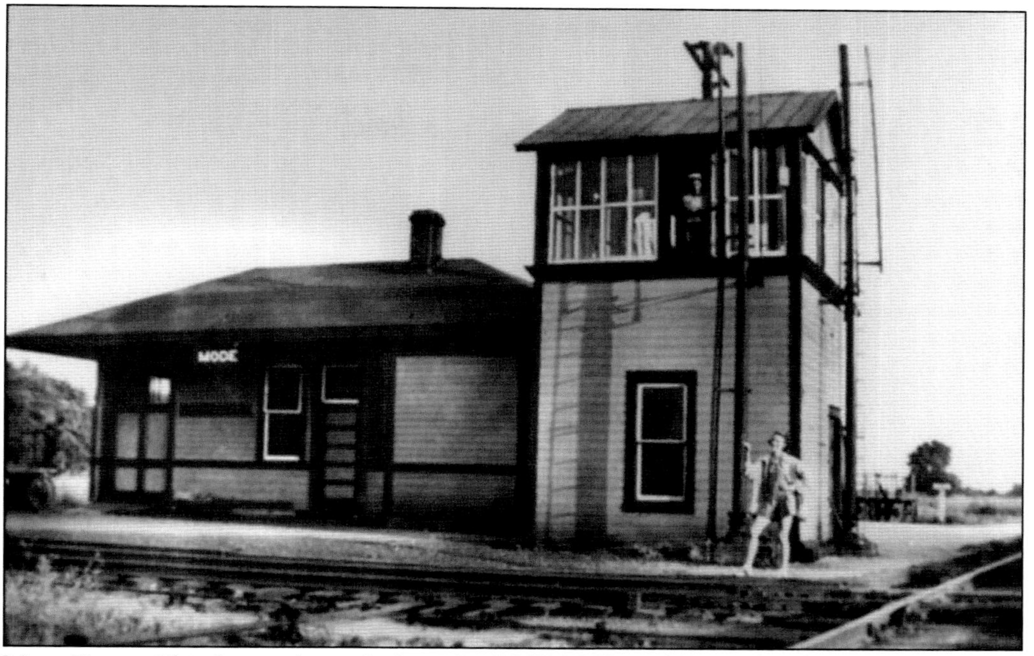

Mode Depot. This depot is located where the C&EI, NYC, and STL railroads intersect. The date of the photograph is unknown, but the man in the train office at the top is Joe Wattenbarger, and the man who is joking around is Gene Rinckstom.

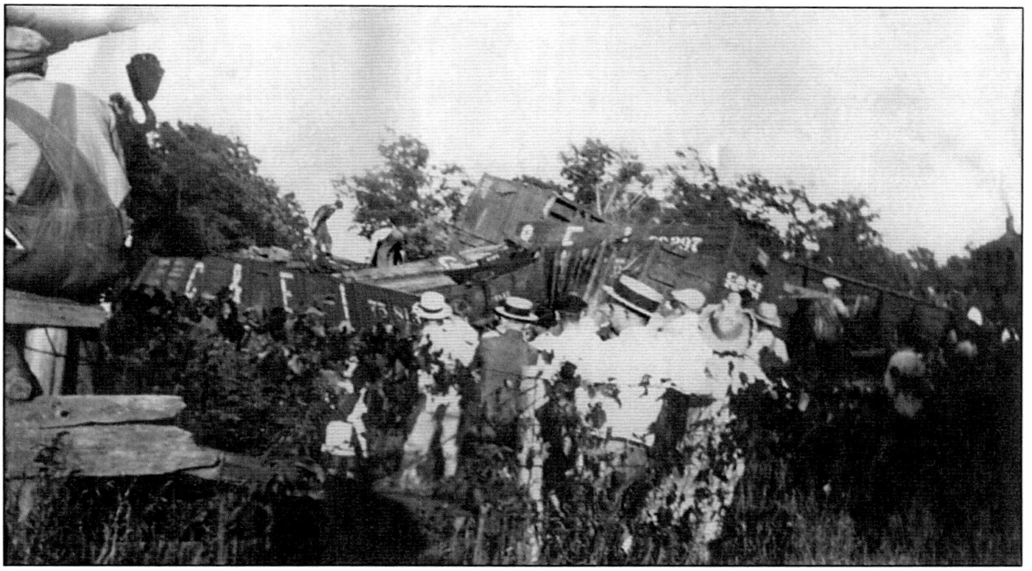

Train Wreck. This wreck occurred just north of Mode in 1922. There was extensive damage and the cleanup crews had to wait for a crane to travel in by rail.

www.arcadiapublishing.com

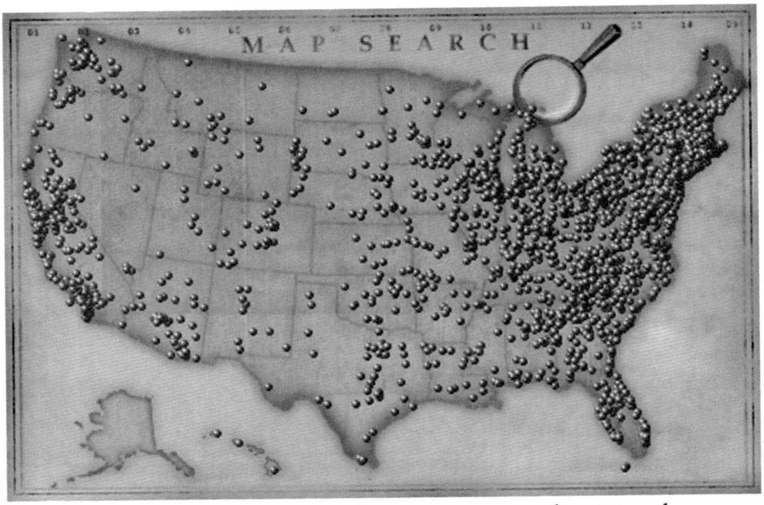

Discover books about the town where you grew up, the cities where your friends and families live, the town where your parents met, or even that retirement spot you've been dreaming about. Our Web site provides history lovers with exclusive deals, advanced notification about new titles, e-mail alerts of author events, and much more.

MADE IN THE USA

Arcadia Publishing, the leading local history publisher in the United States, is committed to making history accessible and meaningful through publishing books that celebrate and preserve the heritage of America's people and places. Consistent with our mission to preserve history on a local level, this book was printed in South Carolina on American-made paper and manufactured entirely in the United States.

This book carries the accredited Forest Stewardship Council (FSC) label and is printed on 100 percent FSC-certified paper. Products carrying the FSC label are independently certified to assure consumers that they come from forests that are managed to meet the social, economic, and ecological needs of present and future generations.

FSC
Mixed Sources
Product group from well-managed forests and other controlled sources

Cert no. SW-COC-001530
www.fsc.org
© 1996 Forest Stewardship Council

Find *Your* Place in History.